2ND EDITION

W9-BNZ-070

MODERNIZE
Your Resume
Get Noticed ... Get Hired

MASTER RESUME WRITERS

**Wendy Enelow &
Louise Kursmark**

Modernize Your Resume
Get Noticed ... Get Hired

Copyright © 2019 by Wendy Enelow and Louise Kursmark

ISBN 978-0-9966803-2-5

 EMERALD CAREER PUBLISHING

Publisher: Emerald Career Publishing
               2265 Walker Road
               Coleman Falls, VA 24536
               www.emeraldcareerpublishing.com
               800-881-9972

Cover & Interior Design: Deb Tremper, Six Penny Graphics
http://sixpennygraphics.com

Distributor: Cardinal Publishers Group
www.cardinalpub.com

Printed in the United States of America

CONTENTS

Introduction

If you're like most job seekers, writing your resume is one of the most daunting tasks in the entire job search process. As your first point of contact with potential employers and recruiters, your resume must instantly communicate *who* you are, *what* you can do, and *how well* you do it.

Everywhere you turn, you read and hear different advice about how to write, format, and design your resume. How do you know what to believe—how to handle the specific circumstances and challenges of your career, best showcase your achievements and most notable qualifications, and highlight what is most relevant to employers?

Further complicating your task are the massive changes that have occurred in how you manage your job search and how employers hire. Specifically:

- **The Internet has fundamentally altered the way we read.** As we consume content online, we are skimming, glancing, and quickly picking up select information. If we are not engaged *instantly,* with just a click or a swipe we move on to something more interesting.

  Our new reading habits have crossed over to traditional print documents, such as newspapers, books, and—yes—resumes. Therefore, you must write, format, and design your resume to reward the way people read *today.*

- **Electronic scanning has revolutionized the job application process.** In many instances your resume will be read by a computer before it is ever seen by a person. Therefore, it is critical that it be written and designed to pass through the Applicant Tracking System (ATS) that a particular company is using.

  ATS technology is largely based on keyword algorithms—rules that establish the importance and weight of certain words and phrases. The plain and simple truth is that your resume must contain the *right* keywords or it will never pass the electronic scan and never be seen by a human.

- **Technology has greatly expanded job search channels.** Today, you can post your resume online, respond to electronic and print job advertisements, upload your resume to recruiter and company databases, email your resume to a prospective employer, and apply for jobs from your phone or tablet computer.

  You must be prepared to work with your resume in all of these different online channels.

- **Technology-based job search has far-reaching impact.** LinkedIn has become a dominant force for job seekers to find opportunities and recruiters to find candidates. Twitter, Facebook, YouTube—and perhaps new tools still to evolve—may also be quite valuable in your search. You'll most likely use your resume, or parts of it, in ways you never imagined even just a year or two ago.

- **Companies screen candidates much more thoroughly.** Just about everyone can be found online, giving hiring authorities the chance to learn more about you—personally and professionally—before you ever get a call for an interview. They will read your LinkedIn profile, look at your Facebook posts, and see what YouTube videos you have uploaded.

  Hiring is a financial investment for any company, and they want to be sure they're making the right decision.

If it sounds overwhelming—relax! We've been writing resumes for decades, and we've kept up to date with all that has changed … and all that has not.

The most important thing that has *not* changed—and most likely never will change—is the value of networking to your job search. There is no activity that you can engage in that will be more beneficial than networking—tried-and-true, in-person, one-on-one relationships as well as online communications and community building.

Of course, the starting point for any successful job search is a resume. In the 2nd edition of *Modernize Your Resume*, we take the mystery and confusion out of resume writing. We show you exactly what you need to know and do to create a modern resume that meets the 3 most critical standards of today's job search market:

- **Content** that is tight, lean, and clean, appealing to the way your resume will be read.

- **Format** that showcases your career and accomplishments while working seamlessly in all of the ways that you'll be using the resume throughout your job search.

- **Design** that distinguishes your resume in a crowded field yet is entirely appropriate for your profession, industry, and level.

We also address a fourth, often overlooked, component: **Mindset.** By helping you frame your career in a way that's valuable to employers, we give you the confidence you need to win in today's competitive employment arena.

To expand the value of this book to an even larger audience, we've added 3 new chapters for people facing unique job search challenges:

- **Career Change**

- **Military-to-Civilian Career Transition**

- **Return-to-Work After Extended Absence**

Always remember that resume writing is not a formulaic process, and there are no rules. That's why this book is so valuable, helping you navigate your way through the complexities of all that is involved in creating a resume that will help you *get noticed and get hired!*

PART I:
The Modern Resume

We get it ... you want a fast, easy process to create a great resume and land a new job.

With this book, we give you everything you need—and more. Looking for inspiring resume samples? Check. Fresh design ideas? Check. Great resume content? That, too. The latest advice on keyword-scanning applicant tracking systems? Of course. It's all included and presented in an easy-to-manage process.

And we go deeper, sharing strategies and techniques that we, and 50+ of our professional resume-writing colleagues, use to create powerful resumes that position today's job seekers for success.

How to Use This Book

Divided into 8 distinct parts, this book provides both quick answers and deeper, more thoughtful explanations for everything you need to know to create your own modern resume.

- **Part I—The Modern Resume.** We tell you and show you what's different about resumes today, explain the various sections in the modern resume, and give you guidelines for your specific circumstances—from graduating student to senior executive and everyone in between.

  We also address Resume Mindset, a factor that's critical to your success, and Personal Branding, a powerful trend that is central to creating a distinctive resume and a focused job search.

- **Part II—Modernize Your Resume Content.** The 6 chapters in Part II discuss, in depth, our 6 Core Principles for writing modern resume content and provide best-in-class resume samples of those concepts in action. You'll learn to:
  - Start with the Wow!
  - Put Your Objective in the Driver's Seat
  - Write with Meaning & Power
  - Write Tight, Lean & Clean
  - Leave the Muscle, Lose the Fat
  - Integrate Your Critical Keywords

- **Part III—Modernize Your Resume Format.** The 6 Core Principles in Part III, along with the accompanying resume samples, guide you through the many decisions you'll need to make as you organize, structure, and format your content so that you can:
  - Showcase Your Career with the Right Resume Structure
  - Pop Your Contact Information
  - Follow the Rules of Good Formatting

- Improve Readability & Skimmability
- Choose a Font that Fits
- Prepare for the Complexities of Online Search

- **Part IV—Modernize Your Resume Design.** Never to be overlooked—or its value underestimated—is the visual presentation of your resume. You'll see unique, eye-catching, and remarkably distinctive resume samples that follow our 6 Core Principles to help you:
    - Capture Attention in a Flash
    - Follow the Practices of Good Page Design
    - Match Design Elements to Your Industry & Profession
    - Match Design Elements to Your Career Story
    - Be Distinctive
    - Embrace Color & Graphics

- **Part V—Resumes for Challenging Situations.** Many job seekers are faced with unique challenges that can make resume writing more complicated or require a different approach. In the 3 chapters in this section, you'll find detailed instructions for how to write and format resumes if you are:
    - Changing Careers
    - Transitioning from a Military-to-Civilian Career
    - Returning to Work after an Extended Absence

- **Part VI—Resume Portfolio.** These 40+ modern resumes, written for job seekers of all levels in a wide array of industries and professions, illustrate the core principles discussed in Parts II, III, and IV. Review the portfolio carefully for new and fresh ideas to write, format, and design your own resume.

    Heartfelt thanks to our professional colleagues who shared their very best resumes with us and with you! Each resume shows the contributor's name and contact information, and we encourage you to reach out to these talented writers if you're in need of professional resume assistance.

- **Part VII—Resources.** As you put theory into action and begin to write your resume, you'll find these tools and resources extremely valuable:
    - **Goal-Setting Worksheet,** a tool that will help you define your career objective.
    - **Career Vault,** a structured guideline for gathering all of your resume information.
    - **Dig-Deep Questions** to uncover, quantify, and write about your accomplishments.
    - **Verbs with Verve,** our favorite list of **403 Resume Writing Verbs**.

- **Part VIII—Index.** Use this easy tool to find resumes that match your profession, industry, or circumstance—career change, military transition, return-to-work, unemployment, and more.

Our Commitment to You

Follow our guiding principles, study the resume samples, and move step-by-step through the necessary preparation, and we promise that resume writing, formatting, and design will be easier, faster, and better.

With a modern resume in hand, you'll be a more empowered job seeker, confident in your qualifications, able to articulate your value, and prepared to outperform your competition and win the job!

CHAPTER 1:
Welcome to the World of Modern Resume Writing

6 Hallmarks of a Modern Resume

- Clear and concise, written and designed to appeal to today's readers
- Laser focused to each individual's job targets
- Rich with keywords that resonate with employers
- Specific in describing achievements rather than general capabilities
- Contemporary in appearance and visually distinctive
- Linked to email, online profiles, websites, and social media

Are you ready to take your first step toward your next great career opportunity? It begins with a shift in mindset—how you think about the process of writing, formatting, and designing your resume.

To begin, you must understand the significant changes that resumes have gone through over just the past few years. Rapidly, they have evolved to meet our modern world of job search—characterized by unprecedented competition; a global workforce; and technologies that have forever changed how we communicate, how we find new job opportunities, and how companies select candidates to interview and hire.

Follow our *Modernize Your Resume* guidelines, and we're certain you'll be one of those candidates!

Modern Resume Content, Format & Design

In a tough job market, you must do everything you can to shine brighter than your competition. To help you do that, we've devoted the 3 major sections of this book to the 3 core elements of the modern resume—**Content, Format,** and **Design**—all of which are essential to help you *get noticed and get hired*.

> **PRO TIP:** First, you need to hook your readers with the design and appearance of your resume; then you can reel them in with content that is powerful, interesting, and relevant.

Before we dive in, let's review some essential guidelines to help you develop a solid infrastructure—a foundation—for your resume.

We'll show you what today's modern resume is all about through guidelines and samples for 3 categories of job seekers: Graduating Students & Young Professionals; Mid-Career Professionals; and Senior Managers & Executives.

After you've reviewed the guidelines that are pertinent to you, don't miss the discussion on page 11 regarding all of the other categories you might include on your resume. They will round out the primary sections to paint a complete picture of all that is unique and valuable about you.

> **PRO TIP: Does your career reflect unique circumstances—Career Change, Return to Work, or Military-to-Civilian Transition?** If so, in addition to the guidelines in this chapter you'll want to devote close attention to Part V (pages 147–66), which includes recommendations and samples tailored to you.

Guidelines for Graduating Students & Young Professionals

- **Professional Skills Profile** (Summary). Start your resume with valuable information that positions you as a strong candidate—a short paragraph, a few bullet points, or a brief listing of your most notable skills, education, and experiences as they relate to your target opportunities.

- **Education:** List your degree, college/university, location, academic honors, leadership activities, sports, and other distinguishing information. This will likely be the meatiest section of your resume because your education is your primary qualification, and employers will want to know what you did both in and outside the classroom.

  Does high school matter? Possibly. It matters if you were valedictorian or at the top of your class, had a unique and important internship or related experience, or attended a private high school whose alumni often look to recruit talent from their alma mater.

- **Internships:** Create a separate section if you've had internship(s) that relate to and support your professional objectives. Be sure to mention if you've interned with impressive companies, held notable responsibilities, or had multiple internships.

- **Project Highlights:** If you have important information that you think will attract prospective employers to you, be sure to include a separate section to showcase notable projects, courses, and assignments that support your current career goals.

- **Employment Experience.** Your work experience may be relatively minor as it relates to your professional job objective, but it communicates that you have a strong work ethic and possess other valuable workplace skills. You can include internships here, rather than in a separate section.

John Newsmith Resume—page 7

John's resume incorporates many of our modern resume guidelines. Following a Summary that clearly identifies his qualifications, the most significant part of his resume is Project Highlights. His class projects are elevated into truly meaningful experience that gives him valuable professional skills and relevant achievements even though they were acquired in school and not "on the job."

JOHN NEWSMITH

Orlando, FL 32300 • 803-888-1234
j.newsmith@gmail.com • LinkedIn.com/in/JohnNewsmith

ACCOUNTING GRADUATE • CPA CANDIDATE

High-performing accounting graduate, prepared to assume role as Associate or Staff Accountant. Energetic professional with a tireless work ethic and determination to excel. Quick to step up and take on leadership roles. Mesh easily with diversified teams to support and emphasize problem solving and project excellence.

- Advanced Analytic Capabilities
- Commitment to Continuous Learning
- Intensive Attention to Detail
- Expert Computer Skills

"Mr. Newsmith has consistently produced outstanding work. He presents excellent communication and interpersonal skills, and he always exhibits a sense of responsibility and integrity."
— Anthony A. Jones, CPA, Faculty Instructor in Accounting, Florida State University

EDUCATION

Bachelor of Arts in Accounting, Florida State University, Tallahassee, FL   December 2018

Honors & Awards
- 3.85 GPA • *magna cum laude* • President's List
- Academic Achievement Award in Business Administration

PROJECT HIGHLIGHTS

Strategic Management 2, Florida State University, Tallahassee, FL   Fall 2018

Led team in capstone consultancy project for a local tech startup. Delivered positive and lasting impact for real-world client.
- Produced 120-page business plan, including new mission statement, short- and long-term goals, and marketing and human resources plans.
- Analyzed revenues and expenses, reviewed financial breakdowns, and proposed new financial processes and procedures.

"John took the lead and acted as the group liaison, facilitator, and main presenter. The group's plan gave the business owner sound strategic concepts that, when implemented, helped the business establish a strong competitive advantage." — Dr. Rick Smith

Strategic Management 1, Florida State University, Tallahassee, FL   Spring 2018

Member of a stellar academic team that produced and presented innovative corporate strategy for ABX Corporation in Orlando, FL. Gained competencies in data analysis, teamwork, audits, and risk detection.

ASSOCIATION MEMBERSHIPS

Students for the Advancement of Management (SAM)
Florida Institute of CPAs (FICPA)

Linda Gibson, M.A., CPRW • Career Helm, LLC • www.careerhelm.com

Guidelines for Mid-Career Professionals

- **Professional Qualifications or Career Profile** (Summary). Begin your resume with a strong overview of the qualifications, achievements, expertise, and other knowledge you have that is unique, distinctive, and memorable.

- **Professional Experience or Employment Experience.** Detail your work experience—job titles, employers, locations, and dates. Briefly summarize your areas of responsibility and, most importantly, highlight the successes and achievements of each position.

   This is the most substantial section of the resume for most mid-career professionals, because your experience is typically your strongest qualification. Be certain readers understand what you've done and how valuable it has been.

- **Education.** List your degree, college/university, location, and distinguishing academic honors, along with relevant training, certifications, licenses, and other professional credentials. Don't waste space with details that don't matter (e.g., played lacrosse), but do include any truly distinguishing information from your academic career if you believe it will work to your advantage.

   High school no longer matters, unless fellow alumni can open doors for you in your job search.

Bradley Smith Resume—pages 9–10

Bradley's introduction is rich with relevant detail—a short Summary, followed by "Areas of Expertise" (keywords), then an impressive "Career Highlights" section that puts his most notable achievements smack in the center of the page. His Professional Experience includes more details of those "Highlights" and is the largest portion of the resume. Notice the Education section for someone who does *not* have a degree.

Guidelines for Senior Managers & Executives

- **Career Profile** (Summary). Use this part of the resume to position yourself, communicate who you are, and share your most distinctive and memorable career achievements.

- **Professional Experience.** For senior managers and executives, this section is the most extensive. Describe your experience—job titles, employers, locations, dates, and scope of responsibility.

   Most critically, highlight your achievements, focusing on the big-picture items … things you've done to improve the company and its operational and financial performance. Your achievements are what will set you apart from other talented senior managers and executives vying for the same positions.

- **Education.** List your degree, college/university, location, and distinguishing academic honors, along with relevant training, certifications, licenses, and other credentials. If you do not have a degree, consider omitting this section entirely.

   High school no longer matters, unless fellow alumni can open doors for you in your job search.

BRADLEY SMITH

Calgary, AB ▪ 403.555.1111 ▪ bradley.smith@shaw.ca

IT PROFESSIONAL ▪ INFRASTRUCTURE EXPERT ▪ TEAM LEADER

~ Supporting Staff Productivity through Inventive and Effective IT Solutions ~

Resourceful system and network professional who consistently improves system performance to remove IT obstacles for staff at all levels. Expert in balancing multiple priorities and conveying complex technical concepts and applications to end users. Proactive problem solver.

AREAS OF EXPERTISE

- ✓ Disaster Recovery Planning
- ✓ Application Support
- ✓ Process Reengineering
- ✓ Hardware Configurations
- ✓ VOIP
- ✓ IT Policy Development
- ✓ Customer Service
- ✓ Network Documentation
- ✓ Troubleshooting
- ✓ Equipment Upgrades
- ✓ Task Automation
- ✓ Service Desk Setup

CAREER HIGHLIGHTS

- **Launched disaster recovery site** in collaboration with third-party contractors; integrated use of storage replication, Vmware Site Recovery Manager, and Global Server Load Balancing.

- Automated level-one service desk tasks to **promote resolution of issues during initial call;** scripted frequent responses and provided training to team members.

- Managed 40+ Citrix Xenapp servers supporting 700+ users on 200+ virtual servers; configured system and **recommended upgrades to improve efficiencies.**

- Orchestrated fibre-optic installation to connect numerous municipal buildings, traffic lights, and water systems; **increased communication speeds and lowered operating costs.**

PROFESSIONAL EXPERIENCE

Urban Utilities – Calgary, AB   2017 – Present
NETWORK ADMINISTRATOR

Recruited to replace numerous contractor services including disaster recovery planning. Manage Cisco VOIP system and gateways including on-boarding, troubleshooting, and call quality. Document WAN network to improve issue resolution. Focus on promoting IT as critical resource in overall company structure.

- Achieved best practices of Nimble Storage in Netapp cluster replacement; reviewed guidelines to improve efficiency and time management.
- Initiated planning phase of 10 gigabyte networking equipment upgrade; provided details of increased capacity benefits to sustain company growth.

Customers:
250 Users

Position Tasks:
Disaster Recovery
VOIP System
WAN Network
Network Upgrades
F5 Big-IP Equipment

Jennifer Miller, CPRW, CRS, CARW • Professional Edge Resumes • www.professionaledgeresumes.com

PROFESSIONAL EXPERIENCE CONTINUED

Factor Group – Airdrie, AB   2014 – 2017
SYSTEMS ADMINISTRATOR

Managed 40+ Citrix Xenapp servers and 200 virtual servers; supported Dynamics NAV for subsidiary company by providing backend troubleshooting. Investigated potential technologies, including HP blade centres and Nimble storage, for datacentre refresh.

Customers:
750 Users

Position Tasks:
Citrix Xenapp Servers
Disaster Recovery
Datacentre Updates
Equipment Upgrades
Help Desk Setup

- Partnered with networking team and infrastructure staff during 10 gigabyte Cisco Nexus 6000 series project.
- Provided support to Town of Airdrie municipal groups during June 2013 floods; managed servers and networking equipment.
- Coordinated Netapp storage systems in production and disaster recovery; implemented Citrix Netscalers and Vmware SRM for disaster planning.

Town of Leduc and Town of Devon – Leduc, AB   2012 – 2014
NETWORK ADMINISTRATOR

Monitored and maintained physical and virtual servers; managed networking equipment including firewalls, switches, and wireless access points. Assessed IBM i5/OS system for company ERP system; configured MS Dynamics GP and Worktech Systems for finance and accounting systems.

Customers:
300 Users

Position Tasks:
Server Management
Network Equipment
ERP System
VOIP
IT Projects

- Implemented VOIP for Town of Leduc, generating $5K savings annually.
- Introduced IT service desk function that improved tracking of inquiries and eliminated duplication of efforts by IT staff.
- Directed wireless WAN project connecting town buildings; improved communication between buildings prior to full fibre-optic project.

Poseidon Energy – Edmonton, AB   2008 – 2012
INFRASTRUCTURE SUPPORT ANALYST

Managed MS Active Directory, Exchange 2003, UNIX-based systems, and in-house datacentre infrastructure – HVAC, UPS, and third-party contractors. Helped manage physical server and Vmware virtual server.

- Conducted migration from Solaris to Oracle RDBMS; purchased, planned, and configured IBM hardware and software during 4-month / $2.3M project.

EDUCATION, CERTIFICATIONS, AND TRAINING

Network Administration Diploma – Northern Alberta Institute of Technology, Edmonton, AB

Microsoft Certified Systems Engineer (MCSE) ▪ CompTIA A+ ▪ CompTIA Linux+ ▪ CompTIA Network+
ITIL Foundations ▪ Sun Certified Systems Administrator (SCSA)

Select Training:
Essentials 201 ▪ Citrix XenApp 6.5 Advanced Administration ▪ Citrix Netscaler Essentials and Networking
Certified Cisco Network Administrator Boot Camp ▪ AIX Systems Administration Problem Management
System Administrator Solaris 10 OS ▪ Netbackup 5.x for UNIX Administration

Matthew Marsh Resume—pages 12–13

For this senior executive, the Summary section accurately identifies his executive level and areas of expertise. It's followed by the Professional Experience section which is appropriately the longest, richest, and most detailed. Many of the achievements are quantified, and the chart on page 1 is powerful and eye-catching. The resume is formatted to include a lot of text in an easily readable presentation. Notice that his earliest positions are just briefly listed, without details, to show his full career history.

Additional Sections—For Your Consideration

Many people have "bits and pieces" of information that don't quite fit into any of the major resume sections. Depending on your unique circumstances, you might find it beneficial to add categories so that you can clearly and fully present your distinguishing and relevant details.

- **Technology Qualifications or Technology Profile.** If you're a hands-on tech professional, demonstrate your technical proficiency by listing your technical qualifications in detail.

- **Honors & Awards—Publications—Public Speaking.** All 3 of these categories represent third-party endorsements of your expertise and are valuable additions to most any resume. Create a separate section for each, integrate into your Summary, or add to the appropriate work or school listing.

- **Project Profile.** If you work in a profession where projects are the mainstay, or if you're a consultant, be certain to include your most notable projects—the name of the project, scope of work, project partners, budgets, and results. You can do this in a separate section or integrate with your jobs.

- **Professional Affiliations.** Your involvement with professional associations relevant to your industry can be extremely valuable. Be sure to mention any leadership roles, committees, or achievements.

- **Community Leadership & Memberships.** These items can be a nice addition to your resume, particularly if you're looking to remain in the same geographic region. Include any leadership roles, committees, achievements, or other notable activities.

- **Languages.** If you speak, read, or write multiple languages, prominently showcase them— particularly if you're looking for a job where they will be important. Mention your language skills in the Summary, for instant recognition, or create a separate Languages section.

- **Personal Profile.** US residents, do not include personal information such as marital status or number of children on your resume, and don't list "interests" if they are not distinguishing. Outside the US, follow the customary rules for the country in which you live or work.

Sometimes, however, select bits of personal information may be valuable—they add a whole new dimension about you and are great points of conversation during interviews. Keep these items brief, as they are extras rather than core qualifications.

MATTHEW MARSH

Englewood, NJ 07631| 201.555.4444 | MMarsh@gmail.com | www.linkedin.com/in/MattMarsh

EXECUTIVE MANAGEMENT

HEALTHCARE | SENIOR SERVICES | NON-PROFIT

KEY AREAS OF EXPERTISE

Restructuring & Revitalization

Joint Ventures & Alliances

Business Development

Negotiations

Startups & Turnarounds

Strategic Planning & Branding

Employee & Labor Relations

Financial Analysis & P&L

Hands-on Director with an empathetic approach to the population served and advocate for the employees needed to deliver high-quality care.

Change Agent with proven history of increasing profitability, rescuing faltering organizations, and find innovative solutions to complex issues.

Business Partner who excels at building collaborative, cross-functional relationships that improve healthcare outcomes, enhance customer experience, and drive up annual profit margins.

Innovative and Compassionate Leader with 20+ years of experience in highly competitive and diligently regulated industries.

CAREER HISTORY

Patterson Healthcare System, Patterson, NJ   2014 to Present
Community-based healthcare provider and continuing care retirement community.
***Total Beds/Units:** 650 |* ***Combined Budget:** $28M |* ***Employees:** 600*
EXECUTIVE VICE PRESIDENT, SENIOR SERVICES
Oversee total operations for Patterson Healthcare. Recruited during leadership transition as organization sought a change agent with strong, strategic, and visionary thinking. Pioneered initiatives to break down silos between senior communities and medical center.

- Propelled Patterson's revenue by $700K in 2017 by conceiving and executing Senior Services post-acute strategic plan that included recognizing need for additional sub-acute beds, a more defined referral process, and better integration of support and clinical services.

- Created system strategy for affiliation with VNA Health Group. Affiliation resulted in the following:

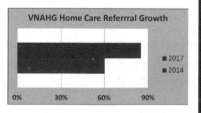

  ⇨ Secured $80K grant from Center for Medicare & Medicaid for nurse coaches to assist patients through continuum of care transition.

  ⇨ Ensured acute care discharges were seen at home within 24 hours.

  ⇨ Increased Visiting Nurses Association Health Group (VNAHG) home care referrals from 60% to 85% in first 3 years of affiliation.

- Led task force in forming Geriatric Fellowship Program in concert with Princeton Medical School. To date, program has graduated 14 fellowship doctors.

Michelle Riklan, ACRW, CPRW, CEIC, CJSS • Riklan Resources • www.riklanresources.com

MATTHEW MARSH | 201.555.4444 | MMarsh@gmail.com | Page 2 of 2

Kaiser Foundation Hospital of New Jersey, Cherry Hill, NJ · 2003 to 2014
NJ-based hospital and part of multiple non-profit health systems providing a continuum of care.
Total employees: *400* | ***Overall Budget:*** *$30M*
PRESIDENT / CHIEF EXECUTIVE OFFICER
Hired to turn around underperforming institution. Initial initiatives included addressing major deficit spending, improving quality of care, revitalizing fundraising, and determining long- term strategy and direction.

- Developed strategic plan and gained consensus from Board of Trustees to downsize from 290 to 220 beds.

- Hired new nursing management team and implemented new quality assurance program. Combined efforts slashed annual NJ Department of Health and Senior Services survey from 15 deficiencies to zero.

- Reduced annual deficit $850K in fiscal year 2008 and $1M in 2011 by reengineering staffing patterns in all departments and reducing overall supply expenses by 5%.

- Increased inpatient sub-acute days 12% by strengthening admissions and marketing departments and streamlining referral process.

- Directed launch of $12M capital campaign in collaboration with Board of Trustees and fundraising consultant. Generated $1.5M in donations through active solicitation of key donor and board contacts.

South Jersey Health System, Ocean, NJ · 1998 to 2003
Integrated delivery system comprising 3 acute care hospitals.
Total beds: *180* | ***Overall Budget:*** *$15M*
SENIOR VICE PRESIDENT, SENIOR SERVICES
Recruited to lead newly formed Senior Service division, a joint effort with 2 hospital systems, and to develop 3 skilled nursing facilities. Merged 2 divergent cultures.

- Oversaw design, construction, policies, budgeting, hiring, regulatory process, and approval to ensure timely implementation of 14-bed, hospital-based, sub-acute unit.

- Consolidated 2 health care systems' senior programs into a single 8000-member organization.

- Integrated acute care rehabilitation department into both outpatient and post-acute services. Process resulted in expense reduction by eliminating use of outside rehab agencies in post-acute setting.

VICE PRESIDENT, SENIOR SERVICES, Northern Jersey Health System, Bergen, NJ

VICE PRESIDENT, OPERATIONS, Little Silver Community Health Services, Little Silver, NJ

ADMINISTRATOR, Southern State Community Health Services, Atlantic City, NJ

PROFESSIONAL ASSOCIATIONS

Board Member, New Jersey Association of Non-Profit Homes (5 years)
American Hospital Association – Long-Term Care & Rehabilitation Governance Council (3 years)
Joint Commission on Accreditation of Healthcare Organizations – Advisory Council (4 years)
New Jersey Hospital Association – Long-Term Care Advisory Committee (9 years)

EDUCATION AND LICENSES

Master of Public Administration, Hofstra University, Hempstead, NY
Bachelor of Arts, Health Education—Minor: Public Administration, Rutgers University, New Brunswick, NJ
Licensed Nursing Home Administrator – New Jersey and New York

The Great Date Debate

Should you include dates on your resume? In most cases, yes. Dates help tell your story and show the progression of your career.

But sometimes, depending on your age, your experience history, and your current career objective, the question is not so straightforward. Let's take a few minutes to discuss several scenarios:

- **You don't want to appear old.** For job seekers 50+, age discrimination is a concern. To show your experience but *not* your precise age, briefly summarize your earliest career experiences *without* dates. If you choose this approach, be certain to also omit your date of college graduation.

- **You don't want to highlight lengthy unemployment.** Instead of using dates, use number of years—for example, "7 years" instead of 1995–2002. Employers will guess that you're currently not working, but you've still communicated that impressive 7 years of employment experience.

- **You want to bring prior experience to the forefront.** Let's say you're making a career switch back to something you did years ago, and your more recent jobs are unrelated. Position that great prior experience prominently—in a Related Experience section that comes before other Professional Experience. If you do that, either omit dates entirely or use the years-only technique.

- **You've heard it's best to delete graduation date.** Sometimes that's true, but be careful that you are not inadvertently aging yourself. Let's say you graduated in 1995 and deleted that year from your Education. Yet you began working that same year—1995—and included that date. Readers will assume there *is* a gap and that you are older than you are or you would have included your graduation date. In that case, include year of graduation *or* summarize early positions without dates.

- **You want to fit in with an older or younger crowd.** Are you targeting startup high-tech companies? Youth is an asset! In other jobs and industries, you don't want to appear young and immature. Understand the culture of the organizations and industries you're interested in, and use the date strategy that positions you appropriately for that audience.

There are no definitive rules about when to use dates and when not. It will depend on your career, the number of years you've been working, your employment history, your college graduation year, and the types of positions you're currently pursuing.

Of course, you should never lie. But neither do you have to bare all. Create the right perception by choosing the best information that supports your current objective.

PRO TIP: In most cases, months don't matter. As a general rule, include years of employment and education. Readers want to see the progression of your career, from one position to another, and the dates make that clean and simple. But don't waste space with months—it's not essential at this point.

In some cases, though, short-term jobs are the norm. For example:

- You're a graduating student with several part-time jobs and internships.
- You're a young professional and are showing a combination of part-time jobs during college and permanent employment since graduation.
- You're an independent contractor with a variety of projects and assignments that overlap and/ or take up only a few months.

If you find that including the months tells a more cohesive story, by all means do so. Make the decision that presents your information in the clearest and most beneficial way for you.

The Modern Resume: Principles in Action

In the chapters that follow we will introduce you to 18 core concepts and share more than 90 resume samples to help you create your own modern resume. As an introduction to everything you'll learn, let's begin with an illustration of how a traditional resume was rewritten, reformatted, and redesigned to align with today's principles that guide modern resume writing.

Peter Belton Resumes—pages 16–17

Look at Peter's "before" resume. By today's standards, it is outdated in both content and appearance:

- He's used a small size in a font (Times New Roman) that is old-school and has been widely overused.
- The resume starts with a Career Objective rather than a Summary.
- At first glance, he appears to be a job hopper—the resume lists 7 distinct jobs. But in fact he has had a very stable and progressive work history with only 2 companies.
- The content is repetitive because so many of his jobs entailed the same responsibilities.
- Peter's email address link is not live, making it impossible for employers to click and connect.

Look at page 17 and you'll see Peter's new, modern resume. You'll notice:

- It includes live links (email and LinkedIn) but does not include a home address—an increasing trend.
- It starts with a powerful Summary that lets employers know exactly what Peter can do for them.
- You can immediately see that Peter has worked for only 2 companies. Job titles are stacked so that you can visually see the progression of his career. The description of overall responsibilities is very short, and bullet points highlight his notable achievements.
- In the Education section, all of the information is on 1 line, and we've included something important he overlooked in his original version—the fact that he was a *cum laude* graduate.
- The visual presentation is much more distinctive and modern.

Before

PETER R. BELTON
10023 Belle River Road, Apt 614, Jacksonville, Florida 33821
(904) 316-9158 * petebelton@msn.com

Career Objective: Position in inventory planning and management with a leading retailer offering opportunities for long-term career planning and advancement.

Professional Experience:

Assistant General Manager and Branch Manager   2018 to Present
Grayson's Furniture Stores, Jacksonville, Florida

Manage a retail sales organization with more than 160 employees at 6 retail stores that produce $35 million a year in sales. Duties include sales, merchandising, advertising, public relations, customer service and satisfaction, profits, product management, merchandising, and all staffing, training and leadership functions. Helped owners redesign purchasing operations, get new suppliers and reduce supply costs by 3.5%.
--Won 2 general manager of the year awards for meeting goals.
--Implemented new computer technology for managing inventory.
--Improved staffing and cut absence rates by 47% and turnover by 35%.
--Sales grew by up to 40% and profits improved by 31%.

Branch Manager   2018
Grayson's Furniture Stores, Charlotte, North Carolina
Managed a large retail store with $12 million in annual sales and 28 employees. Responsible for all store operations, sales, hiring, training, firing, customer service, merchandising, product display, daily accounting and business recordkeeping. Helped regional management to make business decisions on acquiring computer technology, opening new stores and expanding product lines. Won 5 branch manager of the month awards.

Branch Manager   2015 to 2018
Grayson's Furniture Stores, Fayetteville, North Carolina
Managed daily operations of a retail store with $7 million in yearly sales. Same responsibilities as above. Winner of 6 branch manager of the month awards.

Branch Manager   2015
Grayson's Furniture Stores, Durham, North Carolina
Same responsibilities as above for store with $4 million in sales. Earned 1 branch manager award.

Assistant Manager   2014 to 2015
Grayson's Furniture Stores, Newport News, Virginia
Assisted in managing retail store with $7 million in annual sales. Allocated merchandise to maximize square footage with plan-o-grams and market data.

Floating Manager   2011 to 2014
Boater's World, Virginia & Maryland
Managed 13 stores in Maryland and Virginia with 150 employees. Responsible for sales, profits, operations, merchandising, purchasing, distribution, customer service, training and team leadership. Was #4 in sales production out of 214 people and won 3 top sales awards. Introduced new safety product that sold $2 million in a year.

Assistant Manager   2010 to 2011
Boater's World, Newport News, Virginia
Assisted in managing specialty retail operation with 14 employees. Responsible for sales, customer service, product display, store operations and daily store closings.

Education:

Bachelor of Arts Degree in Biology, 2010
University of Virginia, Charlottesville, Virginia

After

PETER R. BELTON

petebelton@msn.com   904-316-9158   linkedin.com/in/peterbelton

RETAIL INDUSTRY MANAGER

Director of Inventory Planning & Management • Branch Manager
9 Years in Progressive Roles with Large Regional Chains • Financial Responsibility to $35M

Merchandise Planning & Allocation	Multi-Site Retail Operations
Inventory Planning & Control	Merchandise Markdowns & Allowances
Vendor Relations & Negotiations	Inventory Shrinkage Control & Management
Financial Planning & Profit Analysis	Employee Training, Development & Leadership

PROFESSIONAL EXPERIENCE

GRAYSON'S FURNITURE STORES   2014–Present

Assistant General Manager/Branch Manager *($35M sales/year),* Jacksonville, FL (2018–Present)
Branch Manager *($12M sales/year),* Charlotte, NC (2018)
Branch Manager *($7M sales/year),* Fayetteville, NC (2015–2018)
Branch Manager *($4M sales/year),* Durham, NC (2015)
Assistant Manager *($7M sales/year),* Newport News, VA (2014–2015)

Promoted rapidly through a series of increasingly responsible management positions based on strong financial, operating, team building, and team leadership performance. Currently manage 160+ employees at 6 regional locations. Notable achievements:

- **Won 14 "Branch Manager of the Month"** and **"General Manager of the Year"** awards for profit and revenue growth.
- Achieved record sales in multiple markets (up to **40% sales growth** and **31% margin increase**).
- **Reduced absenteeism 47% and turnover 35%** with strategies to recruit, train, and retain high-quality employees.
- Implemented **next-generation POS technology. Reduced annual purchasing costs 3.5%.**

BOATER'S WORLD   2010–2014

Floating Manager *(13-store district with 150 employees),* VA/MD Regional District (2011–2014)
Assistant Manager, Newport News, VA (2010–2011)

- **Received 3 "Top Sales Producer"** awards. **Ranked #4 out of 214** sales associates nationwide.
- Launched new safety product in response to regulatory requirements and **sold $2M in first year.**
- Drove sales growth through a strong focus on customer service, merchandising, and teamwork.

EDUCATION

Bachelor of Arts, Cum Laude, 2010 • University of Virginia, Charlottesville, VA

TECHNOLOGY SKILLS

Proficient in Excel, Word, Citrix, Lotus Notes, Bosanova, Fullshot, and Datamatix.

Wendy Enelow, MRW, CCM, CPRW, JCTC • Enelow Enterprises, Inc. • www.wendyenelow.com

Resume Mindset

Now that we've covered the structural fundamentals, it's time to address another vitally important aspect of resume writing and job search: your *mindset.*

A positive mindset is one of the most important assets you bring to the challenge of making a career move, helping you to:

- Focus on the value you bring to your next employer and *not* on any perceived imperfections in your background and qualifications.
- Put yourself in hiring managers' shoes and know how you can help them be more successful.
- Handle the inevitable ups and downs of job search with grace and good humor.
- Accept that you were not chosen for a position without thinking of yourself as a failure.
- Persist when you don't see an end in sight.

> **PRO TIP: In our experience, all too many job seekers focus on the negatives.** They worry about current unemployment, or past job gaps, or lack of the *right* education or credentials. Certainly, some situations present challenges, but they are almost never insurmountable!

In this book, we recommend solutions and strategies for developing a great resume. We always focus on making the most of everything that you have to offer to a new employer. What's more, you can use our recommendations throughout your entire job search by following these strategies for building a positive, confident, and forward-thinking mindset.

- **Think about what you *do* have, not what you don't.** Make your resume all about your assets—your value, contributions, and achievements. Prepare and practice your success stories for use in your resume and during interviews. (Refer to the Career Vault, page 228, for more on success stories.)

- **Match your value to employers' needs.** How will you aid your next employer? Approach resume writing and interviewing from the viewpoint of "I'm here to help." Being helpful makes us feel valuable and in control, and that translates to confidence in the job search and the workplace.

- **Know why you're a great fit for a specific role.** Learn as much as you can about the job, the company, and the industry, and be able to clearly express how your specific skills and experiences fit the need. It's easier to focus on the positives when you really know—and can address—what's involved.

- **Recognize that all candidates have drawbacks.** Guess what: There's no such thing as a perfect candidate! It's easy to fall into the trap of thinking that "everyone else" is more qualified than you. Companies hire candidates who can help them *now,* and they weigh the pluses and minuses of each candidate. Why shouldn't they choose you?

- **Understand "fit factor."** A lot of hiring decisions are based on fit, which is hard to define but easy to feel. Even when you're an ideal candidate, you might not get the job because someone else just fit better into that company's culture. It's outside your control, so accept it and move on.

- **Deal with your demons.** Believe it or not, much of what you might worry endlessly about ends up being a minor point in your job search. Nonetheless, you must be prepared to address it during the interview and hiring process. Put together a plan and prepare a response to whatever might come up. You'll worry less and be much more confident.

Personal Branding & Resume Writing

A current, high-profile trend in resume writing is personal branding. Simply stated, a branded resume tells an interview-attracting story of qualification and success while demonstrating passion, personality, work style, leadership style, and other unique characteristics. It's a bold way of stating definitively—*THIS IS WHO I AM*.

A branded resume generally starts with a strong branding statement at the very beginning. This statement, in conjunction with the headline, communicates your unique value proposition in such a way that it's clear, concise, and recognizable to every recruiter, hiring manager, and decision maker.

Here are 3 examples of resume headlines with their accompanying branding statements:

Information Technology Director

Advancing strategic business goals in a fast-paced marketplace by delivering agile, flexible technology that is highly responsive to user needs.

CHIEF EXECUTIVE OFFICER

Growth Catalyst • Market Strategist • Consummate Relationship Builder • Value Creator

---

RETAIL EXECUTIVE—*Building Multi-State Retail Enterprises that Blow Away the Competition*

> **PRO TIP: Even if you don't start with a specific branding statement, you will still create a branded resume.** Every modern resume is branded because it powerfully communicates *who* you are, *how* you're unique and distinguishable from other candidates, and *why* a company should hire you.

For examples of well-branded resumes, you can look at every single resume sample in this book!

In general, the personal brand of each individual that is announced at the top of the page is reinforced and supported in every other section of the resume. The theme is consistent: This is who I am, what I'm good at, and why you can believe me. This is how I do things and what makes me different from—and better than—other candidates.

Your resume, too, will be clearly branded if you follow our guidelines for resume Content, Format, and Design in Parts II, III, and IV. You'll create your own modern resume with a strong brand that is clearly recognizable, and you will outpace your competition!

Next Steps

Now that you've dipped a toe into the world of modern resume writing, it's time to plunge in wholeheartedly so you can move forward with your job search.

Parts II, III, and IV will guide you through modern resume Content, Format, and Design. The lessons we share about the core resume-development principles, combined with the resume samples, will inspire you to create your own powerful resume so that you will *get noticed and get hired!*

PART II:
Modernize Your Resume Content

The 6 Principles of Modern Resume Content
- **Start with the Wow!**
- **Put Your Objective in the Driver's Seat**
- **Write with Meaning & Power**
- **Write Tight, Lean & Clean**
- **Leave the Muscle, Lose the Fat**
- **Integrate Your Critical Keywords**

A great resume starts with great content. No matter how visually dazzling or neatly structured, no resume will help you achieve your goals unless it communicates your value in the workplace to recruiters, employers, and other decision makers.

One reason that resume writing is so challenging is that most people don't do it very often! You might put together a new resume when you enter the workforce and then every 2 to 5 years when you are looking for a new job. Like anything else, practice improves skill, and the reality is that most people don't get that much practice.

We're here to help. In the following pages you'll learn how to write strong resume content that showcases you—your skills, qualifications, notable achievements, work experience, educational credentials, and all of the other tangible and intangible assets you bring to the employment marketplace.

> **PRO TIP: All of our content principles and guidelines are valuable for everyone**—from the senior executive to the graduating student, from the career changer to the return-to-work mom or dad, from the classroom teacher to the global sales associate, and virtually every other profession, industry, and job search challenge or situation.

We'll teach you what professional resume writers do and we'll show you how we do it so you can apply the 6 Principles of Modern Resume Content to create your own great resume.

CHAPTER 2:
Start with the Wow!

What is the wow? It's what's most impressive, important, and valuable about you as a candidate— the top few things that you want readers to instantly know about you, so they'll be impressed, interested, and eager to learn more.

Your unique "wow factor" information distinguishes you from others with similar skills and qualifications. Be sure to prominently position it on your resume so readers can't possibly miss it and you create an instantly positive first impression.

To clearly demonstrate the difference between the wow and the not-so-wow, here are 2 examples:

> **Not-So-Wow:**
> *Responsible for turning around stagnant sales region and returning it to profitability.*
>
> **Wow:**
> *Grew sales by $34M in first year, a 220% increase over prior year.*
>
> **Not-So-Wow:**
> *Wrote software programs and applications for new technology releases.*
>
> **Wow:**
> *Pioneered next-generation technology architecture for Microsoft's newest suite of laptops.*

As you can see, wow statements are specific—they tell what *you* did, not what someone with a similar job might have done. They make your resume (and you) memorable, and that's step #1 to getting interviewed and hired.

Wow content can go virtually anywhere in your resume, including the following sections:

Summary. When you add wow statements to your Summary, you're starting with your best foot forward. In just a glance, readers will quickly learn what you have accomplished.

Tips for including wow statements in your Summary:
- Limit your items to 3–4. If you have too many, you diminish the impact that you are trying to create.
- Or use just 1 "big wow" and position it right at the top of your resume, either above or below the headline that boldly states *who* you are.

- Try to keep your wow statements to 1 line if possible. Fewer words draw more attention.
- Save details for later. Your wow statement is a "quick hit" of impressive information. If it needs more explanation (and if it's a major career success story, likely it will), you can expand on the achievement in the appropriate section of your resume.

Experience. In most resumes, each position description begins with a summary of job responsibilities. That's important information, of course—but it's not the most interesting.

Instead, consider starting each job description with the #1 achievement of that job. When you do that, you communicate an instant message of success. You can then follow the wow with a brief description of your job responsibilities and other achievements of that position.

Education. If you're a recent college graduate with limited work experience, your education section becomes the showpiece of your resume. Make sure that you wow your readers by highlighting what it is that makes you a uniquely qualified young professional—perhaps your notable academic performance, leadership activities, special projects, internships, or volunteer work.

Honors & Awards. Distinguishing honors and awards are a great enhancement to your wow factor. They can be listed in a separate category—either near the beginning of your resume or at the end; they can be integrated into the Summary—with an "Honors and Awards" subheading; they can be integrated into the jobs where you won them; or they can be highlighted in Education.

Other wow information that may be relevant to some job seekers includes publications, board-of-director affiliations, media mentions, public-speaking engagements, patents … anything that tells readers you are an expert in your field, recognized by your peers, and valued for your contributions and accomplishments. As with honors and awards, this information can be included in separate sections or integrated into your Summary, Experience, or Education.

> **PRO TIP: Ask yourself these questions to help uncover your wow items:**
> - When have I been *first* or *best?*
> - What is the #1 thing I achieved in each position?
> - When did I help turn a failure into a success?
> - Which of my achievements have the most impressive numbers?
> - What have I been publicly recognized for?
> - What major business successes have I contributed to?

Following are 2 great examples of resumes that clearly exemplify the start-with-the-wow technique. The moment you start reading, you're instantly drawn in and impressed with the success of both job seekers.

Sally Clairborne Resume—pages 26–27

Sally's resume includes a number of wow factors that create an immediately positive first impression that is reinforced by the strong content throughout this resume:

- A bold graphic at the top immediately signals that Sally is in the healthcare field.
- The branding statement underneath her headline highlights her success in "practice transformation."
- Shaded boxes set off her summary and concise job descriptions, creating immediate visual distinction between sections.
- Attention-getting headings are set in reverse (white) type in a bold black box.
- Bullet points in the summary and in the experience section are introduced with bold type that draws attention to her expertise and achievements.
- The strong visual impression from page 1 carries over to page 2, where a graphic illustrates her related technical achievements.

Tricia Officer Resume—page 28

Tricia's resume uses several "wow" techniques to capture and maintain each reader's interest:

- A headline instantly describes her as an "Award-Winning Sales Executive."
- An endorsement from her prior manager provides a third-party testimonial to her success.
- The "Career Highlights and Awards" section draws maximum attention to the many times she stood out from her peers.
- A powerful "Revenue Growth" graphic captures the eye and reinforces achievements (numbers) that are highlighted in bold in the bullet points.

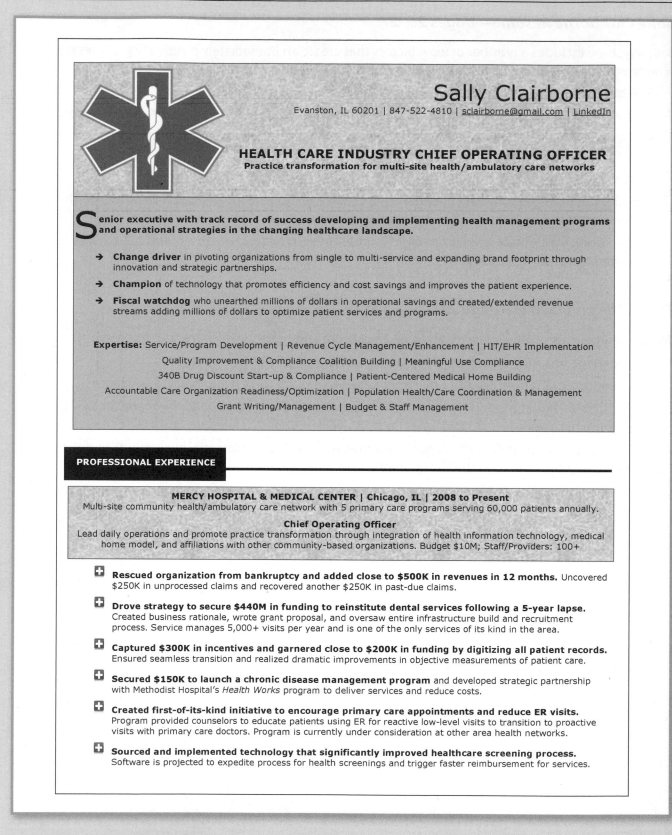

Sally Clairborne

Evanston, IL 60201 | 847-522-4810 | sclairborne@gmail.com | LinkedIn

HEALTH CARE INDUSTRY CHIEF OPERATING OFFICER
Practice transformation for multi-site health/ambulatory care networks

Senior executive with track record of success developing and implementing health management programs and operational strategies in the changing healthcare landscape.

→ **Change driver** in pivoting organizations from single to multi-service and expanding brand footprint through innovation and strategic partnerships.

→ **Champion** of technology that promotes efficiency and cost savings and improves the patient experience.

→ **Fiscal watchdog** who unearthed millions of dollars in operational savings and created/extended revenue streams adding millions of dollars to optimize patient services and programs.

Expertise: Service/Program Development | Revenue Cycle Management/Enhancement | HIT/EHR Implementation
Quality Improvement & Compliance Coalition Building | Meaningful Use Compliance
340B Drug Discount Start-up & Compliance | Patient-Centered Medical Home Building
Accountable Care Organization Readiness/Optimization | Population Health/Care Coordination & Management
Grant Writing/Management | Budget & Staff Management

PROFESSIONAL EXPERIENCE

MERCY HOSPITAL & MEDICAL CENTER | Chicago, IL | 2008 to Present
Multi-site community health/ambulatory care network with 5 primary care programs serving 60,000 patients annually.

Chief Operating Officer
Lead daily operations and promote practice transformation through integration of health information technology, medical home model, and affiliations with other community-based organizations. Budget $10M; Staff/Providers: 100+

➕ **Rescued organization from bankruptcy and added close to $500K in revenues in 12 months.** Uncovered $250K in unprocessed claims and recovered another $250K in past-due claims.

➕ **Drove strategy to secure $440M in funding to reinstitute dental services following a 5-year lapse.** Created business rationale, wrote grant proposal, and oversaw entire infrastructure build and recruitment process. Service manages 5,000+ visits per year and is one of the only services of its kind in the area.

➕ **Captured $300K in incentives and garnered close to $200K in funding by digitizing all patient records.** Ensured seamless transition and realized dramatic improvements in objective measurements of patient care.

➕ **Secured $150K to launch a chronic disease management program** and developed strategic partnership with Methodist Hospital's *Health Works* program to deliver services and reduce costs.

➕ **Created first-of-its-kind initiative to encourage primary care appointments and reduce ER visits.** Program provided counselors to educate patients using ER for reactive low-level visits to transition to proactive visits with primary care doctors. Program is currently under consideration at other area health networks.

➕ **Sourced and implemented technology that significantly improved healthcare screening process.** Software is projected to expedite process for health screenings and trigger faster reimbursement for services.

AWARD WINNER
Modernize Your Resume Contest

Barbara Safani, NCRW, CPRW, CERW, CCM • Career Solvers • www.careersolvers.com

Sally Clairborne | 847-522-4810 | sclairborne@gmail.com | Page 2

METHODIST HOSPITAL OF CHICAGO | Chicago, IL | 2005 to 2008
$110M, 24-site ambulatory care network managing 500,000 patient encounters annually.

Assistant Vice President, Ambulatory Care Division
Planned, developed, and delivered enterprise-wide strategic initiatives. Designed, organized, and implemented new programs and services to increase access to care and achieve organizational growth objectives. Key advisor to senior administration on operational initiatives and regulatory compliance. Budget: $110M

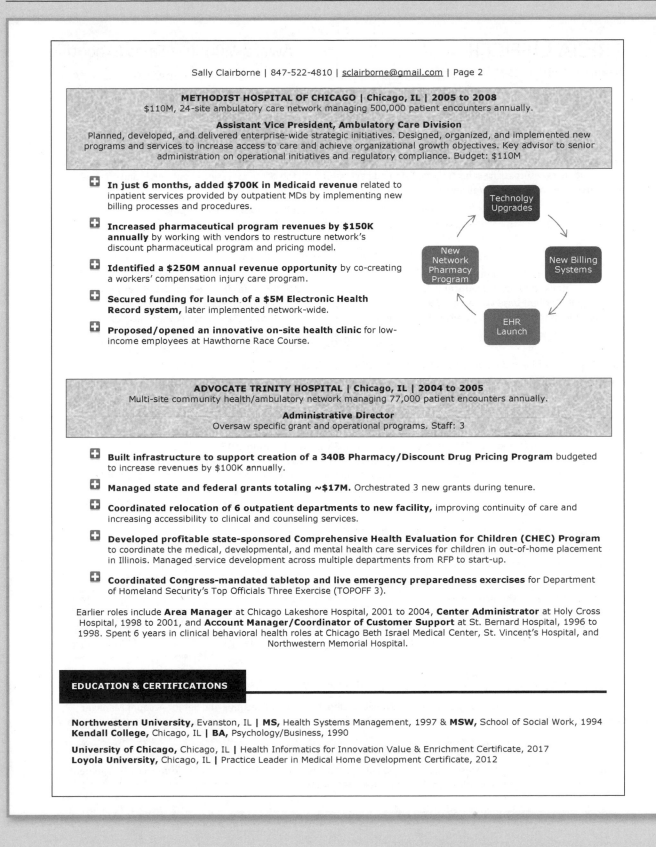

➕ **In just 6 months, added $700K in Medicaid revenue** related to inpatient services provided by outpatient MDs by implementing new billing processes and procedures.

➕ **Increased pharmaceutical program revenues by $150K annually** by working with vendors to restructure network's discount pharmaceutical program and pricing model.

➕ **Identified a $250M annual revenue opportunity** by co-creating a workers' compensation injury care program.

➕ **Secured funding for launch of a $5M Electronic Health Record system,** later implemented network-wide.

➕ **Proposed/opened an innovative on-site health clinic** for low-income employees at Hawthorne Race Course.

ADVOCATE TRINITY HOSPITAL | Chicago, IL | 2004 to 2005
Multi-site community health/ambulatory network managing 77,000 patient encounters annually.

Administrative Director
Oversaw specific grant and operational programs. Staff: 3

➕ **Built infrastructure to support creation of a 340B Pharmacy/Discount Drug Pricing Program** budgeted to increase revenues by $100K annually.

➕ **Managed state and federal grants totaling ~$17M.** Orchestrated 3 new grants during tenure.

➕ **Coordinated relocation of 6 outpatient departments to new facility,** improving continuity of care and increasing accessibility to clinical and counseling services.

➕ **Developed profitable state-sponsored Comprehensive Health Evaluation for Children (CHEC) Program** to coordinate the medical, developmental, and mental health care services for children in out-of-home placement in Illinois. Managed service development across multiple departments from RFP to start-up.

➕ **Coordinated Congress-mandated tabletop and live emergency preparedness exercises** for Department of Homeland Security's Top Officials Three Exercise (TOPOFF 3).

Earlier roles include **Area Manager** at Chicago Lakeshore Hospital, 2001 to 2004, **Center Administrator** at Holy Cross Hospital, 1998 to 2001, and **Account Manager/Coordinator of Customer Support** at St. Bernard Hospital, 1996 to 1998. Spent 6 years in clinical behavioral health roles at Chicago Beth Israel Medical Center, St. Vincent's Hospital, and Northwestern Memorial Hospital.

EDUCATION & CERTIFICATIONS

Northwestern University, Evanston, IL | **MS,** Health Systems Management, 1997 & **MSW,** School of Social Work, 1994
Kendall College, Chicago, IL | **BA,** Psychology/Business, 1990

University of Chicago, Chicago, IL | Health Informatics for Innovation Value & Enrichment Certificate, 2017
Loyola University, Chicago, IL | Practice Leader in Medical Home Development Certificate, 2012

TRICIA OFFICER

Award-Winning Sales Executive

Winston, FL 33815 | 313-575-1519 | tricia.officer@yahoo.com

www.linkedin.com/in/triciaofficer

*"Tricia relocated as Regional Sales Manager to take over an underperforming region … and delivered the **largest revenue growth** and the highest performance to quota, **exceeding quota every month.**"*

– Tyrone Williams, prior supervisor, Records Management Company

Tenacious revenue generator, #1 in the nation 2 years in a row by aggressively developing a continual pipeline of new clients and quickly surpassing sales targets. Talented negotiator with the gift of assessing client needs and offering viable solutions to secure the sale. Well versed in Salesforce, Word, PowerPoint, and Excel.

Strategic Relationship Building | Situational Fluency | Business Development
Market Expansion | Territory Development | Account Management

Career Highlights and Awards

Records Management Company	*Maximum Corp., Inc.*
Ranked #1 sales producer in US.	**Boosted sales from zero to $1.2M in 18 months.**
Built client base valued at $19.7M.	**8-time President's Club Winner.**
Counted in top third of company sales metrics.	**Sales Excellence Award Recipient.**

Career Progression

Director of Sales | Records Management Company, Miami, FL (2011 – 2013)

Managed team of 5 Account Managers and Sales Agents promoting multiple product lines, including data protection support, records management, and shredding services, across regional territory spanning Virginia to Florida. Persevered through multiple restructurings to instill focus and resilience among team, leading to consistent top results.

- Acknowledged as **#1** in country among 18 counterparts, 2011 and 2012, by achieving **112%** of goal.
- Built and maintained a **$9.2M** client portfolio with **2.93%** growth factor in 2013.
- Captured **$1.4M** in new sales (non-recurring) and **$547K** in recurring new sales revenue in 2012.
- Recognized as **#6** across the US in 2012 with quota attainment of **111%** and new sales revenue of **$1.9M.**
- Nurtured client accounts collectively valued at **$19.7M,** yielding a **2.5%** growth factor in 2012.
- Resurrected unfavorable terms and secured **$1.5M** contract with national hotel chain to service 684 locations.

VP of Sales, Southeast Region | Maximum Corp., Inc., Naples, FL (2008 – 2011)

Coached, led, and supervised 15 staff while identifying effective growth strategies and executing profitable marketing solutions to boost revenue at $150M print service bureau.

- Produced **$7.1M** in yearly sales, meeting firm goals with no additional staff despite severely shrinking market.
- Secured **$23M** in retention revenue and earned **#1** position of 5 Regional VPs.
- Generated **$4.3M** within 1 year, achieving **105%** of corporate objective.
- Drove sales from zero to **$1.2M** over 18 months by developing and managing new territory *(see adjacent chart).*

Early Career

Progressively promoted with Maximum Corp. from Billing Clerk to Account Executive and Senior Account Manager. Generated **$1.3M** in sales by targeting and capturing key accounts with industry leaders Equifax and South Bank.

Training & Development

Major Account Planning Process, Dale Carnegie Public Speaking, Solution Selling, High-Performance Management, Power Message Training, Challenger Methodology, Situational Fluency

Melanie Denny, CPRW, CIPCC • www.melaniedenny.com

CHAPTER 3:
Put Your Objective in the Driver's Seat

The #1 reason you're creating a resume is to position yourself for your next job. Of course, your work experience, achievements, education, and other qualifications are all critical resume building blocks, but *how* you include your information, *where*, and *why* should all be dictated by your current career goals.

When you know the jobs you want, you know what skills are in demand and what employers value most. That information becomes the foundation upon which you build your entire resume.

For some people, that's easy. If you're a sales representative looking for another sales opportunity, you can showcase your success in increasing sales revenues *(including numbers and percentages)*, capturing key accounts, launching products, building new markets, and all of the other sales functions of your job.

It becomes more challenging, however, when your current career goals don't directly align with your past experience. Let's suppose in your sales job you spent 20% of your time training new sales associates, and now you want to pursue jobs in training and development. That 20% becomes the primary focus of your resume, showcasing all of your relevant experience in training, mentoring, creating training materials, designing training programs, and performing related activities.

The other 80% … of course you'll include some or even most of that information, but it becomes secondary to all training-related experience and qualifications.

Your goal is to paint the picture of yourself that you want someone to see. You don't want to lie; you don't want to misrepresent. What you do want to do is put the focus where it belongs, minimize or omit what doesn't add value, and align your resume with your current career goals and aspirations.

> **PRO TIP: If you're not certain of your career objective, STOP!** To write a powerful and effective resume, you must have some idea of your job targets. Some options for honing in on a target:
>
> - Look at lots of job postings to find those that interest you the most and for which you have some related skills, experience, or educational qualifications.
>
> - Identify your top skills and interests, and then match them to available opportunities.
>
> - Consult a career coach, who can guide you through a process of career discovery and exploration.
>
> When you've defined your career objective (see page 227 for our Goal-Setting Worksheet in Part VII—Resources), you can move forward to create a well-targeted resume to help you achieve that goal.

Following are 3 approaches that will put your objective in the driver's seat:

- **Write to the future … to your next great job.** A resume is not an autobiographical retrospective (although it does include some of the same information). Rather, today's modern resume is a marketing tool designed to merchandise you as a strong candidate for the jobs you're pursuing.

- **Reweight your skills and experience.** The sales representative who now wants to transition into training and development is the perfect example of when to reweight skills, qualifications, experiences, educational credentials, and anything else you might include in your resume. Put the heaviest emphasis on the things that relate to your objective and the least emphasis on things that do not.

- **Integrate critical keywords.** We address this topic in greater detail in Chapter 7, but it deserves a brief mention here. Keywords are the foundation for all resume-scanning systems, so it is imperative that your resume contain essential keywords for the jobs and industries you are targeting. Using the same sales training example we just discussed, without enough of the right training-related keywords the resume will simply be passed over.

Summary vs. Objective Statement

The final point in this chapter is a discussion of the use of objective statements in today's modern resume.

Bottom line, we don't recommend Objectives for the vast majority of job seekers. When you include an Objective, you're telling employers what you want from them and, frankly, they don't care.

In today's resume, the Summary has largely replaced the Objective. In a Summary, you can tell employers what you can do for them, the value you bring to their organization, your strongest areas of expertise, and other information that should entice the reader to contact you. Instead of writing "this is what I want," you're communicating "this is what I can do for you"—a message that will resonate with employers.

But we don't dismiss objective statements entirely. In select circumstances they can be helpful, particularly for job seekers whose objectives will not be clear from their work experience, skills, or educational credentials. If that's the case, a clean and well-targeted Objective can add value and clarity to the resume:

Objective: Position in Purchasing & Supply Chain Management

With a glance, employers know what this candidate wants—and that's essential information.

> **PRO TIP: There is never an occasion to use an objective that says nothing of value.**
>
> *Seeking a position offering growth and long-term career development.*
>
> What's wrong with that Objective? It's not specific—it tells us nothing about what industry or profession the job seeker is targeting. And it's not employer focused—it says nothing about the value that person brings to a company. It's simply a waste of space.

As you'll see from the samples in this book, we believe a Summary is a stronger, more employer-focused way to begin your resume than the outdated Objective. But even when an "objective" is not overtly stated, in every case the job seeker's specific objective was in the driver's seat, steering the writer's decision-making around every element in the resume.

The following 2 resumes demonstrate this principle very effectively.

Marty Basso Resume—page 32

Marty's functional resume plays up his specific skills and experiences as they relate to his current objective: a position as a Trades Apprentice. His work history is presented very simply, with no details, to minimize the fact that he is returning to the building trades after a gap during which he performed other types of work and served a multi-year prison term.

Alex Rodman Resume—page 33

Your first thought when reviewing Alex's resume is that he is an experienced network administrator. Everything in the resume positions him for that specific goal. It is not until you read his employment section, at the very bottom of the page, that you learn he is actually a supply officer in the US Navy. Everything in the resume is 100% accurate—it simply reweights his network administrator experiences into the most prominent content on the resume, in line with his current career objective. Perfect!

Marty Basso

(860) 749-5611 – Hartford, CT - BassoM@email.com

TRADES APPRENTICE

Diligent Trade Worker offering more than 5 years' electrical and iron work experience in commercial, industrial, and residential settings. Reliable, dependable, and trustworthy.

Strong technical background; able to quickly learn new tasks and troubleshoot problems. Capable of performing in all conditions and environments including inside, outside, hot, cold, tight/narrow, and elevated worksites. Exceptional interpersonal skills; able to professionally interact with customers and work as a team.

Proficient with CAD software, security systems, automated systems, MS Word, Excel, and Adobe Illustrator.

SKILLS SUMMARY

Equipment Expertise		Areas of Strength	
➤ Voltage Meters	➤ Torches/Welders	➤ Equipment Operation	➤ Maintenance
➤ Wire Cutters	➤ Drills	➤ Diagnostics	➤ Blueprint Reading
➤ Benders	➤ Power Tools	➤ Wiring Circuits	➤ Low/High Voltage
➤ Hand Tools	➤ Measuring Devices	➤ Inventory Control	➤ Service Installs

VOCATIONAL EXPERIENCE

Electrical
- Measured, cut, bent, and installed metal and plastic conduits above ground and buried.
- Utilized voltage meters to troubleshoot short circuits and test amperages.
- Installed and wired switches (single, 3- and 4-way), outlets (interior, exterior, and GFCI), fixtures, appliances, safety devices, and equipment.
- Diagnosed and performed electrical repair on energized and non-energized circuits, including industrial high-voltage panels and residential service installations.
- Mounted panels, installed circuit breakers, ran homeruns, buried grounding rods, and labeled wires.

Iron Work
- Utilized welders, torches, grinding wheels, saws, and benders to work with iron.
- Operated lifts, jackhammers, cement mixer, pumps, and heavy vehicles (trucks).
- Designed custom fittings for residential and commercial projects.

General
- Performed work in basements, attics, rooftops, commercial, industrial, and residential settings.
- Maintained inventory by recording parts used and identifying parts needed.

EXPERIENCE

Maintenance Worker	*Garner Institution*, New London, CT	2016–2019
Electrical Apprentice	*Johnny Electric*, Groton, CT	2014–2016
Ironworker	*Roger Wrought Iron*, New London, CT	2010–2014

EDUCATION

3 Semesters of Electrical Apprenticeship, Valley Community College, Essex, CT
Diploma, New London High School, New London, CT

ALEX RODMAN

630-555-5555

arodman@msn.com
www.linked.com/alexrodman

PROFESSIONAL PROFILE

Network Administrator with 10+ years' experience in technical training, project management, computer architecture, and technology operations. Expert in networking, TCP/IP protocol, and network security.

Skilled troubleshooter with attention to detail and ability to work effectively in fast-paced, mission-critical environments. Talented team leader who consistently achieves/surpasses desired results. Top Secret clearance.

TECHNICAL SUMMARY

CERTIFICATIONS

- A+ | Network + | Linux + | LPI | MCSA | CNA
- VMware Certified Professional (VCP)
- Cisco Certified Network Associate, Routing & Switching (CCNA-R&S)

KNOWLEDGE & SKILLS

- Windows 8/10 | Windows 365 | Windows Server 2012 | UNIX | Linux | Exchange Server 2013
- Cisco IOS | TCP/IP | LAN/WAN | BGP | DHCP | DNS | TLS/SSL | Gigabit Ethernet
- VMware vSphere | Data Center & Storage Management Platforms | Cloud Services (SaaS, IaaS, PaaS)

EXPERIENCE HIGHLIGHTS

- **NETWORK ADMINISTRATOR:** Provided workable and proven solutions to maintain various operating environments. Installed, configured, and maintained the network for military training school, achieving zero classroom downtime for more than 3 years. Demonstrated strong diagnostic abilities with attention to detail and ability to work effectively and efficiently in a fast-paced environment.

  Recognized as a competent and credible authority on establishing procedures, conducting tests to verify correct operation of equipment/systems, implementing fault-tolerant procedures for hardware and software failures, and designing audit procedures to test systems integrity and reliability.

- **PROJECT MANAGER:** Managed $3.5M supply inventory and annual budget of $600K. Provided all logistics, including parts issues, contingency purchasing, and emergency field delivery, with no measurable losses.

- **RISK ANALYST:** Identified potential liabilities in computerized military accounting system training program. Analyzed accuracy, usage feasibility, and deficiencies while providing solutions for obstacles.

- **LEADER:** Earned multiple awards for performance excellence. Motivated and inspired organizations ranging in size from 30–400 personnel. Effectively guided and directed associates to achieve their highest potential. Encouraged and supported a teamwork environment that resulted in increased efficiency and productivity.

- **INSTRUCTOR:** Played a major role in design and implementation of self-paced curriculum at military training facility, increasing throughput and retention of more than 150 students per year.

EDUCATION

B.S. Computer Science, Excelsior University, Alameda, CA   2018
A.S. Computer Technology, Empire College, Santa Rosa, CA   2013

EMPLOYMENT

United States Coast Guard   2003–2018

- Supply Officer/Department Head—USCG BOUTWELL (WHEC-719), Alameda, CA, 2013–2018
- Supervisor/Assistant Branch Chief—Maintenance & Logistics Command Pacific, Alameda, CA, 2009–2013
- Instructor—USCG Training Center, Petaluma, CA, 2003–2009

CHAPTER 4:
Write with Meaning & Power

Read these 2 sentences:

> *I was responsible for managing the design, development, and marketing of new biomedical equipment that the company had developed. After the product launch into the market, I helped with $12 million in sales in the first year.*

Now, read this sentence:

> *Championed design, development, and market roll-out of new biomedical equipment that generated $12M in first-year sales.*

Can you tell the difference? Can you *feel* the difference in the strength and impact of the second sentence? Even though both sentences say the same thing, the second one says it with meaning, power, and a real story about that job seeker's performance.

> **Pro Tip: Writing a resume is just like writing any other marketing document.** You have a product—*yourself*—to sell, and the more powerfully you can write about it, the more enticing *you* will be!

What are the elements of that second sentence that make it so strong and effective—instantly capturing a reader's attention and interest? How is it an example of writing with meaning and power?

Professional resume writers use the following techniques to make that happen.

Technique #1: Quantify Achievements

Numbers and percentages are always valuable to include in your resume because they're a measurable indicator of your performance. For example:

- **Cut costs 20%** after redesigning administrative and office procedures.
- **Increased yield $10M** with implementation of next-generation technology.
- Restructured staffing models for 10 locations and **improved productivity 28%.**

The obvious next question is … what if you don't have quantified achievements? A big part of preparation for writing your resume and conducting your job search is recalling your career success stories. It is those success stories that are at the root of quantified achievements. When you dig deep into each story, you can often generate numbers, dollars, and percentages that will instantly add power and meaning to your resume.

Refer to Dig-Deep Questions, on pages 231–32 in Part VII—Resources, for a list of idea-inspiring questions to help you uncover your numbers and other specific results.

> **PRO TIP: Not everything is quantifiable**—we know that, and employers know it too. If you can't quantify many of your achievements, pay special attention to the writing techniques in the rest of this chapter so that your resume content is strong, clear, and specific even if not quantified.

Technique #2: Lead with Strong Verbs

One of the first things you'll notice about the 3 bullet points in the previous section is that each begins with a verb—Cut, Increased, Restructured. Verbs convey action and energy—you *did* something! You will increase the vigor of your entire resume by starting each paragraph and each bullet point with a strong verb—even if that paragraph or bullet point is not linked to a quantified achievement.

Another good writing technique is to vary the verbs that you use. You will quickly bore your readers if you start many sentences with the same word. Choose verbs that clearly and specifically describe what you did.

For example, if you "increased" sales and "increased" profitability and "increased" customer service scores, think of other diverse and interesting verbs you can use to convey the same valuable information:

- **Built** the #1 sales region in the company, **driving** up revenue from $7M to $18M in 2 years.
- **Delivered** profit margins 7% above company average.
- **Reversed** declining service scores and **achieved** double-digit growth in customer satisfaction.

You'll find our very useful list of 403 Resume Writing Verbs on pages 233–34 in Part VII—Resources. In addition, a thesaurus is a gold mine for identifying a variety of words that convey similar meanings.

Technique #3: Write with Umbrella Terms

Umbrella terms are single words or short phrases that cover whole families of words and communicate an entire message just by themselves. Here's a brief illustration of the impact, depth, and dimension that umbrella terms will bring to your resume:

- **Executive.** If you use this word, particularly in your Summary, you're instantly communicating that you perform at a very senior level.
- **P&L.** If you're responsible for profit and loss, you're in a position of significant power and decision-making authority.
- **Operations.** In the manufacturing industry, the single word "operations" communicates that you have vast responsibilities that could range from daily production to output yield, from staffing and training to production technologies, from supply chain to regulatory compliance.
- **Budget.** This word most likely communicates that you manage a budget, allocate funds, coordinate financial reporting, and forecast future years' budgetary needs.

- **Outsourcing.** With this word you communicate that you were likely involved in selecting outsourcing partners and suppliers, negotiating their contracts, managing the quality of their work, and communicating with them on a regular basis.

The number of words and short phrases that communicate vast amounts of information is virtually endless. Determine what words matter most for you and your job targets, and be certain to integrate them wisely into your resume text.

> **PRO TIP: Keywords are also a vital component of writing with umbrella terms and creating strong resume content,** and you'll read more about them in Chapter 7.

Technique #4: Write in First Person … Never in Third Person

First person is the most reader-friendly and the most intimate—you're telling *your* career story. Although it is rare that you would use the word "I" in your resume, it is assumed and understood. For example:

> *[I] direct daily operations for Reynolds' highest-volume manufacturing plant ($18M annual volume, 189 employees, 2K sq. ft. facility).*

Eliminate the "I," capitalize the "d," and you've got a strong and meaningful resume sentence to add to a short paragraph or include as a bullet point within the job description. It even starts with a verb, as we discussed in Technique #2 on the previous page.

Conversely, writing in third person changes the tone and feel of your resume, and *not* for the better:

> *[She] directs daily operations for Reynolds' highest-volume manufacturing plant ($18M annual volume, 189 employees, 2K sq. ft. facility).*

Now the focus is on "she"—someone else—and not on you. Instantly, you've lost ownership of your resume and all of the wonderful content. Don't ever let that happen … not even in your Summary, where sometimes it feels more natural to write in third person.

> **PRO TIP: If you were to write a professional bio to accompany your resume, it can be written in third person, and many of them are.** Bios are a different type of career marketing communication and networking tool, meant as an introduction, an addendum to a business plan, an inclusion in a project portfolio, and for other professional activities—job search related and not.

Technique #5: Eliminate Words, Phrases, and Introductions You Don't Need

Read through your resume and see how many of these terms you have used:

- Responsible for …
- Duties included …
- Achievements included … (followed by bullet-point achievements)
- Skills include … (followed by a double-column listing of your top professional skills)

Now, ask yourself if those words add any value to your resume. Chances are almost 100% that they do not. Delete them and edit accordingly!

Technique #6: Be Specific

Specifics are much more meaningful and memorable than generalities. To see what we mean, compare these 2 sentences from a job seeker's Summary:

> *Accomplished retail manager with 10 years of experience and a track record of increasing sales and reducing labor costs.*

or

> *Retail manager who led 2 different stores to #1 in sales in 20-store Midwest Region while delivering the company's highest profit-per-labor-dollar.*

The first sentence is general: It could be written by many retail managers. The second, however, is specific and unique to a single individual. When you write specifics, your resume immediately stands out and you successfully distinguish yourself from other candidates.

While of course you do need to provide some general career details, too many generalities can weigh down your resume—especially today, when we need to capture attention quickly and provide short bites of information to keep readers engaged.

> **Pro Tip: An added bonus when you write specifics is that you convey essential information.** In the example above, clearly the retail manager from sentence #2 is "accomplished" and has a great "track record." By telling precisely what he has done, we don't need those over-used words. Instead, we convey that message in a way that's much more powerful, distinctive, and credible.

Technique #7: Add Context to Add Meaning

Synonyms for context are "background," "situation," and "frame of reference." Context helps readers understand and appreciate your achievements—making those achievements even more impressive!

Here's an example of an achievement that, at first glance, seems to be clear and strong:

> *Increased territory revenue 26%.*

Yet consider how much more meaningful and valuable that same accomplishment becomes when we provide a frame of reference:

> *Increased territory revenue 26%, twice the company average.*

You can also add context to your job descriptions by describing why you were hired for the job. For example, rather than simply writing:

> *Managed a $12M sales territory and supervised 19 independent contractors who provided daily route service to retail accounts.*

… you can make that job description much richer with information about the situation that existed when you were hired:

> *Recruited to reverse declining sales and improve service to retail accounts. In 1 year, grew revenue from $8M to $12M and created a customer-first culture among front-line service team of 19 independent contractors.*

Another example of how specifics can work for you has to do with company names—names that are *not* familiar to most people. We all know Apple, IBM, Nike, McDonald's, and AT&T. But what about Reymon Manufacturing, Samuelson Stores, and The Gallery? Those company names mean nothing to a reader.

Sometimes that's okay. If you're not looking for a job in the same industry, it's probably best to omit details that will position you squarely within your past industry. However, if your goal is to work in the same or a related industry, sharing specifics about that company is vitally important. You instantly communicate that you know the industry and, maybe, the market, competition, customer base, products, and more.

Be specific, but be succinct! For example:

> *Reymon Manufacturing* ($32M industrial equipment manufacturer/distributor)

The 2 resumes that we're showcasing in this chapter, for Bernard Henry and Taj Gupta, are both great examples of all 6 of the writing techniques in this chapter. They:

- Have quantifiable achievements.
- Are written in first person.
- Lead with strong verbs.
- Use meaningful umbrella terms.
- Avoid unnecessary words and details.
- Are very specific throughout.
- Include context that adds meaning and impact.

Let's look more closely at each.

Bernard Henry Resume—pages 40–41

Bernard's resume includes:

- A Summary with specific details about his career accomplishments.
- Succinct company descriptions that help us understand his work environment.
- Specific achievements highlighted in bold numbers and eye-catching graphics.
- Precise verbs, umbrella terms, and other high-impact language.
- Context information to tell us why he was hired for each job.
- Just enough information to help us understand his career successes without drowning in detail.

Taj Gupta Resume—pages 42–43

Taj's resume showcases:

- Specific industry expertise (online travel) in the Summary, with clear headline and powerful graphic.
- An impressive and one-of-a-kind endorsement.
- Strong verbs that paint a colorful picture of his career and achievements.
- Umbrella terms and other relevant keywords that emphasize his broad and deep expertise.
- Concise descriptions of the scope of each position—budget, direct reports, and focus of the job.
- The context around each position—why he was chosen for that job.
- Quantified achievements, with numbers and other results highlighted in bold.

BUSINESS TURNAROUND ➲ CUSTOMER FOCUS ➲ RAPID IMPLEMENTATION

BERNARD M. HENRY

Tulsa, OK 74115 ➲ 918-838-5000 ➲ bhenry@wordright.com

INDUSTRY EXPERTISE Manufacturing ➲ Supply Chain ➲ Warehouse Management ➲ Shipping

VP | DIRECTOR SUPPLY CHAIN MANAGEMENT ▶▶ VP | DIRECTOR ENTERPRISE RESOURCE PLANNING [ERP]

INFLUENTIAL, TOP-PRODUCING BUSINESS EXECUTIVE, expert in leading rapid implementations, transforming performance, and driving profitability. Recognized for collaboration, teamwork, negotiation, influence, and relationship-building. Dozens of impeccable end-to-end business process conversions completed on time and on budget.

MBA BOSTON UNIVERSITY | APICS AND ICCP CERTIFICATIONS | MULTIPLE INDUSTRY AWARDS

CRITICAL COMPETENCIES

- Process Reengineering | Implementation
- P&L | Capital Investment Decisions
- Business Continuity Planning
- Negotiation and Influence
- JDA | Oracle | Server Technologies

- Proprietary Systems Migration
- Business Intelligence
- Team Development | Mentorship
- WMS | Manufacturing Platforms
- Enterprise Change Management

- Customer Service | Support | Retention
- Product Design | Development | Marketing
- System-Oriented Architecture
- Warehouse and Inventory Management
- Integration Solutions (FTP, EDI, XML)

PROFESSIONAL EXPERIENCE

CHIEF TECHNOLOGY OFFICER	Tele-Enterprises Incorporated	2016 – Present

*Cloud-based **$67M** multi-functional supply chain management software and ERP company with 275 employees.*

Reporting to CEO and Owner, recruited to drive sales and product marketing in preparation for the imminent sale of the firm.

- Led product demand-sensing pilot project that led to major contract and product usage expansion with **$12.7M** identified savings.
- Drove winning presales engagements by developing proposals and detailed Statements of Work (SOW) with 3 international Fortune 500 clients.
- Led sales strategy for Force One Global (won **$5M+** contract) and Braxton, Inc. (secured **$2.5M** extension of existing contract).

DEMAND SENSING PROJECT: $12.7M IN SAVINGS OVER 3 QUARTERS

CHIEF INFORMATION OFFICER (CIO)	Public Employee Retirement Plan (PERP)	2009 – 2016

$39B public pension plan formed from American Public Employees' Pension Plan and American Teachers' Retirement Plan.

Recruited by CEO to improve plan performance, transformed it to best-in-class from most poorly performing fund in US history. Reengineered business technology processes, revitalized underperforming teams, and restored accountability, trust, and confidence among governing bodies.

Managed **$88M** budget, 6 direct reports, and 250 total staff in IT, Operations, and System Design.

> **SPEARHEADED INTEGRATION OF 2 MULTIBILLION-DOLLAR PENSION ADMINISTRATIONS AND CONSTRUCTED WORLD-CLASS IT OPERATIONS.**

(PERP continued)

- Transformed services-level retirement processing from **77%** late to **80%** on time.
- Decreased costs by **$5M** and increased internet usage from **300K to 16M+** annual views by designing and implementing "Plan Interactive" application that improved web-based client service.
- Negotiated **$110M** technology renewal plan by state Boards of Directors for 4-year industry-standard IT operations strategy to build mission-critical and sustainable technology infrastructure.

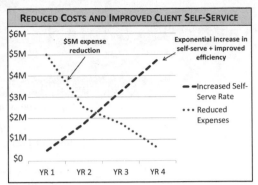

REDUCED COSTS AND IMPROVED CLIENT SELF-SERVICE

CREATED PMO, LEADING 110+ PROJECTS ANNUALLY WITH 88%+ ON-TIME, ON-BUDGET DELIVERY.

- Catapulted APERP to an unqualified audit position and implemented a disaster recovery and business continuity plan, mitigating risk and building organizational capacity and resilience.
- Orchestrated 2-year **$3.5M** data cleanup project to restructure 300,000 member accounts, enabling real-time provision of online retirement calculations and pro-forma statements. Results cleared the path for outsourcing of the 401k pension portion.

SENIOR DIRECTOR	High Volume Technologies, Toledo, OH	2013 – 2016

*Global supply chain management software and services company acquired by IMF Software Group in 2010 with a market capitalization of **$2.2B** and **200** employees.*

Reporting to VP Global Sales, directed a team of 39 staff, 7 direct reports, and **$11M P&L**. Company grew from **$4M to $1.1B**. Recruited by CEO for reputation of stellar results at 2 Fortune 100 companies.

Grew product marketing for pharmaceutical, metals, oil and gas, and chemical business units. Implemented business plans and product vision.

- Achieved **$11M** revenue by optimizing productivity and restoring regional divisions to peak performance.
- Drove revenue by **250% to $1.4M** and achieved stretch quota goals from **11% to 39%** in 2 quarters. Captured **88%** market share for domestic metals industry.
- Coordinated and integrated engineering function, staffing, products, and marketing post-acquisition of Turner Technologies and Ironworks.
- Achieved **$52M** sales quota by generating e-trading sales wins.
- Produced top software-selling region by combining 2 regions, reducing headcount **44%,** and implementing strategies to reach **$15M** sales target.

PRIOR EXPERIENCE

Progressed through supply chain and operations management roles with Ryder Dedicated Logistics and UPS.

EDUCATION, CERTIFICATIONS, AND INDUSTRY AWARDS

Master of Business Administration | New York University
Bachelor of Science in Industrial Management | Wharton School of Management
5 President's Club Honors Awards for Excellence in Leadership | High Volume Technologies

Bernard Henry, Tulsa, OK 74115 ☎ 918-838-5000 ✉ bhenry@wordright.com

Taj Gupta

20 Years of Experience Shaping the Online Travel Industry

Strategic Leader - Executive Director - Online Travel Industry Expert

277-333-6655 – taj.gupta@coldmail.com – www.linkedin.com/tajgupta – Atlanta, GA 30303

"Taj brings expertise in both the online travel industry and executive management that allows our business to be at the forefront of our industry." - CEO, quickbeds.com.

Internationally experienced, **commercially focused Executive Director** positioned to drive responsible progression and authentic results. Depth of experience encapsulates **financial management, strategic leadership,** and **key stakeholder engagement**. Authority in advancing controls and transporting business forward by leveraging emerging technologies.

- Key Value Offerings -

- **Respected Executive** with more than **20 years of experience** leading innovation and setting precedence within the **online travel industry.**

- A passion for **shaping organizations** and **building capabilities** complemented by proven results in **implementing systems**, developing emerging leaders, and driving **cultural change to achieve positive financial growth.**

- Reputed for **outstanding negotiation** skills, **leadership,** and **communication talents** that achieve results in multifunctional teams.

☑ Board Reporting	☑ Financial Management	☑ Risk Management
☑ Change Management	☑ Quality Controls	☑ Strategic Planning
☑ Compliance Controls	☑ Board Reporting	☑ Team Leadership

- Key Career Highlights -

Executive Director, quickbeds.com, Atlanta, GA   2017–Present

Approached to undertake the multifaceted role managing the complete strategic functions of the group. Showcased a commitment to stakeholder engagement and achieved unprecedented buy-in to initiatives while positioning the business as a leader in the industry.

Team: 23 Executive Direct Reports	**Budget:** $10M	**Focus:** Positioning as Industry Leader

Shaping Industry: Leveraged cutting-edge innovations to position the business at the forefront of industry and **awarded National Leader in Emerging Technologies in 2018** by Travel, Inc. This was as a direct result of spearheading the introduction of Virtual Credit Cards to pay suppliers, providing a more efficient process as well as untapped revenue.

Systems Improvements: Spearheaded functional enhancements to reflect the expedited business growth of **20% year on year** and removed dependency on legacy back-office systems.

Asian Regional Growth: Expedited the global direction of the business by **driving 48% growth in the Asian region** as a result of migration to standardized group financial systems.

Business Growth: ⇧ 20%	**Regional Growth:** ⇧ 48%	**Performance Rating:** 5 Star

Kylie Chown, CMRW, CERM, CARW • Kylie Chown Consulting • www.kyliechown.com.au

277-333-6655 – taj.gupta@coldmail.com – www.linkedin.com/tajgupta – Page 2

- Key Career Highlights (Continued) -

Chief Executive Officer, quickbeds.com, Atlanta, GA — 2012–2017

Prominent leadership role in a period of significant change. Complete responsibility for the strategic functions of the group. Clarified business model to take the business forward. Demonstrated loyalty and dedication with a commitment to achieving results.

Team: 15 Executive Direct Reports | **Budget:** $9M | **Focus:** Strategic Business Growth

Process Management: Elevated multi-site compliance **from 80% to 95% within 12 months.** Project standardized all financial processes and disciplines of the group and improved internal controls.

Executive Team Leadership: Unified a consistent executive management team over a 24-month period that reduced **attrition rates by 20%.** Mobilized the team in developing organizational capabilities and optimizing the headcount that ensured quality outputs reflective of the changing requirements.

Financial Management: Heightened accuracy and expedited **budget process from 8 hours to 2 hours** by developing an integrated and streamlined budget model.

Business Development: Acquired **20% of new business** as targeted clients. Initiated a hands-on approach towards organic and inorganic growth reflective of long- and short-term strategic objectives.

Risk Management: Lessened critical incidents reported by 20% over 12 months. Consolidated all risk management functions and implemented strategies to mitigate negative impact.

Business Growth: ⇧ 20% | **Compliance:** ⇧ 95% | **Performance Rating:** 5 Star

Operations Director, quickbeds.com, Los Angeles, CA — 2011–2012

Identified as a high performer and rapidly promoted to Operations Director to manage the business at a strategic level. Delivered business improvements that increased business performance to unprecedented levels.

Team: 10 Executive Direct Reports | **Budget:** $7M | **Focus:** Improvements and Cost Reduction

Continuous Improvements: Accelerated **increases in turnover by more than 25% in 12 months.** Identified labor-intensive processes that were then retooled for maximum efficiency and reduced costs.

Cost Reductions: Identified opportunity and **renegotiated service contracts for a 74% reduction in cost.**

Best Practices: Maintained 100% compliance to best practices, identified as a competitive advantage. Performed continued business analysis to refine processes and procedures.

Business Growth: ⇧ 22% | **Compliance:** ⇧ 100% | **Performance Rating:** 5 Star

- Education -

MA Economics, University of California, Los Angeles, CA — 2012
BS Business, University of Southern California, Los Angeles, CA — 2007

Resume of **Taj Gupta**

CHAPTER 5:
Write Tight, Lean & Clean

Writing tight, lean, and clean refers to techniques that impact every single item on your resume, from minor things like locations and contact information, to major items such as job descriptions, achievement statements, project highlights, educational credentials, professional affiliations … everything.

To write a modern resume, not only must it be powerful in its content, it must also be written in such a way that it's easy and relatively fast to read. Today's modern resume is:

- **Written succinctly to match readers' short attention spans.** Rather than intricate sentences, lengthy lists of bullet points, and long-winded paragraphs, capture that same information in a tighter, more telegraphic writing style and ditch the words that don't matter.

  Ask Yourself: Does every word I've written on my resume mean something and have value?

- **Designed for skimmers rather than readers.** Be certain that critical information is noticeable in just a quick glance to instantly capture the attention of recruiters, hiring managers, and other key decision makers.

  Ask Yourself: Can someone skim my resume in just a few seconds and immediately understand who I am?

The over-arching strategy of these 2 concepts, and the challenge you face, is to:

Tell your whole career story in half the words.

In the pages that follow, we're going to show you how that's done.

Eliminate the Little Words

You'd be amazed at how much space words such as "a," "an," "the," "by," and others take up on a page. Although they might seem insignificant, when you delete them from your resume—unless you feel a particular need to include one in a sentence here or there—all of your sentences, paragraphs, and pages become shorter and tighter.

Eliminating these little words creates a tight writing style that is perfect for resumes. You convey the needed information without requiring space or attention for words that do nothing to enhance meaning or value.

Ditch the Details that Don't Matter

Although your tendency might be to include everything you did in each of your jobs, don't. Certain details simply don't matter. Ask yourself:

- If you are an office manager and one of your responsibilities is to order paper, is that resume-worthy? (Probably not.)
- If you're a customer service agent, do you need to mention that you interact with customers? (It is understood from your job title.)
- Isn't it enough to state that you direct operations at 12 telemarketing centers in Michigan … do you really need to list the name of each city? (Probably not.)
- Must you list the name of every product you sell or every customer you service? (Generally, only the products or companies that are widely recognized or directly related to your current search objectives are appropriate to include.)

In another example, consider the project manager who has performed the same functions for 20+ different projects. Does that job seeker need to include the same level of detailed information about each project? *(No!)* Instead, he can write it once and then showcase the single most notable achievement for each project—at least the most noteworthy projects. The reality is that he's not going to include all 20 projects, shouldn't include them all, and doesn't have the space to do so.

Review your resume very closely to identify where there is too much insignificant detail and hit delete!

Edit Widow Lines

How many times have you written a paragraph—whether in a resume, marketing brochure, or business correspondence—where the last 1 or 2 words are "widowed" on a line by themselves? Those widow lines are a prime opportunity to shorten content, reduce text density, and diminish paragraph length—all good things in today's modern resume.

Our best advice for eliminating widow lines—in paragraphs or bullet points—is to ruthlessly edit the entire section, deleting all words that are not critical to the content and meaning. Often just a minor edit will move the widow up to the prior line so the paragraph becomes tighter. Sometimes, you'll have to edit more extensively to shorten that section of content, and that's a valuable use of your time.

Use Abbreviations

You can easily abbreviate certain words and be confident that everyone will know what those abbreviations stand for. State names are an excellent example. It is passé to write out their full names—even the United States Postal Service (USPS) doesn't do that.

Job seekers in the US, use 2-letter state abbreviations; job seekers in Canada, use 2-letter province abbreviations. Those in other countries, use whatever abbreviations are most common.

College degrees are also prime areas for abbreviation. There is no need to spell out Associate of Arts, Bachelor of Science, Master of Business Administration, and other well-known degrees. The abbreviations AA,

BS, and MBA are universally known. If you have a less-known degree from outside North America or the major universities in Europe, spell everything out so you're certain to communicate important information and not shortchange yourself.

> **PRO TIP: Two key benefits from using abbreviations are that they save space and they stand out on the page** because they are usually written as all capital letters.

You will find many instances when an abbreviation is the right option—when you can use the quick term and feel sure that readers will understand your meaning. A few of the countless examples:

- Cities (NYC—New York City)
- Countries (US or USA—United States)
- Technology terms (PC—personal computer)
- Financial terms (CFO—chief financial officer)
- Manufacturing terms (OEM—original equipment manufacturer)
- Banking terms (ATM—automatic teller machine)
- Company names (IBM—International Business Machines)
- Job responsibilities (P&L—profit and loss)

Use Acronyms

The Oxford Dictionary states that an acronym is "an abbreviation formed from the initial letters of other words and pronounced as a word." Using the right acronyms in your resume can save a great deal of space.

Consider these very common acronyms:

- AIDS—Acquired Immunodeficiency Syndrome
- NATO—North Atlantic Treaty Organization
- OPEC—Organization of the Petroleum Exporting Countries
- Scuba—Self-Contained Underwater Breathing Apparatus

Other acronyms are very specific to certain industries and professions. For example, everyone in manufacturing knows that FIFO means First In, First Out; everyone in the medical field knows that JCAHO is the Joint Commission on Accreditation of Healthcare Organizations; everyone in technology knows that FIOS is Fiber-Optic Service.

When writing your resume, always consider your audience when deciding to use acronyms, as these examples illustrate:

- If you're a quality manager looking for other opportunities in manufacturing, you can use the acronym SAP in your resume and feel confident that anyone reading it will know what it means.

- Conversely, if you are making a career shift from quality management into training and development, you'd want to spell out Systems, Applications, and Products because the SAP acronym might not be recognizable to most readers.

A good basic rule: *When in doubt, spell it out!*

If you do spell it out, use the word first, followed by the acronym: *Earnings Before Income Tax (EBIT)*

You can then use the acronym in the rest of your resume, because now everyone knows what it means.

> **PRO TIP: Keyword searches typically include both the acronym and the spelled-out version of the term.** Employers don't want to miss out on good candidates by searching for "consumer packaged goods" but not its common acronym, CPG. Therefore, you can safely use common acronyms in your resume and still pass the screening scans.

Write & Then Edit

Tight, lean, clean writing requires good editing! Don't expect to produce a masterpiece in a single sitting.

First, use our Career Vault tool on pages 228–30 in Part VII—Resources to assemble all of the information you will need.

Next, write your resume, capturing all of the details that you think you want to include. This may take several sittings to accomplish, so don't berate yourself for not doing it faster. Resume writing is a multi-step process—even for very experienced professional resume writers!

Then, take time to read it slowly and carefully. What words have you written that don't need to be there? What details don't add value and, in fact, obscure the meaning of more important information? Delete everything you can. Edit ruthlessly, without cutting anything that's relevant, important, or distinctive.

If you follow the guidelines in this chapter, you'll produce a resume that is powerful, memorable, and effective. You can see how well that has been done in the 2 samples that follow.

James Earlington Resume—pages 48–49

Notice how much of the content of James' resumes is presented in just 1 or 2 lines. This draws quick attention to the resume and makes for easy skimming. Even paragraphs that are a bit longer (4 lines maximum) are tightly written and provide essential details—nothing wasted, nothing extra. The resume is clean and lean, with a few distinguishing design elements (shadowed font for his name at the top, shaded box for key competencies, borders throughout) that are attractive and appropriate.

Timothy Walden Resume—pages 50–51

Timothy's resume conveys urgency and action through the use of strong verbs, bold type, and high-impact statements. The only paragraph that is longer than 3 lines is "Areas of Impact" in the Summary. That section is packed with keywords—great for electronic scanning.

James T. Earlington

☎ 248-555-3210
✉ jearlington@gmail.com
⌂ Southeast Michigan/Greater Detroit
in www.linkedin.com/james.earlington

FINANCE AND BUSINESS PLANNING EXECUTIVE

Global Operations

P&L Management

Budget Management

Strategic Planning

Sales and Pricing Management

Acquisition Integration

Corporate Restructuring

Quality Systems Implementation

Versatile leader and change agent with extensive experience directing global financial and planning functions for a $2B technology company. Rewarded with multiple promotions for leadership and performance.

Accomplishment Highlights

Drove revenue and profit growth by creating a metrics-based business planning framework and establishing best practices for sales.

Led seamless integrations, divestitures, and restructuring initiatives.

Fostered a culture of high expectations—allowing top performers to flourish and leveraging their individual strengths to accomplish goals.

PROFESSIONAL EXPERIENCE

COMPUWARE CORPORATION—Detroit, Michigan   2002–present
A $2B+ software and technical services company. Customers include 80% of Fortune 500 companies worldwide.

Vice President—International Finance (promotion, 2012–present)

Hand-picked by the CFO to orchestrate global finance operations in 24 countries. Lead international teams of 100+ finance professionals in revenue recognition, A/R, A/P, payroll, and tax preparation. Accountable for compliance with internal controls, GAAP, audit requirements, and statutory rules in 24 countries. Manage a $10M budget. Facilitate global pricing strategies.

- Led a global corporate restructuring initiative that identified $50M in annual cost savings.
- Orchestrated worldwide pricing strategies and business practices across 20 currencies and multiple business units amidst an ever-changing product portfolio and revenue recognition environment.
- Led the deployment of multiple global financial systems (Oracle) in 26 countries around the globe. Deployed dozens of flawless launches on a compressed, three-year schedule.

Vice President—Integrations and Change Management (2010–2012)

Led corporate change and integration—orchestrating the assimilation of all processes, data, and systems. Reported directly to the CFO.

- Seamlessly integrated four acquisitions ($70M) into Compuware.
- Facilitated an $80M divestiture as Compuware representative and buyer liaison.

Page 1 of 2

Deborah Schuster, CPRW • The Lettersmith Resume Service •
www.thelettersmith.com

James Earlington · 248-555-3210

COMPUWARE CORPORATION, Continued

Vice President—Program Management Office (promotion, 2004–2010)

Promoted to direct multiple functions in a Chief-of-Staff role, reporting directly to COO. Led a 100-person, multi-disciplinary operations team. Assisted the COO in all operational areas with fact-based, data-driven decision making and policy setting. Managed a $9M consolidated budget and P&L for a $12M operation.

Led a 50-person North American Inside Sales organization and a 20-person Telemarketing organization.
- Established best practices, forecast process, and a commission plan aligned with sales goals.
- Achieved *100% Club* in the first year of leadership, delivering $12M in sales.

Directed the Sales Administration Support department.
- Created global pricing strategies for the deployment of business systems.

Managed Quality Planning department.
- Co-developed and launched the Compuware Quality Management System—achieving ISO and Ford QOS quality certifications and retaining preferred vendor status with Ford.

Orchestrated corporate-wide reorganization.
- Coordinated a corporate-wide restructuring, ensuring that all processes, systems, and marketing communications were revised to align with the new organization.

Director—Corporate Planning (2002–2004)

Led global business planning and forecasting, reporting to the CEO. Provided decision support to operations leadership. Managed a corporate budget of $1.8M. Key member of the corporate Executive Committee. Directed a team of planning managers and financial analysts.

- Built corporate-wide, metrics-based annual operating plan, aligned with revenue and profit growth targets.
- Achieved 118% growth in professional services and 41% growth in product revenue as a key member of the leadership team.

EARLY CAREER

GENERAL MOTORS CORPORATION—Detroit, Michigan
Global Budget Manager (promotion, 2000–2002)
Senior Financial Analyst—Corporate Finance (1999–2000)

EDUCATION

Master of Business Administration (MBA)
UNIVERSITY OF MICHIGAN—Ann Arbor, Michigan

Bachelor of Business Administration (BBA)
MICHIGAN STATE UNIVERSITY—Lansing, Michigan

TIMOTHY WALDEN

New York, NY | (201) 887-4223 | timothy@timothywalden.com
www.linkedin.com/in/timothywalden.com

EXECUTIVE PROFILE

Performance-driven leader providing vision for profitable growth strategies, products, services, and new market entries. Delivered tens of millions of dollars in revenue at technology companies.

Experience...	P&L accountability for multimillion-dollar technology businesses Startup and new venture leadership
Technology Expertise ...	Data Analytics	Cyber Security	Cloud Infrastructure	Unified Communications	Contact Center
Areas of Impact ...	Strategy. Business turnarounds. Spotting emerging opportunities. Product development and management. Complex mergers and acquisitions. Business development/partnering with startup technology companies. Securing funding for new ventures. Creating investor returns in early-stage and mature organizations. Exit planning. Hiring and leading top IT and business development talent.

Vast national and regional contacts: angel investors, VCs, and senior technology executives.

CAREER MILESTONES

Steered strategy, marketing, product, and technology initiatives in 6 companies that resulted in multimillion-dollar impact on revenues, cost reductions, or enterprise value. Examples:

- **Turned around, grew revenues, and boosted net income 20% at IT solutions business (Tech Institute).**

- **Secured $15M in venture funding from the board and $45M partnership agreement; landed anchor customer to launch business; set stage for company's successful IPO (Morrow, Inc.).**

- **Brought deal to SA Communications and developed business plan to enter contact center software market with potential to generate $35M in Q4 2015.**

- **Steered 100% cash exit for $19.7M, returning 4X to investors at ecommerce startup (CPT Advisory Group).**

PROFESSIONAL EXPERIENCE

SA COMMUNICATIONS, New York, NY • 2018 to Present

VICE PRESIDENT, CORPORATE DEVELOPMENT

Hired to create a new managed services business and lead corporate development at a provider of on-demand, cloud-based communications services for businesses and contact centers. Authored business plans; researched MS Lync-based contact center software companies and ecosystem. Modeled economics of perpetual licensing vs. subscription models.

➢ **Within 30 days, presented business plan** that identified key positioning opportunities and entry strategies.

➢ **Delivered 2 strategic business opportunities valued at $5.3M,** following preparation of customer pitch and product package for flagship offering.

➢ **Developed business plan for entering contact center software market**; qualified, negotiated, and presented an acquisition candidate that fit 100% of board's screening criteria.

➢ **Authored fundraising pitch and differentiation strategy**—based on strategic, technical, financial, and market conditions—to secure a new round of venture funding.

➢ **Closed a strategic partnership** and implemented solution to enter hosted unified communications and hosted contact center markets.

Louise Garver, CERM, CJSS, CPRW, CCMC, IJCTC, CMP, MCDP • Career Directions Intl, LLC • www.careerdirections.com

TIMOTHY WALDEN – PAGE 2   (201) 887-4223 | timothy@timothywalden.com

CPT ADVISORY GROUP, New York, NY • 2011 to 2018

PRESIDENT

Built a business focused on strategy, commercialization, and operations consulting. Created company's operational infrastructure and grew business to $8.5M/annual. Selected engagement highlights:

➢ **As Interim CEO of Torrington, LLC (2016 to 2017),** took over a financially troubled data protection and backup business, lowered debt service 95%, and enabled company to begin reestablishing market position. Streamlined accounting and operational processes, resulting in 75% greater sales capacity and 50% faster sales-to-cash intervals.

➢ **Led development of a trademark clearinghouse critical to supporting launch of global top-level domains for next-generation technology initiative program ($150M+ revenue).** Worked with often competing stakeholders to gain consensus in a first-of-its-kind initiative.

➢ **Analyzed commercialization potential of a cyber security research portfolio for Tech Institute.** Mapped out supply chain, developed forecast model, and outlined pursuit plan for commercialization.

➢ **Conducted due diligence leading to successful funding ($24M) for a tech startup.**

TECH INSTITUTE, New York, NY • 2007 to 2011

VICE PRESIDENT, IT SOLUTIONS & KNOWLEDGE MANAGEMENT

Recruited to drive business development and reestablish growth trajectory for division of world's largest non-profit research and development organization. Within 60 days, selected to lead the $50M IT solutions business unit to energize and inspire 250 employees through 6 direct reports. Held full P&L and operations management accountability.

➢ **Revitalized IT solutions business; grew revenues and increased net income 20%** without increasing overhead.

➢ **Defined strategy, added 3 new practice areas** (knowledge management, information assurance/security, enterprise architecture), restarted IP development to create differentiation, and secured CMMI level-2 certification.

➢ **Created new strategy for effective enterprise-wide knowledge sharing** by leveraging influencing skills to garner support of major knowledge and information purveyors across company.

MORROW, INC., NEW YORK, NY • 2005 to 2007

VICE PRESIDENT, IP SERVICES

Brought on board to develop strategy and launch plan for a new convergence business unit. Established strategic direction, goals, and priorities for new entity. Staffed business unit and managed $10M budget. Led IP development project that introduced Morrow's SIP-based number translation service in the market.

➢ **Created a funded, sustainable new business by securing $15M in venture funding from the Morrow board.**

➢ **Helped legitimize company in a nascent market and generate $250K in revenue immediately** by securing level-3 rating as an anchor customer.

➢ **Negotiated $45M agreement** to partner on identity management product with an IT industry leader.

GLOBAL SYSTEMS, NEW YORK, NY • 2004 to 2005

PRESIDENT, GLOBAL ALLIANCES & PARTNERSHIPS

Served on senior management team that developed and presented strategic plan for the first pan-European broadband telecom company and one of the largest Tier-1 Internet service providers in Europe.

➢ **Built business plan for entering web hosting business.** Executed co-marketing deals with 2 technology companies.

EDUCATION

COLUMBIA UNIVERSITY, New York, NY
Master of Business Administration | Bachelor of Science, Computer Science

CHAPTER 6:

Leave the Muscle, Lose the Fat

It's a catchy phrase, but what does it mean? Simply put, it refers to the fact that you want to eliminate all unnecessary details (the fat) and focus on what's most important to prospective employers (the muscle).

Following are our favorite 8 strategies to sharpen your writing, tell the whole story in half the words, and visually draw the reader's eye to what's most important.

In addition, we've included samples that demonstrate how to transition lengthy content into short, concise, easy-to-skim bites while still retaining critical information. These samples are more complex examples of what it means to write tight, lean, and clean, as you read about in the previous chapter. They take that concept to a deeper and even more meaningful level.

Strategy #1: Transform dense Summary paragraphs into short branding statements.

The most important consideration when writing or tightening your Summary is to keep the information on point and on brand. The easiest way to accomplish that is to identify and then focus on the 2 or 3 things you want readers to instantly know about you.

In this example, we've replaced an entire paragraph of relatively generic information (the traditional version) with 2 sharp lines that highlight this executive's unique value (the modernized version).

Example #1: Traditional

Global Corporate Development Executive
Senior Operating Executive / VP, Sales & Marketing

Bilingual (English/Spanish) Leader with demonstrated achievement including both top- and bottom-line growth in domestic and international markets. Effective business builder and mentor with a keen insight to solving business problems and creating synergies that drive multimillion-dollar growth regardless of economic environment. Tenacious at identifying new revenue opportunities, securing customer loyalty, and forging solid relationships with external and internal business partners.

Example #1: Modernized

Global Corporate Development Executive
Senior Operating Executive / VP, Sales & Marketing

Bilingual (English-Spanish) Business Leader
Delivering Top- & Bottom-Line Growth in Multinational Markets Since 2003

Strategy #2: Transform long bullet-point Summaries into short, easy-to-read paragraphs with a headline as a bonus.

A bullet-point Summary is often a great way to present a lot of different information clearly and concisely. But when the list becomes too long, readers quickly tune out. In this example for a new graduate, we've transformed a long bullet list into a headline, subheading, and simple 2-line summary paragraph that communicates what's most important.

Example #2: Traditional

- Master of Science in Accounting Student at Baruch College (2018 graduation).
- Bachelor's Degree in International Economics & Trade.
- Strong analytical and mathematical talents. Won national and provincial awards in native China.
- Superior ability to learn and use accounting, statistical, office, and design software.
- Teamwork experience and record of working effectively on both group and individual projects.
- Proven ability to set and achieve goals, adapt to new challenges, devise effective solutions, and support/encourage people of all ages, professionally and personally.

Example #2: Modernized

ACCOUNTING & FINANCE PROFESSIONAL
Passion for International Business

MS in Accounting and **BS in International Economics & Trade**—an award-winning analyst with multicultural background, fluency in English and Mandarin, and deep interest in the global economy.

Strategy #3: Trim the fat from company descriptions.

Of course, it's important to provide details about the companies where you've worked, but make them brief to keep the focus on you. In this example, the company description went from 3 lines to 1 by eliminating unnecessary detail.

Example #3: Traditional

RYDER DEDICATED LOGISTICS (HQ—Dallas, TX) — 2013–Present
$420 million transportation and dedicated logistics company with 20,000+ customers around the world and 100,000+ employees working in 106 countries throughout North America, South America, Europe, Asia, and Africa.

Example #3: Modernized

RYDER DEDICATED LOGISTICS (HQ—Dallas, TX) — 2013–Present
$420M transportation and dedicated logistics company; 20K+ clients; 100K+ employees in 106 countries

---

Strategy #4: Transform dense job descriptions into 1-line job scope summaries.

When you're writing about your experience, you want to focus attention on your actions and achievements, and not the mundane duties of every job. A modern technique that you might try is to replace full sentences and paragraphs with short phrases describing job scope and responsibility. See how this strategy removes fat from the following job description.

Example #4: Traditional

Galaxy Air Lines, Houston, TX   2012–2016

Senior Account Manager
Managed $300M territory, servicing Fortune 500 accounts such as Dell Computer, Exxon, and Shell as well as large regional travel agency accounts. Used solution-selling approach to drive continuous market share increases in a challenging and competitive environment. Built strong customer relationships based on performance and trust. Presented to and negotiated at all levels, from purchasing agents and travel managers to senior executives. Overcame objections and devised creative strategies to retain business in an environment of severe cost competition and travel alternatives.

   • (followed by accomplishment bullets)

Example #4: Modernized

Galaxy Air Lines, Houston, TX   2012–2016

Senior Account Manager
$300M territory | Solution selling to Fortune 500 (Dell, Exxon, Shell) | C-level presentations & negotiations

   • (followed by accomplishment bullets)

Strategy #5: Focus on the big-picture story and results and not day-to-day minutiae.

Readers are not really interested in reading job descriptions that could be identical for everyone who ever held a similar job. Keep that information to the minimum and focus on what's unique about you.

Example #5: Traditional

Senior Website Designer • BAY STATE COLLEGE, Boston, MA (2014–Present)

Design websites and manage day-to-day site maintenance. Determine design goals and specifications based on user requirements, marketing input, and comparative research. Prepare schedules and requirements documents; coordinate with marketing, content administrators, programmers, and others to deliver final product. Create mockups, final designs, templates for content developers, Flash timelines, and other special features. Test content for cross-browser compliance. Provide technical support for content providers and end users.

- (followed by accomplishment bullets)

Example #5: Modernized

Senior Website Designer • BAY STATE COLLEGE, Boston, MA (2014–Present)

Built award-winning web presence for 25,000-student college. Provide end-to-end site management to ensure maximum functionality, uptime, ease of use, and responsiveness to changing needs of students, faculty, and administration.

- (followed by accomplishment bullets)

Strategy #6: Sharpen bullet points to make impact and results jump off the page.

In the "traditional" example below—for that same web designer—it's hard to quickly find and focus on the great results she achieved. The bullet points are long and in many cases the results are hidden at the end of the sentence.

The "modernized" example presents sharp, 1-line bullet points that lead with results and provide only enough detail to create context for the achievement.

Example #6: Traditional

- Redesigned organization's website (www.baystatecollege.edu) and earned customer accolades and recognition by Northeast Education Consortium as "best college website" in 2017 and 2018.

- Served as designer on team that delivered project for remake of organization's main, 4000-page website 2 months ahead of schedule; met deadlines on all other projects.

- Enhanced quality of sites through improvements in architecture, elimination of redundancy, and incorporation of user-friendly design; maintained quality and consistency by developing and implementing style guidelines.

- Developed "canned procedures" for frequently asked questions, thereby increasing productivity of website support services.

Example #6: Modernized

- Awarded "Best College Website" by NE Education Consortium (165 universities), 2017 and 2018.

- Designed and delivered—2 months early—a total remake of primary, 4000-page website.

- Improved architecture, eliminated redundancies, and added user-friendly style guidelines.

- Increased staff productivity by creating consistent procedures for FAQs.

Strategy #7: Condense content and tighten presentation.

Even in your Education section, you may be able to save space that you can put to good use elsewhere.

Example #7: Traditional

Bachelor of Science Degree in Finance & Economics, 2010
UNIVERSITY OF VIRGINIA, Charlottesville, VA
Cum Laude Graduate
Dean's List—6 semesters

Example #7: Modernized

BS—Finance & Economics, *Cum Laude,* University of Virginia, Charlottesville, VA, 2010

Strategy #8: Put like with like and improve skimmability.

Example #8 shows a hefty list of education, certifications, and other credentials. The information is important, but it's hard to skim and read.

Simply grouping like items together and adding a bit of white space makes all the difference, as shown in the modernized version.

Example #8: Traditional

Master of Business Administration, YALE UNIVERSITY, December 2016
Certified Concierge, AMERICAN CONCIERGE ASSOCIATION, August 2014
Certified Hospitality Manager, AMERICAN HOSPITALITY ASSOCIATION, June 2013
Bachelor of Science in Hospitality Management, VILLANOVA UNIVERSITY, May 2013
Certified Front Desk Manager, AMERICAN HOSPITALITY ASSOCIATION, April 2011
Licensed Private Pilot, AIRCRAFT OWNERS AND PILOTS ASSOCIATION, December 2010

Example #8: Modernized

MBA, YALE UNIVERSITY, 2016
BS Hospitality Management, VILLANOVA UNIVERSITY, 2013

Certified Concierge, AMERICAN CONCIERGE ASSOCIATION, 2014
Certified Hospitality Manager, AMERICAN HOSPITALITY ASSOCIATION, 2013
Certified Front Desk Manager, AMERICAN HOSPITALITY ASSOCIATION, 2011

Licensed Private Pilot, AIRCRAFT OWNERS AND PILOTS ASSOCIATION, 2010

To further demonstrate the many ways to save the muscle and lose the fat, look at the 2 resumes on the following pages.

Gerald Jackson Resume—page 58

Gerald's resume is a concise 1 page. It begins with a 1-line summary that touts his record of operational efficiency. His company description is 1 line. His job descriptions are short paragraphs, and each bullet point is no longer than 2 lines.

Charles Martin Resume—pages 59–60

Charles's resume begins with a headline, followed by a subheading that instantly conveys the 3 key points he wants readers to know first. Under each job title is a single line with short phrases describing his job scope. His bullets are 1 or 2 lines long, and his entire 2-page executive resume is easy to skim and read.

GERALD JACKSON
Holiday, FL 34690 • (727) 334-4544 • gjackson@yahoo.com

PRODUCTION MANAGER

Maximize operational efficiency and cost control through exemplary management of people and processes.

Core Strengths

- **Manufacturing / Production:** Experience guiding a wide range of operations, including quality control and improvement, scheduling, distribution / transportation, and shipping / receiving.

- **Innovation / Leadership:** Track record for designing and executing production improvements to optimize resource planning / management. Six Sigma Green Belt with lean manufacturing capabilities.

- **Team Building:** Strong communication skills and ability to supervise and motivate shift crews to perform at high levels through training, mentoring, and setting of clear productivity expectations.

Outstanding performer and colleague with strong listening skills and commitment to helping others succeed.

CAREER HIGHLIGHTS

ABSOLUTE PHARMACEUTICALS, Holiday, FL • 2013–2019
Company that manufactures injectable drug components and delivery systems for distribution globally.

Area Manager • 2016–2019
Ensured high quality and efficient production operations, monitoring various processes for problems and identifying improvements. Proficiently executed full range of supply chain functions, such as shipping / receiving, distribution / transportation, raw material management, and logistics support. Led completion of special projects.

- Strengthened production staffs' performance through stellar supervision, training, and coaching.

- While serving as sole manager on night shift, took initiative to learn full range of production operations, including tool / dye, quality assurance, and machine mechanic processes.

- Gained reputation as a hands-on, highly communicative manager and supervisor, often serving as intermediary between line staff and senior management on HR and work-related issues.

- Earned respect and trust from subordinates by leveraging production experience and active listening / participatory management style.

- Saved company $5K+ through design of Kanban system to avoid over-production of raw materials.

Press Operator • 2013-2016
Operated production machinery in manufacture of medical caps, setting up and monitoring operations to identify and resolve cap defects and minimize waste and downtime. Worked closely with quality assurance staff.

- Performed effectively within press operations team employing 3 staff and 8 presses to manufacture approximately 1M medical caps daily.

- Groomed by senior management to assume role as Area Manager; given opportunity to participate in numerous corporate-sponsored training seminars within high-level leadership and management areas.

EDUCATION / CERTIFICATION / COMPUTER SKILLS

Associate's Degree in Communication, Stephenson University, Irvine CA
Six Sigma Green Belt
Microsoft Office Suite (Word & Excel) and Kronos Scheduling Software

CHARLES MARTIN

212-730-9168 | charles.martin@gmail.com | linkedin.com/in/charlesmartin | New York Metro

SENIOR EXECUTIVE: CEO / CHANGE MANAGER

Growth Catalyst | Turnaround Architect | MBA

Executive repeatedly promoted to lead strategic expansions and turnarounds. Consistently drive revenue growth, transform culture, and improve operations. Bring focus, drive, and energy critical to building businesses. Excel at developing strong teams of top performers while creating and executing marketing and branding strategies.

Strong analytical skills with sharp focus on the bottom line. Responsive. Direct.

EXPERIENCE & ACHIEVEMENTS

Hercules Investment, New York, NY   2015–2019
Company invests in small to medium-sized unlisted companies with intent to grow them long-term.
MANAGING DIRECTOR

$600M revenue | 5 portfolio companies | 600 employees

- **Turned around 2 subsidiaries** (Bilbao and Volva).
- Delivered **37% EBITDA** on the portfolio, more than 2X average of the S&P 500.
- Acquired $50M, 50-staff engineering company in 2012 and sold at **73% ROI** in 3 years.

Star Group, Seattle, WA   2013–2015
Family-owned grain products business. $850M revenue, 500 employees, 16 production units in USA, Canada, Europe.
MANAGING DIRECTOR, Star Group North America
BOARD MEMBER, Star Group

$600M revenue | 5 companies + subsidiaries | 7 production units

- **Reversed 3 years of sliding performance,** turning around 4 of the 5 companies through assortment analysis, rationalizations, and workforce reductions.
- **Increased North American revenues 28% and profits 35%** in 2 years.

Northern Food Products, Dallas, TX   2010–2013
NASDAQ-listed food company. $15B revenue, 5000 employees.
GENERAL MANAGER, Northern Food Retail

$400M business unit | 8 production units | 1400 employees

- **Grew company in stagnant market**, achieving positive results every year and increasing business unit profits **40%.**
- **Launched Northern Food into the burgeoning Fast Casual channel,** striking deals with Panera and Qdoba.
- Led smooth integration of Premier Foods into Northern. Doubled retail business unit from **$200M** to **$400M.**

Venture Corporation, Seattle, WA   2005–2010
Leading food company. NASDAQ-listed, $2B revenue, 500 employees.
SALES DIRECTOR, Venture Cheese & Dairy, 2006–2007

$900M revenue | 28 employees

- Member of the management team involved in company-wide strategy setting and decision making.
- **Refocused sales team.** Outlined and implemented key account manager structure, new business programs, and profitability strategies that together led to **18% jump in sales revenue and 34% surge in profits.**

Birgitta Moller, ACRW • www.cvhjalpen.nu

MARKETING DIRECTOR, Venture Cheese & Dairy, 2004–2006

$30M marketing budget | 7 employees

- Recruited to build marketing and products organization from ground up when 2 business entities merged.
- **Dethroned market-leading company** and increased market share radically when cutting-edge concept was launched and **became category captain.**
- **Increased brand awareness 6 percentage points.**

MARKETING MANAGER, Venture Food Partner, 2002–2005

$300M revenue | 3–person marketing organization

- **Built and grew** range of products for newly launched partnership.
- **Architected business plan** from scratch covering marketing and branding strategies.

Comida XYZ, Madrid, Spain   **2012–2005**

Group owned by Hola, leading supplier of branded consumer goods. Turnover $34B, 12,5000 employees.

PRODUCT MANAGER

$250M revenue | 1 direct report

- Launched new fast-food concept in Spanish market. **Grew revenue from $0 to $60M in 2 years**.
- Directed process of replacing all equipment and products at 260 units in Europe.
- Created business plan for concept, assortment, branding, and marketing.

Promoted out of Management Development program **in 6 months** and appointed **Comida's** Product Manager in Spain.

BOARD POSITIONS

Chairman of the Board/Acting CEO, Upstart XYZ (Food Technology)	2018–Present
Chairman of the Board, YourHealthNow (Medical Technology)	2017–Present

LANGUAGES

English (native), **Spanish** (fluent), **German** (conversational)

EDUCATION

Executive Master of Business Administration (MBA)	London School of Economics, London, England
Bachelor of Science in Business and Economics	Xavier University, Cincinnati, OH

CHAPTER 7:
Integrate Your Critical Keywords

Keywords are the backbone of all electronic resume-scanning technologies and applicant tracking systems (ATS). Nearly all companies and recruiters use keywords as the primary method to identify qualified candidates, and they are *the* words that will help you get found online and make the cut.

To understand how critical keywords are to your search, consider a recruiter seeking a candidate with supply chain experience. Maybe you have all of the core skills—purchasing, logistics, inventory control, and other related activities—but you've never used the exact words "supply chain" in your resume.

When that recruiter does a search using those words ("supply chain") as the #1 keyword, your resume will probably be overlooked even though you have precisely the experience the recruiter seeks. Most recruiters and hiring managers use multiple keywords to identify candidates, but you never know.

> **PRO TIP: In online and database searches, candidate selection has evolved into an almost entirely technical function.** Know the keywords for the jobs you are targeting!

Now, think beyond just job skills and consider the hiring manager who is recruiting an electrical engineer for a company in Cincinnati. It's easy to do a search for an electrical engineer, but the company only wants candidates in Cincinnati, so that word becomes a searchable keyword term. Zip codes can also be used.

Employers often look to recruit candidates from competitor companies. Some are interested only in graduates from Harvard and Yale. Others might be searching for a rare technical skill. The specificity of a keyword search can be deep, so you *must* focus every word in your resume on information that matters most.

Keywords and searchable terms have greater range and diversity than you might think. They encompass:

1. **Hard Skills & Facts**

Job Titles	Areas of Expertise
Professional Skills	Industry-Specific Language
Technology Qualifications	Project Highlights

2. **Soft Skills**

Communications	Interpersonal Relationships
Organization	Collaboration and Teamwork
Prioritization	Personal Traits and Attributes

3. **Educational & Training Credentials**

College/University Names	College Degrees, Majors, and Minors
Professional Credentials	Training Programs and Training Organizations
Professional Licenses	Internships and Fellowships

4. **General Information**

Company Names	Professional Affiliations
Product Names	Cities, States, and Zip Codes
Foreign Languages	Countries and International Details

If you're currently working in a job that's similar to those you are targeting, you're in luck. The single most valuable resource in identifying keywords for your industry and profession is you! The duties and functions that you perform every day (hard skills) and the manner in which you do your job and the way that you perform (soft skills) are precisely the keywords you will want to feature in your resume.

For others who are seeking positions with greater responsibilities, changing careers, graduating from college, returning to work, and in other situations, keyword identification might not be quite so easy. Here's a wealth of resources to help you identify your most critical keywords, particularly your hard and soft skills:

- Online job postings
- Company websites (job postings, "About Us," or "Mission")
- LinkedIn Group conversations, job postings, and company pages
- Social media engagement and multimedia sources
- Professional associations (newsletters, meetings, conferences, and networking)
- Formal job descriptions
- Books, trade journals, specialized industry dictionaries, and other online and hard-copy publications

Integrating keywords is a crucial part of modern resume writing. Perhaps the quickest and easiest technique is to create a "key skills" or "core competencies" list as part of your Summary. Load that list with all of your top keywords to paint a picture of someone who is well qualified for the positions you are targeting.

But don't stop there. Ideally, your keywords should be incorporated into all areas of your resume. In essence, you are using the language of your profession to describe your activities and achievements. See how it's done in the 2 resumes that follow.

Sally Johnson Resume—page 63

Sally's resume starts with a headline (keywords), Summary with keyword-rich bullets, a keyword skills section, and job summaries that are concise yet descriptive. The core achievement of each job—positioned directly below the title—also includes keywords for her field of Public Relations.

Gwen Morgan Resume—page 64

In Gwen's resume, you'll see a keyword list immediately below the headline, then a second list of her technology expertise that is loaded with searchable terms. Even the Education section includes keywords via the course listings. The well-written bullets in the job description integrate still more keywords.

SALLY JOHNSON

https://www.linkedin.com/in/sallyjpr

Open to Relocation ♦ 737.995.6463 ♦ sallyjohnson@mac.com

PUBLIC RELATIONS / COMMUNICATIONS

Dedicated and creative new professional with an eye for detail poised to excel in the communications field. Proven track record as a social media innovator, gaining loyal followers and building brands to boost company profits.

- ♦ Strategic communicator who successfully pitched stories and ideas to bloggers and journalists.
- ♦ Confident public speaker spurring others to action. Impeccable organizer for high-profile events.
- ♦ Publisher of articles circulated to 40K+ students within campus community through social media tools.

Social Media Management | Event Planning & Management | Blogging | Research | Email Marketing | Publicity | Editing | Press Releases | Media Alerts | Photoshop & InDesign | AP Style | MS Office | Google Analytics

PUBLIC RELATIONS EXPERIENCE & INTERNSHIPS

Fashion Public Relations Intern, 2018–2019 ♦ BEVERLY SHAW IMAGE CONSULTING AGENCY, Orlando, FL

Selected out of 3 interns to deliver styling advice as part of high-profile event for 450 socialites.

Sought out new business opportunities and partnerships for fashion consultancy re-engaging with audience after a 1-year hiatus. Researched, targeted, and identified 12+ local events and drafted and disseminated proposal letters to introduce services. Developed promotional campaigns, pitch sheets, and press kits using InDesign.

Public Relations Chair, 2018–2019 ♦ DELTA SORORITY, Orlando, FL

Planned a community-service mentoring event for 6 junior high schools in Orlando.

Established local chapter presence of national service-based organization with 50K+ members. Managed social media presence (Facebook, Twitter) and increased website analytics 60% from prior year. Carried out publicity, organized 10 donation events, and coordinated charity clothing drive collecting 300 apparel items in just 3 days.

Public Relations Intern, 2018 ♦ KEY BRIGHT COMMUNICATIONS, Washington, D.C.

Pitched branded Look Book, an idea that increased sales within 30 days of implementation.

Drafted press releases, wrote media pitches, developed communication strategies, and authored web content for 8 clients as part of virtual internship. Built trust with CEO and audience, increasing social media presence by 365 followers within 5 months. Diagramed and sketched website wireframes during business rebranding process.

Director of Publicity, 2017–2018 ♦ ON-CAMPUS COUNCIL, Orlando, FL

Introduced new cinemagraph technique, Flixel, for promoting campus events.

Brought on to turn around low social media following. Collaborated with 10 event directors and organized brainstorming sessions with executive directors. Coordinated celebrity comedy events and concerts.

Social Media Intern, 2016–2017 ♦ SOCIAL SAVVY, Cocoa Beach, FL

Pitched paper products line, an idea that was successfully implemented in Fall 2016.

Created social media presence for event management firm. Grew Facebook page to 852 fans. Researched speaking engagements and managed photo shoots for annual social media conference.

EDUCATION

BA in Communication, Public Relations Concentration, 2019 ♦ SUNSHINE COLLEGE, Orlando, FL
Dean's List ♦ Member of Public Relations Society of America

GWEN MORGAN

gwen.morgan@gmail.com ▪ 860.675.5555

INFORMATION TECHNOLOGY SPECIALIST

CCNA Training	Operations Analysis	Troubleshooting
Data Control Functions	Diagnostic Procedures	Customer Service
Computer Programming	Installation / Maintenance	System Evaluation

Results-driven and Cisco-certified technical professional offering deep knowledge of information technology systems. Highly effective communicator with strong presentation, project management, and networking skills. Natural problem solver and efficient troubleshooter; detail oriented and skilled in testing programs. Outgoing representative with expertise in customer service.

Project Management InsightIQ, Operations Manager, Analytics, Oracle Enterprise Manager, MS Visio, MS Project

Network/Infrastructure VLans, Trunking, LAN/WAN links, NAT, PAT, TCP/IP, ACL, Routing

Languages/Frameworks PostgreSQL 8, HTML, JAVA, Visual Basic, C++, Ruby

Software Proficiencies Oracle ZFS, Hitachi HCP/HDI, Dreamweaver, Flash, Microsoft Office Suite: Word, Excel, PowerPoint, Publisher, Outlook

PROFESSIONAL EXPERIENCE

FREEDOM CLAIMS AND LIFE INSURANCE, Springfield, MA
Network System Analyst   2016 – Present

Reduced ticket issues 35% by training users and developing "Troubleshooting FAQ Guide," a user-friendly, self-directed, online resource manual.

- Monitor network to ensure network availability to 75 system users and perform maintenance.
- Provide technical support on-site or remotely through analysis, testing, and troubleshooting.
- Diagnose and resolve hardware, software, and other network and system problems while informing users of necessary changes, issues, and timelines.
- Perform network maintenance to ensure optimal network operation.
- Install, configure, and support local area networks.

CERTIFICATION & EDUCATION

Cisco Certified Network Associate – 2018

Bachelor of Science – Information Technology Systems – 2016   New York University, New York, NY

Coursework included...
Workflow Diagrams, Database Management, Information System Ethics, Project Management, System Analysis & Design, Desktop Build & Installations

VOLUNTEER SERVICE

HARTFORD HIGH SCHOOL, West Hartford, CT
Head Track Coach   2016 – Present

Erica Tew, CPRW • CT Department of Labor • www.ct.gov/dol

PART III:
Modernize Your Resume Format

The 6 Principles of Modern Resume Formatting
- Showcase Your Career with the Right Resume Structure
- Pop Your Contact Information
- Follow the Rules of Good Formatting
- Improve Readability & Skimmability
- Choose a Font that Fits
- Prepare for the Complexities of Online Search

Format—the structure and layout of your resume—matters, and it matters a lot!

In Part III of this book, we shift our focus from writing great resume content to selecting the resume format that best showcases everything you've written about yourself and your career.

Decades ago, selecting the right resume format was easy. Resumes were basically chronological listings of where you worked, what you did, and the dates of your employment. Of course, your education was also included, as well as your personal information.

On occasion, job seekers who faced unique challenges—such as returning to work after years of unemployment or transitioning from military service to the corporate world—used a functional format to put the focus on their skills and qualifications with just a brief mention of their work experience. Read Part V of this book for detailed explanations and samples for several of these situations.

Guess what? Not all that much has changed! There are still only 2 basic resume formats, but there are hundreds of things that you can do within those formats to highlight what is most important to present your skills and experience and capture the interest of prospective employers.

CHAPTER 8:
Showcase Your Career with the Right Resume Structure

Which resume format is right for you—Combination or Functional? Let's explore both so you can determine the format that works best to showcase your career.

Combination Resume

Today's modern resume combines the best of the 2 traditional formats: the structured presentation of your work history and education (the largely now-defunct pure chronological format), along with a strong emphasis on your core skills, qualifications, and achievements (the functional format).

> **PRO TIP: 90% of all great modern resumes are combination resumes.**

Combination resumes generally include 3 critical content sections:

- **Summary** (Career Summary; Professional Profile; Qualifications Profile; Core Competencies)
- **Experience** (Work Experience; Professional Experience; Employment Experience)
- **Education** (Education & Professional Credentials; Training & Education; Degrees & Licenses)

> **PRO TIP: If you're a young college graduate, Education is your #1 selling point** and will probably come before Experience. For all others, stick with the order as outlined above.

Other sections that may be appropriate to include in your combination resume, based on your own experiences and career path, include the following:

Technology Qualifications or Technical Skills
Professional Credentials
Professional Affiliations
Board of Director Appointments

Community & Civic Memberships
Languages
Public Speaking
Publications

You'll find that the majority of resumes in this book are combination resumes. Why? A combination resume allows you to tell your career story in a way that employers can quickly scan and easily understand. At the same time, it gives you many opportunities to share your specific successes, valuable contributions, and unique qualifications. It offers immense flexibility in an easy-to-follow structure.

> **Pro Tip: Your resume does not have to be 1 page**—that's one of the great myths of resume writing. It needs to be long enough to state your qualifications and tell your career story in a readable, attractive format. For some, that can be accomplished in 1 page; for others, 2 pages are needed—and that's fine!
>
> As a general rule, graduating students and young professionals will have a 1-page resume. More experienced managers and executives will often need 2 pages to include all of the relevant information. All of the examples in this book are rich and deep in content, yet well organized and tightly written so that everything fits on 1 or 2 pages—as appropriate for that individual.
>
> With our modern emphasis on lean content and tight writing, we rarely create 3-page resumes, even for very senior executives. But, on occasion, the content may warrant a third page.
>
> The bottom line is that there is no rule about resume length. You should first write the content, edit carefully, format for visual appeal and readability, and make final adjustments for good page layout.

Goldie Norman Resume—page 71

Goldie's combination resume clearly organizes the information to showcase her experience, achievements, and education.

A few things you'll notice:

- This resume begins with a headline (Operations Manager) rather than a heading such as the word "Summary." Many of the resume samples in this book use the headline technique because it is so powerful. With just a glance, every reader knows *who* this candidate is and *what* she can do.
- After a short paragraph, the Summary continues with a list of core competencies—the all-important keywords that are relevant to Goldie's target positions.
- Employer names, dates of employment, and job titles are clearly shown.
- A short paragraph describes the scope of Goldie's responsibilities, and then 2 to 4 bullet points showcase the most important information in this resume: her unique achievements.

Functional Resume

Just like the combination, the functional resume also includes all of your skills, qualifications, achievements, and important and distinguishing information. But it is structured in a way that separates all of that content from when and where it happened.

The advantage to a functional resume is that it can disguise situations such as gaps in employment, an unrelated job history, absences from the workforce, and other challenges faced by some job seekers: career changers, job hoppers, people returning to work after caring for family, people transitioning from military-to-civilian careers, and ex-offenders. As such, it can be the right format for some. If you fall into any of these categories, be sure to read Chapters 20, 21, and 22 for more specific information and samples.

Because a functional resume makes it hard to determine exactly what you did when and where, many employers prefer the combination resume, which gives them the information they seek in a more predictable format. However, if a combination resume is going to instantly share information that is *not* to your advantage, you may find the functional format a better choice.

Pro Tip: Only about 10% of job seekers need functional resumes. Unless you are faced with a challenging situation, a combination resume is most likely your best option.

A functional resume does include a work experience section, but it's generally at or near the bottom of the resume and includes little or no detail—because all of the valuable information has already been presented earlier in the resume to showcase skills, projects, achievements, and other qualifications.

The functional resume typically includes 4 key sections—the same 3 primary sections found in a combination resume (Summary, Experience, Education), plus one more critically important category that contains the majority of the content.

That fourth section, which showcases your most noteworthy and relevant experience, should have a headline that communicates the value of the information that follows. Here are a few examples that have worked for job seekers in creating effective functional resumes:

- Career Overview
- Key Accomplishments
- Experience Summary
- Experience Highlights
- Skills and Achievements
- Core Competencies
- Project Highlights

Or you can create a heading for that section that most closely aligns with your skill sets. For example, a "Technology Innovation" heading might work well for those in IT, new media, social media, and related industries and professions.

Functional resumes can include additional sections, just like the combination resume, if those sections are relevant to the specific job seeker. Just as a reminder, those sections include the following:

Technology Qualifications
Professional Credentials
Professional Affiliations
Board of Director Appointments

Memberships
Languages
Public Speaking
Publications

Ned Sung Resume—pages 72–73

To see how a functional resume is structured, take a look at Ned's resume. You'll notice:

- It begins with a headline and a strong Summary paragraph.
- Ned's Leadership and Technical Competencies are positioned in an easy-to-skim format toward the top of the page—a quick reference for hiring managers looking for a specific skill set.
- The third section, titled "Key Accomplishments," is the meatiest and most important part of Ned's resume. His rich experience and strong achievements are explained in some detail, grouped under headings that highlight his key areas of expertise.
- On page 2, Ned's Career History is listed without detail, followed by his Education and Training.

Ned's functional resume clearly positions him for his career goal in IT management while minimizing 2 potential negatives: He has never held a formal managerial role and he has been unemployed for more than a year. Now you see how well a functional format can work!

Brooklyn, NY 11230 • LinkedIn.com/in/GoldieNorman
(212) 932-8567 • goldienorman@gmail.com

OPERATIONS MANAGER

Reputation for Delivering Superior Results:
Cutting Costs, Improving Operations & Executing Innovative Solutions

High-impact Senior Operations Leader with 14 years' experience in quality control and business management. Catalyst for building high-performing teams, streamlining operations, and optimizing productivity.

- Inventory Control
- Data Collection & Reporting
- Relationship Management
- Quality Assurance

- Conflict Resolution
- Training & Supervision
- Systems & Controls
- Project Management

- Database Management
- Logistics
- Cost Reduction Measures
- Risk Management

PROFESSIONAL EXPERIENCE

RILEY ENTERPRISES, New York, NY, 2015–Present
Operations & Logistics Manager
Oversee and supervise logistics department, develop and execute on-boarding procedures, and establish and manage staff training program.

- Increased **450** customers / **16** direct reports / **14** routes to **1300+** customers / **29** direct reports / **24** routes.
- Saved **$250,000** to date by implementing fuel-tracking program.
- Captured **$40,000** cost reduction by overhauling SOPs, prompting insurance policy revisions.
- Launched company's drug-free workplace (DFW) program, resulting in additional **5%** insurance savings.

WENDELE ENTERPRISES, INC, New York, NY, 2009–2015
Field Operations Manager
Managed 75 direct reports and 15 indirect reports. Oversaw scheduling, performance, and payroll. Directed quality control, corrective action, conflict resolution, hiring, training, and termination.

- Implemented comprehensive quality assurance program that reduced customer complaints **74%**.
- Executed training program to include classroom presentations, field education, and training videos.
- Managed and coordinated all inbound and outbound sales programs and professional development.

GASWIRTH NATIONAL LEASE CORP., New York, NY, 2001–2009
Terminal Manager
Directly supervised 19 commercial tractor-trailer drivers and managed interstate and intrastate dispatch of 30 to 50 commercial drivers for load tracking and emergency response. Administered new hire training, safety inspections, driver surveillance, scheduling, and payroll. Oversaw security concerns for 18 locations.

- Received "Top Performance" awards for 5 consecutive years (2003–2008).
- Reduced security costs more than **65%**. Increased employee performance standards **41%**.

THE SECURITY CORP., New York, NY, 1995–2001
Custom Protection Officer & Supervisor
Handled armed security and supervision of security officer teams for public schools, international airports, state and federal courts, and high-security non-government and government offices.

- Awarded recognition for consistently superior performance and team improvement.
- Lowered security costs **53%** in public sector and **27%** in private sector.

EDUCATION

Bachelor of Science in Business Management – **FIVE TOWNS COLLEGE**, Nassau County, NY

Question:	*What piece of your IT Management Team is missing?*
Answer:	NIEN "NED" SUNG
Solution:	Contact Ned at 917.345.8645 or NSung@gmail.com

BUSINESS-FOCUSED IT PROFESSIONAL

Unique blend of **conceptual/visionary thinking** towards improving business processes, **analytical skills** to define objectives, and **hands-on technical acumen.** Able to rapidly comprehend complex environments and communicate effective improvements to both technical and non-technical staff at all levels. Long-standing record of delivering IT projects on time and under budget despite staffing and organizational challenges.

LEADERSHIP AND TECHNICAL COMPETENCIES

- Team Leadership & Motivation
- Project & Program Management
- Process Improvement
- Client Relationship Management

- Vendor Sourcing & Management
- Contract Negotiation & Cost Control
- Demand & Change Management
- Strategic & Tactical Planning

- Business Analysis
- Technology Infrastructure
- Enterprise Application Integration
- Technology Deployment & Evaluation

Skills & Languages:	UML, Data Modeling, XML, XSLT, ESQL, SQL, Java, C, VB, COBOL, EDI X12, SWIFT
Tools:	SalesForce.com, MOSS 2007, Internet Information Services (IIS), WebSphere, MQ, WebSphere Message Broker, WebSphere Business Integrator, WebSphere Transformation Extender, QPasa, ETI*Extract, Business Objects
Databases:	DB2, SQL Server, Oracle
Operating Systems:	Windows Servers, AIX, MVS/TSO
Software:	Microsoft Office Suite (including Vision and Project)
Version Control:	PVCS, Librarian

KEY ACCOMPLISHMENTS

BUSINESS LEADERSHIP

- Identified serious data quality problems in SalesForce CRM system that contributed to unnecessary operational risks. Gained support of business units and presented information to senior management, leading to executive authorization for a cleanup effort across multiple branches.

- Recommended combining database server with web server, ensuring data security and reducing costs by $100K.

- Drove consolidation of cross-department projects, recognizing similar needs and eliminating repetitive work. New application reduced processing time by 50% and could be easily scaled to add new departments.

TEAM LEADERSHIP & STAFF DEVELOPMENT

- Directed team of 2 senior WebSphere MQ engineers managing messaging infrastructure of North American organization, with daily responsibilities for monitoring operational support of 15 production queue managers and 50+ development queue managers on various platforms, including Z/OS, AIX, Solaris, Tandem, and Windows servers.

- Coached, mentored, and motivated underperforming systems officer through weekly one-on-one sessions. Employee became engaged in performance process and empowered to take ownership for expected responsibilities.

PROJECT MANAGEMENT

- Managed e-fax project team with 7 IT staff, 1 telecom vendor (MCI/Verizon), and 3 business people; oversaw $140K budget. Used existing resources and infrastructure to deliver project by 10% below budget.

Michelle Riklan, ACRW, CPRW, CEIC, CJSS • Riklan Resources • www.riklanresources.com

PROJECT MANAGEMENT (CONTINUED)

- Led migration of antiquated intranet to MS SharePoint technology. Obtained buy-in from 25+ business units via internal marketing efforts and proactive communications. Planned and executed project following strict guidelines for vendor management, budget control, development, testing, training, and migration.

- Led technical team to rebuild infrastructure for 4 Internet sites, including cash management and trade finance.

- Assembled and led project team for e-gateway that proved to be a revenue-generating project: $100K in first year.

ARCHITECTURE/DESIGN

- Developed 50+ integrations based on asynchronous message broker architecture, utilizing EAI patterns that included pipes and filters, dynamic routers, splitters, aggregators, request-replies, and canonical data models.

- Created e-gateway application to leverage EDI VAN capabilities for external file transfers. Dynamically routed internal files using WebSphere MQ and the WebSphere Message Broker, providing data transformation services as needed. Designed both the user interface (written in VB6) and messaging architecture.

- Developed e-fax application and outbound fax gateway, replacing legacy system with a high-fail delivery rate. Designed both the web UI (written in C# and ASP.NET 1.1) and messaging architecture well ahead of schedule.

CAREER HISTORY

BANK OF JAPAN, New York, NY   2000 to 2018
Largest bank in Japan, providing a broad range of domestic and international services around the world.

Senior Architect – CRM / Business Intelligence, 2016 to 2018

Project Manager – Web Development / Web Hosting, 2013 to 2016

Manager – WebSphere MQ Administration, 2011 to 2013

Lead Architect – Enterprise Application Integration, 2004 to 2011

Programmer – Comptroller's Group, 2000 to 2004

EDUCATION AND TRAINING

Master of Science, Information Systems Major, New York University, New York, NY
Bachelor of Business Arts, Finance Major, Adelphi University, Garden City, NY

Training: Business Objects Web Intelligence Report Design ▪ Apex and Visualforce Controllers (DEV-501)
SharePoint Technologies Comprehensive Introduction ▪ New Manager Training

Languages: Fluent in Chinese (Cantonese)

CHAPTER 9:
Pop Your Contact Information

The contact information on your resume must jump off the page! In just a few lines, you let employers know how to reach you and how to find out more about you. Here are 5 guidelines:

- **Put your contact information at the top of your resume.** While it's possible to position this information at the bottom, on the side, or in the middle of a clever design, we don't recommend it. Your goal is to get a response—an email or a phone call. Make things easy for your readers.

- **Pop your name.** Place your name boldly and distinctly so people know who they are contacting, and to immediately distinguish your resume from all others. Don't make readers search for your name in the upper-left corner in 10-point type!

- **Use only 1 phone number and 1 email address.** No one is going to call multiple phones or send numerous emails in an effort to contact you.

  Use your mobile number, so you're instantly accessible, along with a professional email address (e.g., marysmith@gmail.com and *not* marylovescats@gmail.com).

- **Determine whether to include your mailing address.** Not everyone needs to include a street address, city, state, and zip on their resume. Ask yourself if every time you upload your resume or respond to a job posting, you want all of those eyes to know where you live? With the massive surge in online identity theft, it is something to be considered.

  The only time we recommend you include your address is if you're looking for a job in the general area where you currently live and work. Companies will see that you're a local candidate, and that can work to your benefit. Even then, you may choose not to list your street address but merely your city, state, and possibly zip code.

  If you are willing to relocate—or will at least consider it—don't lead with the fact that you live out of the area. You might instantly exclude yourself from consideration. First, let employers see that you're a qualified candidate and give yourself a chance. When the time is right, they'll ask where you live.

- **Think linkability.** Be sure that you include live links to your email address, LinkedIn profile, website (if you have one), and other social media or contact information. You want to make it easy for people to instantly click through to contact you or learn more about you.

Here are 4 sample contact sections that show a variety of ways to present this critical information at the top of your resume so that it is easy to see and easy for employers to connect with you.

Roberto Diaz

212-498-1107 • robdiaz@mac.com
www.linkedin.com/in/robertodiaz • @RobDiaz

LAURIE WILSON

Denver, CO 30039 ❧ lauriewil@mac.com ❧ linkedin.com/in/lauriewilson ❧ 443.629.8362

DANA CASPER

New York Metro
212-604-2910

danacasper@nyc.rr.com
www.danacasper.com

CYNTHIA WILLIAMS

Winston-Salem, NC 27105
336-949-1101 — cynwilliams@gmail.com
http://www.linkedin.com/in/cynthiawilliams

Use the resume samples on the next few pages and in Part VI—Resume Portfolio as a resource to find a contact heading format that you like and that works best with the information you're including.

On the following pages are 2 resumes, both great examples of how to include contact information.

Jane Brown Resume—page 76

Jane's resume includes her phone, email, and location (city and state) at the top of the resume. In addition, in the gray box on the right you can see links to her Twitter account, Pinterest page, LinkedIn profile, and personal website. Employers who are so inclined can learn much more about her and easily get in touch!

Mimi Thornton Resume—pages 77–78

Mimi's resume uses an efficient 1-line format to quickly and clearly convey her relevant contact information (email, phone number, LinkedIn URL). Her city and state are included, but not her full address.

JANE BROWN

215.555.7654 – JBROWN@GMAIL.COM – PHILADELPHIA, PA

SOCIAL MEDIA MANAGER

- Expert in social media platform functionality, engagement, analytics, scheduling, and search engine optimization.
- Direct, concise, compelling communicator.
- Key contributor and project leader who clearly executes creative direction, brings new ideas to the team, and thrives in highly collaborative environments.

EXPERIENCE

MMO Gaming, Inc., Allentown, PA   2018–Present
Community Manager

- Lead team of 60 social media specialists to provide online customer assistance to **4.3M subscribers globally**.
- Eliminated phone wait times to customer lines through introduction of weekly Twitter chat (#MMONews) to brief customer base on changes from latest expansions or patches, **saving company $1.2M** annually in staffing hours and operating costs.
- Collaborate with IT, UX, and executives as tester on development team to ensure mobile, PC, and tablet accessibility.

E-Gaming Accessories, Philadelphia, PA   2014–2018
Social Media Manager

- Increased follower base **85% within 4 months** by optimizing website for searchability and reporting out on activity analytics.
- Initiated online promotions to improve in-store traffic, resulting in **35% quarterly sales increase**.
- Managed and coordinated monthly blog to share news and product updates from owners.

Datacom Industries, Trenton, NJ   2012–2014
Social Media Specialist

- Drafted posts for corporate blog and social accounts.
- Researched industry trends and presented topics at monthly meetings.
- Corresponded with public across accounts using various management tools and analytics.

SKILLS

Core Competencies: Strategic Planning, Engagement, Community Management, Search Engine Optimization (SEO), HTML

Software & Platforms: Proficient on both Mac & PC. Skilled in design for promotional content using Photoshop, Prezi, Illustrator, Dreamweaver, InDesign, Canva.

Social Media: Twitter, Facebook, LinkedIn, Vimeo, Instagram, Snapchat, Pinterest, WordPress, Vine, Blogger, Google+, YouTube

Management Tools: Tweepi, Hootsuite, Tweetdeck, Google Analytics, Klout

Microsoft: Word, Excel, Project, Outlook, PowerPoint

FOLLOW ME ONLINE

WWW.JBROWN.COM   /JBROWN

/IN/JANEBROWN   /JBPINNING

EDUCATION

University of Pennsylvania – **Bachelor of Arts Degree in Communication** – 2012
Concentration in Journalism and Marketing

Erica Tew, CPRW • CT Department of Labor • www.ct.gov/dol

MIMI THORNTON

970.260.7635 ◆ mimi3T@hotmail.com ◆ LinkedIn.com/in/MimiThornton ◆ Charlotte, NC 28212

Office Manager

SUPPORTING TEAMS AND DRIVING OPERATIONAL EFFICIENCY SINCE 2002

Loyal professional dedicated to managing projects, handling details, achieving daily productivity results, taking initiative, supporting employees and customers, and responding to challenges.

Microsoft Office Suite
Adobe Photoshop
SalesForce
ACT! CRM
Swiftpage
SharePoint
HTML / CSS
WordPress
Apple Productivity Suite

❖ **Contributed to 25% branch office profit increase in 8 months** by analyzing customer interactions and company processes, resulting in enhanced procedures focused on customer requirements and support.

❖ **Increased branch office productivity 56%** through process transformation, communication, and support for customer needs.

❖ **Reduced travel expenses, saving 70+ hours of employee monthly travel time,** by implementing cloud-based teleconferencing options.

Project Management ~ Operation Efficiency ~ Research Analysis ~ System Improvements ~ Process Updates
High-Quality Customer Care ~ Issue Resolution ~ Teamwork ~ Resource Allocation ~ Budget Coordination

EXPERIENCE

Treptow & Sellers Attorneys and Counselors at Law

2008–Present

National tax law experts with 12 national branch offices generating approximately $14 million in annual revenue

Branch Manager, 2016–Present

Lead process efficiency, productivity, and customer care. Travel as needed to provide field support. Manage logistics and project needs, set priorities and schedules, and analyze outcomes.

◆ **Direct complex office projects** with budgets ranging from $5,000 to $40,000 by identifying gaps, making quality decisions, increasing efficiency, and supporting goals.

◆ **Maintain 75+ annual attorney and client case projects** by communicating information, coordinating schedules, anticipating issues, and providing solutions.

◆ **Reduced costs 15% in 2015** by implementing advanced telecommunications solutions, including iPad Skype, HDMI connection, and Panasonic cloud-based system.

Resolve Issues — Connect Staff, Customers & Prospects — Answer Inquiries — Optimize Efficiency

Administrative Assistant, 2012–2016

Ensured branch office efforts were aligned and integrated with firm operations, while following procedures. Traveled as needed. Contributed to staff success, set priorities, and met deadlines.

◆ **Managed daily office operations** by developing client correspondence, conducting research and analysis, assisting staff, and streamlining processes to support team efforts.

◆ **Grew annual revenue** through marketing efforts that included print, online, and television advertisements, press releases, and social media posts.

Ruth Pankratz, NCRW, CPRW, MBA • Gabby Communications • www.gabbycommunications.com

- **Assisted executive team** with issue resolution, weekly meeting minutes, and strategies to support organizational goals.
- **Strengthened human resources efforts** by organizing performance evaluations, researching healthcare provider services, and capturing accurate data.

Receptionist, 2008–2012

Welcomed guests, attorneys, and staff. Supported marketing, IT, logistics, office management, corporate housing, and accounting teams. Ensured inquiries, prospects, and clients were provided with accurate and timely information.

- **Supported 1,400+ clients annually** as first point of contact and maintained client confidential data, resulting in increased client satisfaction, repeat business, and referrals.
- **Created and implemented policies and procedures** that aligned branch efforts with firm headquarters procedures, ensuring consistent client interactions.
- **Increased client response time and quality of support** through daily communications. Generated repeat business, sustained client confidence, and built trusting relationships.

EDUCATION & PROFESSIONAL DEVELOPMENT

Bachelor of Arts, English, Loyola University of New Orleans, 2007

WORKSHOPS:

The Future of Business, Small Business Association, 2018
The 7 Habits for Admin, Franklin Covey, 2017
Innovation Network: Advancing Solutions, SkillPath, 2015
Managing Projects, Project Management Institute, 2014

INTERESTS

Host, Airbnb–welcomed 45+ international visitors since 2016

Certified Open Water Scuba Diver, 2015

Writer/Blogger, 2015–Present

"Mimi's administrative and office management skills truly shone through at a time when the organization decided to take on a monumental task to move the branch office across town. Mimi's positive attitude made the overall experience calm, painless, and organized." – A. Rays, Senior Attorney, Treptow and Sellers Law Firm

CHAPTER 10:
Follow the Rules of Good Formatting

Going beyond the content of your resume, you must devote the time and attention needed to ensure the integrity of your page format and resume structure.

What do we mean by integrity? One definition is "a sound, unimpaired, or perfect condition," and a synonym is "incorruptibility." Good format integrity makes your resume (and you) appear more professional and more attentive to detail. And it keeps glitches to a minimum on the receiving end—very important when you are emailing or uploading a resume to people who can hire you … or not!

We've compiled 5 guidelines that will ensure the integrity of your resume format.

Guideline #1: Space once after punctuation. Modern keyboarding does not require the extra space after periods and other punctuation—that's a holdover from typewriter days!

But if you were taught to type with 2 spaces, it can be a hard habit to break. One thing that helped us immensely is the "Find & Replace" function in MS Word. Search for 2 spaces and "replace all" with 1 space. In just a few seconds you'll have corrected the spacing throughout your entire resume.

Guideline #2: Use the tab function correctly. Most people rely on default settings and simply hit "Tab" repeatedly to move text over on the page. But the tab feature is one of the most versatile and useful tools in MS Word. You can use tabs to position text precisely where you want it and know that it will never move even if you change the font, adjust the font size, add new content to a line, or edit existing content.

In a resume, the most valuable use of tab settings is to place dates flush right. Set a right tab at the right margin, hit the Tab key once, and, like magic, the dates will all line up perfectly and stay in position.

Tabs are also quite important if you're formatting information in columns. When you create a multi-column list of keywords, for example, you want everyone who reads it to see this:

- *Sales Management*
- *Negotiation & Sales Closing*
- *National-Level Profit & Loss*
- *Training and Development*
- *Sales Reporting & Analysis*
- *Budget Management*

… and not this—a view that can occur on the receiving end when default tab settings are used:

- *Sales Management*
- *Negotiation & Sales Closing*
- *National-Level Profit & Loss*
- *Training and Development*
- *Budget Management*
- *Sales Reporting & Analysis*

If this concept is new to you, Google "how to set tabs in MS Word" to find text and video tutorials that will walk you through the process.

Guideline #3: Be consistent. Consistency of font and font size, spacing between items and sections, and the way that you present certain types of information adds to the professionalism of your resume and aids in reader understanding.

For example, all of your job titles should be formatted identically, in the same font, font size, and font enhancement (e.g., bold, italics, underlining). All of your section headings should look the same. All of the dates should be positioned similarly.

> **PRO TIP: Consistency provides visual cues** that help your readers quickly absorb the information in your resume.

Guideline #4: Call attention to the *right* information. When you glance at your finished resume, what stands out? Your format should spotlight the things that are most important and help guide your readers through the document.

Headings should be large and clear and achievements prominent. Your career chronology should be easy to find and skim—unless you want to downplay a choppy work history or period of unemployment. In that case, *don't* call attention to your career chronology and employment dates. Rather, focus on what's most advantageous to you—education, skills, or achievements.

Guideline #5: Proofread very carefully. Sloppy formatting, inconsistent punctuation, grammar mistakes, misspellings, and typographical errors—all send a message of carelessness and lack of attention to detail. And yes, some recruiters and employers will nix your resume if they spot a mistake. Proofread … many, many times!

> **PRO TIP: Put periods at the end of bullet-point statements.** Often debated by resume writers and job seekers is whether a bullet point is a sentence and needs a period at the end. Our take: If it's a complete thought, it needs a period—even though it's written in "resume style" that omits the subject (I). Here's an example of resume bullets that need periods at the end:
>
> - Saved $50K in first year of implementing new purchasing guidelines.
> - Increased department productivity 25% by training staff on advanced software functions.
> - Brought major renovation project in on schedule and 8% under budget.
>
> In contrast, you would not use periods at the end of bullets that are simply lists of items, such as a Core Competencies list:
>
> | | | |
> |---|---|---|
> | • CCNA Training | • Operations Analysis | • Troubleshooting |
> | • Data Control Functions | • Diagnostic Procedures | • Customer Service |
> | • Computer Programming | • Installation / Maintenance | • System Evaluation |

To see great examples of strong formatting, review the 2 resumes that follow. In both, the consistent use of borders, boxes, and shading distinguishes different kinds of information and calls attention to the *right* information.

Fred Johnson Resume—pages 82–83

- Endorsements section takes center stage of the Summary and the whole resume.
- Bullet points in both bulleted sections of Summary are aligned.
- Space between bullets in Summary and Professional Experience significantly enhances readability.
- Lines under major headings and above company names provide visual cues that you're moving on to a new section.

Mark Vandermere Resume—pages 84–85

- In the Summary, format of headline, branding statement, bullets, and core competencies commmunicates he is a qualified biomedical engineer.
- Prominent positioning of Education draws instant attention.
- Relevant Coursework & Project Highlights, much like a functional resume, puts a heavy focus on his most important areas of skill and achievement.
- Computer Skills offers a visually brief and easy-to-read presentation of his most valuable software and applications knowledge as it relates to his current search.

Fred Johnson

LinkedIn Profile | 857-554-4444 | fred.johnson@gmail.com

Sales Manager – Specialty Foods
Commodity Food Items — Major Food Categories — Imported & Domestic
Fluent in English & Italian

- Transformed stagnant revenue stream into a thriving $14M+ business.
- Closed 6-figure deals while maximizing profitability.
- Drove rapid company growth through consultative, relationship-based sales.

Endorsements

Fred is dedicated and excellent at his sales job. He has in-depth knowledge of all his customers' buying patterns and has great perception on price in the marketplace.
- Sarah Seaborn, **Field Sales Manager at MB Food Distributors**

His passion for food and knowledge is quite extensive. He has been a great help in providing and sourcing items. Fred is a "get the job done" kind of guy.
- Richard Garcia, **Foodie's Urban Market**

He is delightful to work with. Customer oriented, responsive, detailed and thorough. Perfect!
- Keisha Jones, **Downtown Food Emporium**

Areas of Expertise

- Solution Selling
- Revenue Generation
- Profit Optimization
- Relationship Building
- Rapid Growth & Expansion
- Customer Service
- Account Management
- Contract Negotiations
- Promotion Planning

Professional Experience

MB Food Distributors, East Boston, MA
Wholesale distributor, selling more than 24,000 ingredients to the bakery and supermarket industries.

Sales Director *(2015 – Present)*

Report directly to owner while managing all aspects of sourcing, pricing, and selling both commodity and specialized food items. Sell to a portfolio of 250+ accounts comprising restaurants, wholesalers, distributors, and hotels. Process daily orders ranging from $200 to more than $100K, perform pricing analysis, develop revenue forecasts, and anticipate market trends to create new sales opportunities.

- Boosted overall revenue stream from $3M to $14.5M, accounting for 23% of $60M annual income.
- Consistently generated the highest gross margins among entire sales force of 30 since second year of tenure.
- Single-handedly expanded product line from 12 commodity items to 200+ specialty food items including non-GMO, gourmet pastries, and organic foods.
- Cultivated lucrative partnership with a major account by eliminating contracts, simplifying pricing structure, developing buying incentives, and offering seasonal promotions.
- Earned *Supplier of the Year Award* for Foodie's Urban Market, becoming their preferred vendor in 2017.

Continued...

Fred Johnson

Chelsea Foods, Inc., Chelsea, MA
$50M specialty foodservice distributor, specializing in high-end hotels and restaurants

Customer Service Sales Representative *(2008 – 2015)*

Serviced customer accounts, ensuring product offerings aligned with customer needs to build trust and loyalty. Enhanced product line by introducing imported specialty items, ultimately improving profit margins.

- Launched and directed specialty cheese division, achieving up to 40% margin versus 20% among colleagues.
- Expanded market reach and generated $8M in revenue by leveraging relationships with industry suppliers.

Boston Wholesalers, Boston, MA
One of the largest importers and distributors of fresh produce and specialty foods in Northeast and Mid-Atlantic.

Sales Representative *(2005 – 2008)*

Recruited to expand regional produce sales. Recognized opportunity to tap into dairy space and lobbied new dairy sector to company president.

- Gained approval to start and run entire dairy division from the ground up.
- Expanded facility to store inventory within 2 months.
- Leveraged industry contacts to pre-sell $20K–$30K in cream cheese on day 1 of department opening.

Prior

Served as Quality Control Manager at International Food Corporation, ensuring the accuracy and quality of incoming and outgoing orders of specialty imported foods, particularly limited production international cheeses.

Education

University of Massachusetts, Boston, MA
Bachelor of Science in Business Administration – Concentration in Food Science

MARK VANDERMERE

Dubuque, IA 52003
563-444-2345
mark.vandermere@email.com

BIOMEDICAL ENGINEER

Enthusiastic recent graduate eager to utilize and expand upon knowledge of microfluidics, bioinstrumentation, nanomedicine, and the engineering design process.

- **Highly motivated professional** with significant interest in drug discovery and delivery as well as strengths in project management, prototype development, and lab-on-a-chip (LOC) technology.

- **Quick study** with solid understanding of technical papers, drawings, and specifications, excellent drafting capabilities, and proficiency in wiring and programming.

- **Valued contributor** to engineering projects through excellent communication and troubleshooting skills, collaborative attitude, and commitment to innovation and process improvement.

Core competencies include:
- Data Analysis
- Mechanical Testing
- Thermal Systems
- Computer-Aided Design (CAD)
- Leadership & Teambuilding
- Report Generation
- Installation & Maintenance
- Recordkeeping

EDUCATION

BS – Biomedical Engineering (Focus in Nanotechnology), University of Iowa, Iowa City, IA (2019)

Honors: Contribution and Enrichment of the Arts Award, Presidential Scholarship

Activity: Treasurer – Biomedical Engineering Society

RELEVANT COURSEWORK & PROJECT HIGHLIGHTS

Biomedical Engineering / Nanotechnology Coursework

Bioinstrumentation ▪ Biosensors, Bio-Microelectromechanical Systems (BioMEMS) & Nanomedicine ▪ Biomedical Thermal Systems ▪ Engineering Physiology ▪ Biomechanics ▪ Biofluid Mechanics ▪ Product Development & Innovation

Robotic Surgery Simulator

Supplied mechanical, electrical, and physiological knowledge to aid in production of simulator to be used for educational purposes to display the advantages/disadvantages of robot-assisted surgery.

- Formulated and installed rotational support system to reduce jitter by 90%.

- Authored future work plan to ensure project completion in organized fashion.

- Delivered presentation at Northeast Bioengineering Conference (NEBEC) in April 2015 and published in subsequent NEBEC article.

Kidney Protection Application

Developed application to calculate risks of kidney stones in patients, using Objective-C to program system to compile information regarding beverage intake and dietary needs.

- Improved accuracy 72% by devising a method that updated the application on continuous basis.

Freddie Rohner, CARW, CRS+AF, CRS+HR • iHire • www.ihire.com

MARK VANDERMERE

563-444-2345 ▪ mark.vandermere@email.com

Project Highlights, continued

Thermo-Modulating Container

Incorporated temperature response system into point-of-care device container to control power to Peltier cooler, using microelectromechanical systems for design of thermo-modulating package.

- Provided valuable leadership throughout group project, spearheading programming of output response to high and low temperature by toggling power of the Peltier cooler.

LOC Detection of Rotavirus in Infants via Saliva

Contributed to team that employed LOC technology to develop rotavirus detection system using microfluidics.

- Created 3 plans in plant design management system (PDMS) to test mixing/separation of particles.
- Constructed and tested device compatible with optical output and fluid transport with centrifuge.

PROFESSIONAL EXPERIENCE

ENG Design, Inc. – Dubuque, IA   2018 to Present

Engineering Supporter

Brought on board to decrease project delays by addressing issues with change processes. Function as central point of contact for several departments, creating/incorporating change orders and investigating critical problems with purchasing, engineering, and production teams as well as vendors. Implement corrective action reports (CARs) and non-conformance reports. Interface with machine shop personnel to re-work current parts in stock as needed.

- Volunteered to complete diverse tasks from several different supervisors to cut release time by 50% (2 months).
- Gained in-depth understanding of ERP system within 1 month and assisted purchasing and engineering departments in preventing duplicate part numbers.
- Work closely with CTO to develop design solutions for new and current product lines; chosen to attend and participate in design review meetings.

ABC Co. – Pleasant Valley, IA   2016, 2017 to 2018

Assistant Design Engineer/Intern (2017 to 2018) ▪ **General Laborer & Polisher** (Summers 2016 & 2017)

Originally hired for general labor position polishing dandy rolls used for paper machines and assisting with plumbing for waste removal and finishing/installation of dandy rolls. Earned promotion based on knowledge of SolidWorks and received instruction on AutoCAD Inventor, completing drafts needed for key projects within short timeframe.

COMPUTER SKILLS

Autodesk ▪ SolidWorks ▪ ICAPS ▪ Minitab ▪ LabVIEW ▪ MATLAB ▪ Simulink

LibreOffice ▪ MS Office Suite ▪ Windows OS ▪ Linux Mint Cinnamon 17 "Qiana"

CHAPTER 11:
Improve Readability & Skimmability

Be wise about how people read today. Whether reading online or on paper, we skim, we glance, we move quickly from item to item, seeking to pick up information quickly.

Make sure that your resume is formatted to reward this reading style. You will keep your readers engaged if you feed them meaningful information in small bites. Specifically:

- **Write short paragraphs**—3 or 4 lines at most. If you have more to say, break your paragraph into 2 or create a paragraph plus bullet list to convey the information.
- **Add white space between paragraphs and bullets.** White space provides "breathing room" for readers to absorb one bite of information before moving on to the next.
- **Limit your bullet lists** to 3 to 5 items in each list. Too many bullets creates a large block of text that is very easy for readers to skip over.
- **Use headings and subheadings to segment and introduce information.** This is a great technique to improve the skimmability of your resume.
- **Follow the rules of good page design** in Part IV and the font recommendations in Chapter 12 as you build a resume that is both very readable and pleasing to the eye.

Of course, you don't want to shortchange yourself by omitting valuable information just to keep your content short! Here are 3 techniques that work well when you have too many bulleted achievements.

Technique #1: Divide and Conquer. You've written 8 bulleted items for your current job. All of them are important because they represent your most significant accomplishments over the past 5 years. When you first write your resume, those bulleted items might look like this:

- Produced $50M+ revenue from previously untapped states and large districts.
- Exceeded revenue target by $16M and attained 97% of margin against plan.
- Boosted market share from 39% to more than 50% of the US.
- Delivered YOY margin improvements since 2015 in a difficult environment; in 2 largest states, beat plan by $6.2M (30%) in 2018.
- Improved win percentage 45% through process changes that enabled team to respond to 25% more bids.
- Secured $145M in key contracts through competitive bids with state agencies in TX and FL.
- Reduced customer-facing errors 25% and liquidated damages $14M within first year of implementing new cross-functional leadership model.
- Led division's achievement of first ISO certification in 2017.

Even though those items are bulleted, it still looks like a large clump of text … almost like one huge paragraph … so it's very easy for a reader to simply pass over it.

If you group those achievements under subheadings, look at how much cleaner the presentation is and how much easier it is to read. By using subheadings that are directly relevant to your job objective, you increase your keyword count and draw further attention to your core areas of expertise and achievement:

Revenue, Profit & Market Growth

- Produced $50M+ revenue from previously untapped states and large districts.
- Exceeded revenue target by $16M and attained 97% of margin against plan.
- Boosted market share from 39% to more than 50% of the US.
- Delivered YOY margin improvements since 2015 in a difficult environment; in 2 largest states, beat plan by $6.2M (30%) in 2018.

Operational Performance

- Improved win percentage 45% through process changes that enabled team to respond to 25% more bids.
- Secured $145M in key contracts through competitive bids with state agencies in TX and FL.
- Reduced customer-facing errors 25% and liquidated damages $14M within first year of implementing new cross-functional leadership model.
- Led division's achievement of first ISO certification in 2017.

Technique #2: Sub-Bullet. Use sub-bullets to break large items into more easily digestible bites.

For example, let's say you have a meaty bullet point that looks like this:

- Revitalized stagnant organization through a fresh look at partnerships, sponsorships, and community initiatives. Grew subscriber base 5% and sponsor/advertiser base more than 15%. Targeted and captured high-profile new sponsors—Pepsi, Subway, KFC, NASCAR, Old Spice. Forged strong, sustainable relationships with partners and affiliates.

By breaking it into a primary bullet with sub-bullets, you instantly make the content more readable:

- Revitalized stagnant organization through a fresh look at partnerships, sponsorships, and community initiatives.
  - ✓ Grew subscriber base 5% and sponsor/advertiser base more than 15%.
  - ✓ Targeted and captured high-profile new sponsors—Pepsi, Subway, KFC, NASCAR, Old Spice.
  - ✓ Forged strong, sustainable relationships with partners and affiliates.

Technique #3: Create Columns. When a bullet list or paragraph contains many short items—such as a skills list—consider using a double- or triple-column format to save space while keeping readability high.

For example, let's look at 3 different approaches for presenting a skills list for a sales manager.

First, we see skills clumped into a single paragraph, which is dense and hard to read:

Skills include business development, account management, team leadership and supervision, sales prospecting, client sourcing, sales closing, budget development, cost-benefit analysis, ROI forecasting, territory and account management, sales training, contract negotiations, and exceptional customer service.

Second, a double-column bullet list is easier to read but takes up more space on the page:

Professional Skills:

• Business Development	• Account Management
• Team Leadership	• Staff Supervision
• Sales Prospecting	• Client Sourcing
• Sales Closing	• Sales Training
• Budget Development	• Cost-Benefit Analysis
• ROI Forecasting	• Territory and Account Management
• Contract Negotiations	• Exceptional Customer Service

Third, the triple column is efficient, attractive, and easy to peruse:

Professional Qualifications:

• Business Development	• Team Leadership & Supervision	• Account Management
• Client Sourcing	• Sales Prospecting & Closing	• Sales Training
• Budget Development	• Territory & Account Management	• ROI Forecasting
• Contract Negotiations	• Exceptional Customer Service	• Cost-Benefit Analysis

On the next few pages you'll see 2 examples of well-written resumes that are also beautifully formatted for readability and skimmability.

Travis Washington Resume—page 89

Travis's resume, in a sharp-looking 1-page format, clearly highlights the skills, education, and experience that this new graduate brings to the workplace. Pay particular attention to the headline, followed by a branding statement that conveys both his skill and his passion. Also note how key areas of activity are succinctly listed in a gray-shaded box under each job title to enhance both the content and visual appeal.

Sarah Monroe Resume—pages 90–91

Sarah's resume covers more than 20 years of experience in a format that is clean and easy to skim. It doesn't get bogged down in excessive details but focuses on what's really important and makes her achievements easy to spot and easy to absorb.

Travis Washington, MGIS

555-555-3455 • travis.washington@gmail.com • Web Portfolio

GIS Specialist • GIS Data Technician • Mapmaker

Merging the art of mapmaking with the science of data management to create solutions that eliminate barriers, form connections, increase human interaction, and solve problems for people and communities.

Professional Experience

Web Designer | Social Media Manager | LEISURE INDUSTRIES, INC., Alexandria, VA (Remote)   May 2016–Present

Website Redesign | Website Updates | Social Media | Interactive Application Development | Graphic Design | Document Design | Photography

- Took on increasing levels of responsibility and initiated new projects to support the company's digital presence.
- Conceived idea and created GIS-based interactive site maps for company campgrounds—the foundation for a fully interactive reservation system.

GIS Transportation Intern | PENN STATE TRANSPORTATION SERVICES, State College, PA   May 2018–Dec 2018

Enterprise GIS | Data Curation, Editing & Updating | Database Operations | Map Setup | GPS | Querying | Metadata Documentation

- As lead intern, mentored and tutored 3 interns and served as GIS expert to department heads.
- Created best practices and work flows for handling data and managing all of the university's transportation assets.

GIS Intern | HARRISBURG CITY OFFICES, Harrisburg, PA   May 2017–Dec 2017

Field Data Collection | GPS | Post-Processing | Data Maintenance & Curation | App Development | Parcel Data Updates | 3-D | Spatial Analysis

- Pioneered GPS mapping for Harrisburg, launching the city's first up-to-date and accurate GPS data resource—a critical tool for planning projects, projecting costs, and protecting assets.
- Created an interactive story map and app-based tour of city gardens—melding annual citywide competition into an easily accessible attraction for tourists and citizens. U-Spatial Best Use of Maps award, 2017.
- Developed a customized "base map" for the city, drawing city-specific features and adding detailed information on streets, parks, buildings, wetlands, woods, and other sites.

Education

Master in Geographic Information Science, 2019 | PENN STATE UNIVERSITY, State College, PA
- GPA: 3.8

Bachelor of Arts in Multimedia Arts and Sciences, 2017 | CARNEGIE-MELLON UNIVERSITY, Pittsburgh, PA
- Emphasis: 3-D Animation | Minor: Applied Mathematics
- Capstone Project: "Music in Motion," recognized as one of the year's most compelling multimedia pieces

Technical Skills

- **Adobe Suite:** Photoshop, Illustrator, Acrobat, After Effects, Flash, Dreamweaver, Media Encoder
- **ArcGIS Online and Desktop:** Map, App-Builders, Catalog, Database, Globe, Presentation Builders, Server
- **Autodesk:** Maya, AutoCAD, Inventor, Revit, Solidworks
- **GIS Software:** OSM, CartoDB, Java API, SimplyMap, QGIS
- **Google:** Sketchup, Plus, Docs, Sheets, Drive, Keep, Sites
- **GPS:** Trimble, ArcGIS Collector, ArcPad, LIDAR
- **MS Office:** Word, Excel, Publisher, Access, PowerPoint
- **Web:** HTML5, CSS, Javascript, Python

Interests and Activities

- **Musician** (piano, vocals, percussion)—Penn State Chorale, Select Chorus, and Jazz Bands
- **Volunteer**—Habitat for Humanity, Lutheran Campus Ministries, Community Emergency Services
- **Mapmaker**—GISSO, Maptime, STIF (Students Today Leaders Forever): Planned logistics, mapped, and chronicled 3 annual bus tours bringing students to community service projects across the country.

Louise Kursmark, MRW, CPRW, JCTC, CEIP, CCM • Best Impression Career Services • www.louisekursmark.com

Sarah Monroe

New York Metro •••• 201-908-4566 •••• sarah@sarahmonroe.com

Operations Management Executive
Bilingual English / Spanish

COO with a passion for transforming and building profitable software companies (Fortune 500 and VC-backed) that surpass revenue targets and shareholder expectations.

Vibrant operations strategist who guides business growth to the next level with consistent record-setting results. Skillfully manage organizational change, spearhead turnarounds, and steer merger integrations with milestone accomplishments:

- ✓ **$40M to $250M in 3 years at Sanders PLC.**
- ✓ **$320M to $780M in 4 years at RNA, Inc.**
- ✓ **$0 to $5M within first year of PT Solutions' startup.**

Experience and Results

SANDERS PLC, New York, NY   2014 – Present
$450M global provider of customer experience management software solutions serving 42 of top 50 global brands.

CHIEF OPERATING OFFICER – TECHNOLOGY DIVISION (2016 – Present)

Merged and transformed 5 underperforming divisions to create a new division representing 65% of company's total technology revenue. Manage all functions driving revenue generated globally (Asia Pacific, Europe, Middle East, Americas) in software, marketing, sales, services, and education. Lead 200 total staff, including 16 direct reports in pre-sales, sales, marketing, professional services, and customer support.

Signature Achievements:

- Grew business from **$40M to $125M** in 18 months, achieved profitability in 1 year, and laid groundwork for **30% growth** in 2016.
- Steered 4 acquisition integrations that achieved **60% growth** in 18 months, including seamless assimilation of a Dutch management technology company and a German mobile technology company.
- Delivered **8 strategic partnerships**, including all of company's major deals.
- Led team to deliver largest transaction **($4.5M)** in company history.

GENERAL MANAGER – NORTH AMERICA (2013 – 2016)

Recruited to jump-start flat revenue and expand market share. Transformed division's opportunistic sales model into a sustainable business. Managed P&L for North America sales organization (60 sales, pre-sales, field marketing, professional services, and customer support staff). Built and developed team focused on surpassing business goals. Broadened customer base with Fortune 100 companies (Unilever, Walmart, and HP).

Signature Achievements:

- **Doubled revenue** division-wide in 18 months and increased profitability from **59% to 75%** by developing leadership team, communicating expectations, and leveraging company's resources.
- Grew profits to **31%** of professional services business by restructuring team and introducing best practices.
- Spurred team to set a new company record, closing company's first **multimillion-dollar** deal in 2015.

Louise Garver, CERM, CJSS, CPRW, CCMC, IJCTC, CMP, MCDP • Career Directions Intl, LLC • www.careerdirections.com

Sarah Monroe ···· Page 2   201-908-4566 ···· sarah@sarahmonroe.com

PT SOLUTIONS, INC., New York, NY   2010 – 2013
VC-backed security software company developing network content capture, replay, and analysis solutions.

CHIEF OPERATING OFFICER

Piloted startup and growth of North American business. Directed P&L, brand management, product modification for US market, GTM strategy, and partner development. Positioned company for sale in 2013.

Signature Achievements:

- Established and grew US business from **$0 to $5M** in 1 year.
- Led sales team to win **$55M** in 10 US government and private sector contracts.
- Developed and closed company's largest (**$15M**) and most strategic new product transaction ever.

RNA, INC., New York, NY   2000 – 2010
One of the world's largest private software corporations.

Overview: Promoted through increasingly responsible executive roles building unrivaled sales organization in France and then expanding the business to Europe, US, and Asia.

EXECUTIVE VICE PRESIDENT/GENERAL MANAGER – MID-ATLANTIC REGION (2007 – 2010)

Reenergized and expanded company's largest sales organization following transition back to a regional, cross-product model. Took business ownership, managed P&L, and generated new customer acquisition programs. Assembled the right team and led 430 sales executives through 7 VP direct reports.

Signature Achievements:

- Delivered **30%** sales increase over 2 years: **108% of quota ($214M)** in products and services in FY 2005 and **120% of quota ($245M)** in FY 2006.
- Generated **double-digit** increases in new product revenue by capturing competitor replacement business and initiating strategic partnerships with 3 technology industry leaders.
- Maintained **highest customer satisfaction rate** by ensuring world-class service.
- Led smooth integration of a **multibillion-dollar acquisition while retaining entire customer base.**

EXECUTIVE VICE PRESIDENT – ENTERPRISE MANAGEMENT SOLUTIONS (2006 – 2007)

Launched a new sales and customer interaction business model, focusing region on solution selling and customer satisfaction. Directed team of 5 regional sales VPs with 210 indirect reports.

Signature Achievements:

- Delivered **25% product-line growth to $250M in 1 year**—largest division in new product revenue.
- Led team to **produce 60%** of revenue target in North America for all Enterprise Management Solutions.
- Division **won recognition for highest new product revenue generation** in 2004.

SENIOR VICE PRESIDENT – NEW YORK REGION (2003 – 2006)

Grew sales 45% ($66M) YOY from single digit to record-setting 31% of company sales. Achieved top percent revenue growth out of 20 regions company-wide. Led multibillion-dollar acquisition.

Prior positions at RNA, Inc.: Global Director, Corporate Sales (2004 – 2007); Sales Manager (2000 – 2004)

Education

Bachelor of Science in Management, Honors Graduate – NEW YORK UNIVERSITY, New York, NY

CHAPTER 12:

Choose a Font that Fits

Three factors influence your font selection:

- Universal fonts
- Space considerations
- Image and appearance

Universal Fonts

Recruiters, hiring managers, and other decision makers will be looking at your resume electronically—whether you send by email or upload to a database. Either way, you want to be sure that it is entirely readable and looks just the way you formatted it. You don't want your resume to open with a garbled font, a strange replacement font, or another glitch that affects readability or creates a negative first impression.

The best way to achieve this goal is to use a *universal font*—one that is found on just about every Windows and Mac computer system.

Recommended Universal Fonts

Arial	Bookman	Georgia	Palatino Linotype
Arial Narrow	Calibri	**Impact** (Headings)	Tahoma
Arial Black (Headings)	Cambria	Lucida Sans	Trebuchet
Book Antiqua	Garamond	MS Sans Serif	Verdana

> **PRO TIP: You'll note that Times New Roman is not on the list,** although it is certainly a universal font. In fact, it has been universal for so many years that it has become widely overused. In our opinion, it appears outdated and predictable, so we do *not* recommend it.

Of course, many more fonts are available, and you may not want to limit yourself to these safe choices. The font you choose has a huge impact on the overall appearance and image that your resume presents, so be sure that it communicates the *right* message about who you are and what you can do.

A word of caution: If you do use a non-universal font, we recommend saving your resume in PDF format to be sure it transmits properly to everyone. Choose the option to "embed" fonts in your PDF, and be certain to test your file by emailing to yourself and friends.

Bottom line, it's more important to create a resume that's readable than to use your favorite (non-universal) font.

> **Pro Tip: For ATS scanning purposes, font is no longer a prime consideration.** When scanning systems were capturing information by physically scanning a page of text, it was important to use a clean, safe font. Now systems read the underlying code rather than text on a page, so your font choice is immaterial.

Space Considerations

Font selection and sizing have a huge impact on not only how your resume looks but also how much information you can fit on a page. Look at the 2 following sentences, both in a 12-point font. The first is in Arial Narrow; the second in Bookman.

> Recruited by Pepsi to capture new customers and build sales volume in the stagnant OH region.

> Recruited by Pepsi to capture new customers and build sales volume in the stagnant OH region.

Look at the difference in how much space they use. Therein lies your challenge—to find the *right* font that works well with the content you've written.

> **PRO TIP: If your resume looks crowded or hard to read, try a different font.** You might be surprised at how much less space a different font requires—even though it is in the same font size—or how dramatically it changes the overall look of your resume.

The size of your font also has an enormous impact on readability. Because fonts are so variable, we don't have a universal recommendation regarding font size.

In the following examples, we show 4 fonts in the same size. You can see how different they are:

> Modernize Your Resume: Get Noticed … Get Hired (9-point Garamond)
> Modernize Your Resume: Get Noticed ... Get Hired (9-point Calibri)
> Modernize Your Resume: Get Noticed ... Get Hired (9-point Trebuchet)
> Modernize Your Resume: Get Noticed ... Get Hired (9-point Verdana)

Above, only Verdana is comfortably readable in 9-point size.

> Modernize Your Resume: Get Noticed … Get Hired (11-point Garamond)
> Modernize Your Resume: Get Noticed ... Get Hired (11-point Calibri)
> Modernize Your Resume: Get Noticed … Get Hired (11-point Trebuchet)
> Modernize Your Resume: Get Noticed ... Get Hired (11-point Verdana)

At 11 point, Garamond is now readable, and both Calibri and Trebuchet would work well. Verdana, however, now appears too large—almost elementary.

Of course, when your resume is read on screen, the reader can enlarge the view if needed. But that is not the case for your printed resume, which still has a significant and important role in your job search—for interviews, networking meetings, and other in-person job search activities.

> **PRO TIP: Print your resume** to be sure that the font selection, font size, and overall presentation are attractive and readable. Do not rely entirely on your computer screen!

Image and Appearance

In many ways, font selection is—and should be—a matter of personal preference. What do you like? What font, in what size, creates a resume that you think looks great and conveys a professional image that is appropriate to your field, function, and role?

Some people find *serif* fonts—such as Bookman and Cambria, with small embellishments to the basic lines of each character—to be more readable. Others feel just the opposite—that *sans serif* fonts such as Tahoma and Arial are more readable. Interestingly, studies have "proven" both statements to be true!

Given this lack of agreement, you can safely choose a font that you like—one that you find readable and attractive—without worrying about legibility.

A final consideration in font selection is *contrast*. How much contrast is there between the bold and non-bold type? With some fonts, the difference is extreme:

Tahoma / Tahoma Bold • Bookman / Bookman Bold

With others, it's less noticeable:

Calibri / Calibri Bold • Palatino Linotype / Palatino Linotype Bold

If you are using a lot of bold type in your resume, a too-heavy bold may appear overpowering. Conversely, if your resume is relatively text-heavy, use the very bold contrast to improve readability.

> **PRO TIP: Consider using 2 different fonts in your resume:** a primary font for text and a second font for headings. Try Arial or Arial Narrow with Arial Black for headings, or Calibri text with Cambria headings, or another combination that you find adds impact and interest.

Font Enhancements

Bold type is not the only way to enhance a font. When designing your resume, experiment with the many ways you can vary the appearance and impact of your text on the page and on screen.

- ALL CAPS can help you create contrast and send a consistent message—for example, you might put company names in ALL CAPS and job titles in **Bold**. Headlines are another great application for all caps. But just as all caps equates to SHOUTING in an email message, blog post, or tweet, the same is true in your resume. Use ALL CAPS for emphasis but not for narrative content.

- SMALL CAPS is a distinguishing younger cousin of ALL CAPS! Similarly, it should be used for consistency and emphasis in titles, headlines, and more, but not for large bodies of text.

- *Italics are very useful for content that should be understated, such as company descriptions. Avoid using italics for large blocks of text or for any material that's really important because it tends to blend in rather than stand out.*

- **Colored or shaded fonts**, when used consistently, send a subtle message to readers and help them identify different types of content in a resume. Make certain that any colored text is highly readable on screen or if printed on a black-and-white printer.

Your ultimate objective in choosing a font for your resume is to create a distinctive, professional, appropriate image while conveying all of the information you want to share with prospective employers. The following 2 resume samples are very different, but each is an outstanding illustration of a font selection that perfectly supports the job seeker's objective and creates the *right* professional image.

Cherie Rasmussen Resume—pages 96–97

Cherie has chosen Comic Sans, a font that's universal but not commonly used for business documents. However, it works extremely well in her position as an elementary school teacher. The school bus and scissors graphics are also perfect for her.

Justin Lang Resume—page 98

Justin is a Marketing and Sales Executive. His resume is written in Cambria, an attractive modern font that conveys a progressive and professional image. The mix of bold and italic fonts differentiates the various kinds of information in the resume.

CHERIE RASMUSSEN

Relocating to Portland, Oregon
406.829.0999 ▪ CRasmussen@gmail.com

ELEMENTARY TEACHER: GRADES K-3

National Science Teachers' Council ▪ Teachers of Mathematics Society ▪ Montana Educators' Association

Caring, energetic teacher who creates stimulating learning environments, promotes scholastic and social development, and helps children enhance their unique potential for academic and personal success. Patient educator able to blend cooperative learning, classroom management and innovative teaching to create a foundation for lifelong learning. New graduate excited to begin a full-time teaching career in Portland as a ...

- ✎ **Student Motivator:** Creating learning environments respectful of cultural diversity, physical limitations, gender differences, and religious affiliation to meet all students' needs.

- ✎ **Classroom Manager:** Initiating early academic intervention to promote positive reinforcement, mutual respect, and individual responsibility.

EDUCATION & CREDENTIALS

UNIVERSITY OF MONTANA High Honors Graduate, May 2019
Bachelor of Arts in Elementary Education – Reading, Mathematics, and Science Endorsements
K-8 Montana Elementary Teaching Certificate – SEID #12345

Trained in . . .
Dynamic Indicators of Basic Early Literacy Skills (DIBELS)
Adult, Child, and Infant First Aid and CPR, American Heart Association
Reading Well, National Center on Student Progress Monitoring (NCSPM)

TEACHING EXPERIENCE

✂ **2nd Grade Teacher Candidate**
Seeley Lake Elementary, Seeley Lake, Montana, Spring 2019

- Created a warm, exciting atmosphere where children learned and played to strengthen reading mechanics, math readiness, and technology familiarization while developing friendships and social skills.

- Developed a stimulating classroom for 23 students, including 5 receiving Title I services, with a focus on surpassing assessment standards, improving classroom behavior, and building academic confidence.

- Orchestrated IEP in collaboration with mental health counselor, in-class para-educator, and special education teacher for student with obsessive-compulsive disorder and oppositional defiant disorder.

- Verified count of Economically Disadvantaged Students to report yearly progress per No Child Left Behind Act by assessing student records to determine those eligible for or receiving free/reduced-price lunch.

Cherie has chosen Blackboard, a font that is not commonly used for business documents but works extremely well for an elementary school teacher. The school bus and scissors graphics are also perfect for her.

Cheryl Minnick, M.Ed., Ed.D., NCRW, CCMC · University of Montana-Missoula · www.umt.edu

CHERIE RASMUSSEN

✄ K-5 After-School Program Instructor
Franklin Elementary School and Hawthorne Elementary School, Missoula, Montana, 2016 – 2018

- Developed unique after-school outdoor and fun in-class educational activities to support students' social and academic achievements by building peer relationships through play and learning.
- Awarded *Volunteer of the Year 2017* for outstanding contribution and instructional excellence.
- Taught small-group educational games and outside play for a community program targeting at-risk youth.
- Worked in harmony with parents, staff, teachers, and administrators to deliver an outstanding program.
- Invited Humane Society staff to host a "Show 'n Tell" focused on puppy and kitten care.

✄ Private Preschool Tutor and Full-Charge Nanny
Missoula and Seeley Lake, Montana, Summers 2016 – 2018

- Trusted by a high-profile celebrity couple to care for their preschool children, manage an established budget, and shuttle children to/from lessons in the family vehicle.
- Collaborated with live-in housekeeper and cook for meal planning, supply purchases, laundry services, birthday and holiday celebrations, and play-date preparation.
- Cared for children during parents' extended business travel, providing tutoring, medical treatment, and transportation services. Traveled internationally with the family.
- Encouraged children to learn through hands-on educational activities and outdoor games, teaching phonetics, math, and reading readiness in a positive, nurturing environment.

COMMUNITY VOLUNTEERISM

K-3 Adventure Instructor
The Adventure Club, Seeley Lake, Montana, Summer 2015
- Expanded school boundaries beyond four walls to augment classroom learning by immersing students in outdoor adventures with focus on touch, see, smell, hear, and taste. Led students on hikes, rafting adventures, and bird watching trips. Taught "Bear Basics" focused on safety in bear country.

K-4 Soccer Coach
Missoula Public School District, Missoula, Montana, Falls 2015 – 2017
- Introduced children to soccer basics, creating a foundation for enjoyment of physical activity and competition. Taught teamwork, sportsmanship, safety, and rules of the game.

Foster Mom
Western Montana Humane Society, Missoula, Montana, 2013 – 2014
- Provided loving, in-home medical care and socialization to underage, elderly, disabled, sick, and recovering kittens and puppies to prepare them for adoption.

Volunteer Receptionist
AniMeals, Missoula, Montana, 2013 – 2014
- Offered reception service to respond to adoption and donation inquiries at a no-kill shelter and animal food bank. Promoted the shelter at fundraising events and helped gather 9000 lbs. of donated pet food.

JUSTIN LANG

☎ 305-345-1234 ✉ justinlang@gmail.com

MARKETING DIRECTOR
STRATEGIC BUSINESS PLANNING ~ BRAND MANAGEMENT ~ NEW MARKET DEVELOPMENT

Market Share Growth
Positive Earnings Impact
Cost Control/Reduction
Lead Generation
Fiscal Management
Process Improvement
Cross-Team Collaboration

Innovative, profit-oriented leader with demonstrated success increasing market share and earnings, reducing costs, and improving client satisfaction.

Expert in analyzing competitive landscape, conducting market research, and aligning product offerings with customer needs.

Change agent with ability to analyze problems, formulate continuous process improvements, and integrate business system for efficiency and cost management.

Collaborative communicator skilled in building and strengthening relationships across functions to drive cohesive, strategic operations.

CAREER PROGRESSION

PALM BEACH COUNTY MEDICAL ASSOCIATES • Royal Palm Beach, FL

DIRECTOR OF MARKETING

2015–2019

Spearheaded marketing strategy and programs for 350-physician practice group. Managed 2 Marketing Associates and $4M annual budget.

- **Marketing Strategy.** Refocused marketing toward visibility and relationship building.
- **Event Marketing.** Launched innovative health and wellness fair, attracting 50+ national vendors and 500+ attendees.
- **Social Media.** Added Twitter account, Facebook page, and blog; maintained active schedule of articles and posts, with contributions from 60% of medical staff.
- **Community Presence.** Represented practice on Health and Wellness Committee of Palm Beach Chamber of Commerce.

HIGHLIGHT

Eliminated $500K annual advertising expense while doubling rate of new patient acquisitions.

AUBURN INSURANCE, INC. • Lake Worth, FL

DIRECTOR OF MARKETING

2013–2015

Recruited as first Director of Marketing for 100-year old property insurance company.

- **Marketing Strategy.** Created the company's first formal marketing strategy and plan.
- **Program Innovation.** Started radio program dealing with the process of evaluating property claims. Built relationships by featuring local contractors as expert guests.
- **Brand Building.** Uncovered company's core values – customer focus, integrity, expertise – and built marketing, branding, and advertising campaigns to promote them.

HIGHLIGHT

Built brand recognition through educational marketing on the value of insurance.

WEST PALM DEVELOPMENT CORP. • West Palm Beach, FL

MARKETING MANAGER

2010–2013

Played a key role in launching new residential development. Assisted buyers in selecting lots, choosing finishes, and completing the process from pre-sale through closing.

- **Marketing.** Developed brochures, print advertisements, and other marketing materials.
- **Event Marketing.** Generated dozens of prospects by creating "Community Confabs" that drew large groups to learn more about homes in a non-sales environment..

HIGHLIGHT

Sold all 37 homes a year ahead of projection.

EDUCATION

BS BUSINESS ADMINISTRATION, University of Florida, Gainesville, FL • 2010

Katrina Brittingham, CPRW • VentureReady LLC • www.ventureready.net

CHAPTER 13:
Prepare for the Complexities of Online Search

Is your resume readable for both the human eye and the electronic eye?

Today's modern job search demands that you share your resume through various online and offline channels. The unique requirements of each may call for different formats or small edits to your existing format:

- **Print:** Make sure that the print version of your resume is attractive and highly readable, because you'll need it for interviews and other in-person meetings—and you want it to impress! Print your resume on nice paper (not plain copy paper), and always take multiple copies to an interview.

- **Email:** We recommend that you attach your resume as a Word or PDF file and write your message as an e-note, in the body of the email. An e-note is the modern version of the traditional cover letter.

- **Upload:** When applying to a job online or uploading your resume to a database, read and carefully follow the directions to ensure that your resume content is entirely readable.

For uploads, often both Word and PDF files are acceptable. And while every Applicant Tracking System (ATS) has its own methods for reading text, these systems are continuously being improved so that most can now handle a wide variety of formats.

Here is a simple process for creating an ATS-friendly resume.

FIRST: Understand that keywords are the foundation for electronic resume scanning. If your resume doesn't have the right keywords and phrases, you won't get a second look from human eyes.

When applying to a posted position, take the time to peruse the job description and cross-check your resume to be sure you've included most or all of the keywords that you identify—as appropriate to you and your experience. See Chapter 7 for a thorough discussion on keywords.

> **PRO TIP: Keep your resume—in multiple file formats—readily available for sharing.** For emails and applications on the go, have those files accessible through your mobile device.

SECOND: Follow these guidelines to be sure that all of the content of your resume will be captured:

- Introduce each section of your resume with a heading that clearly identifies the content that follows. For scanning purposes, it's better to have an individual section for each category rather than grouping multiple items under a catchall heading such as "Additional Information." For example, if your resume includes Affiliations, Publications, Presentations, and Community Service, list each of these separately with its own heading.

- Avoid "clever" headings and stick with words that the scanner will recognize and understand. If you use "Career Narrative" or "Success Snapshots," for example, and the ATS does not recognize this as your "Professional Experience," it may discount or completely pass over and ignore the information in that section.

- If you are beginning your resume with a Headline, as you'll see in many of our sample resumes, there's no need to add a "Summary" heading above it. ATS have learned to recognize the content in an introductory section on a resume without the need for a heading.

- In your Experience section, use a chronological (not functional) format. A best practice is to include the company name for every position, along with your job title and dates of employment, even if you've held multiple positions at the same company. Repeating the company name will ensure that the resume scanner matches that experience to the right company and time frame.

> **PRO TIP: A functional resume is _not_ appropriate for ATS scanning.** Scanners seek to tie job activities to specific employers and time frames. When you separate them, as you do in a functional resume to highlight all of your relevant experience in one section, you confuse the scanner and most likely will not get credit for your expertise, experience, and achievements.
>
> If using a functional format, for uploads you will need a second version that puts all your experience within the chronological work history. Include all of your job titles, employers, and dates.

- Do not use MS Word's text boxes anywhere in your resume. Content in text boxes cannot be read by ATS scanners and therefore nothing you include in a text box will be recognized or read. By "text boxes" we mean using Word's "Insert Text Box" tool to create discrete sections of text. Instead, find a formatting workaround that allows you to position your content where you want it—but in a way that will be read by resume scanners.

> - **PRO TIP: Use the Tables feature in Word to simulate text boxes.** For example, to create an offset box, simply insert a 2-cell table and use 1 cell for your "boxed" information and the other for the regular text that will appear alongside it. You can adjust the width of each cell to best match the contents, and you might experiment with adding borders, shading, and color to distinguish your boxed information from the rest of the resume text.

- If you use Columns (created using Word's "Layout Columns" tool), be aware that the scanners will read down an entire column and then back up to the top of the next column. Make sure that your content will make sense when read this way. Or, you might prefer to use a Table, which will be read left-to-right across a table row and then down to the next row.
- You can safely use colored text, borders, and shading in your ATS resume. Robots are no longer physically scanning the page; rather, they are reading the code and the content of your resume.
- It's fine to leave graphics, charts, and other visual objects in your resume. The scanner will skip right over them, and they will not affect the readability of the rest of the resume. Just make sure that any facts conveyed in your graphic are also described in words so that important achievements are not overlooked.

If your resume is highly designed or unusually formatted, create a second version in a much plainer format to use for your online search activities. Save the creative, great-looking version for emailing and in-person meetings, and use the plainer, ATS-friendly version to be sure that your resume passes the keyword scan.

As you'll see in the following 2 samples, ATS-friendly does not have to mean plain or boring.

Nicholas Bauman Resume—page 102

Nicholas's resume, written in the universal font Arial, is well designed and attractive. Notice the section headers and structure of the employment listing that promote ATS readability. Also note that the "Education" heading doesn't contain college or university information but does list his apprenticeship and secondary school (high school) education. Both are appropriate to list for this skilled technician.

Javier Rodriguez Resume—pages 103–04

Javier's resume mixes 2 different fonts to create a distinctive look without adding anything that will compromise ATS readability. Notice the "Skills" section in the Summary, always a great addition to beef up those all-important keywords.

Nicholas Bauman

514-345-8610   nickbauman@gmail.com

Heavy Duty Equipment Technician

Fluent French and German | Proficient English

Physically Fit | Able to Lift 100 Pounds | Prefer Working Outdoors

Ten+ years of diverse experience, mainly with diesel engines, forestry equipment, large agricultural machinery, and construction vehicles. Forklift certification.

Exceptional mechanical inclination and up-to-date knowledge of changing technologies through courses and independent study. Experience and knowledge in:

- Fuel injection systems, lubrication systems, installation and alignment of engines and machinery
- Mechanical and hydraulic transmissions, hydraulic-operated working attachments, and winches
- Troubleshooting and equipment inspection, detecting malfunctions, and determining repairs
- Mechanical and electrical repairs

PROFESSIONAL EXPERIENCE

Grand Mechanic, Montreal, QC
Heavy Machinery Mechanic and Machine Operator (2012 – current)
Work as both a mechanic (40% of the time) and machine operator (60% of the time).

- Operate a CAT digger, working mainly outdoors on construction sites.
- Repair equipment onsite, completing contracts that last from 2 days to 5 weeks.
- Attend safety meetings held for all equipment operators. Maintain excellent safety record.

Garage de l'Excellence, Quebec City, QC
Auto Mechanic (2009 – 2012)
Held responsible role with well-established garage that repairs all makes of cars, automatic and standard.

- Performed service and repairs for domestic and imported cars, small trucks, and large equipment.
- Assigned major engine rebuilds and complex machine repairs; used computerized diagnostics.

Ultimate AG, Zug, Switzerland
Service Technician (2006 – 2009)
Travelled to conduct on-site service and repairs of bulldozers, excavators, and other Caterpillar machinery associated with new road construction and gravel pits.

- Acquired comprehensive theoretical and practical training to carry out contracted service work.

Gut Brands, Zug, Switzerland
Technician, Demonstrator, and Sales Associate (2004 – 2007)
Employer is main Swiss importer of Kawasaki ATVs and sells cranes and cable winches for forestry.

- Completed sales training and while demonstrating machinery also conducted sales.
- Built newly purchased machines according to customized orders.

EDUCATION

Apprenticeship: 3.5 years Agricultural Machine Mechanic, Reinhardt & Cie., Zug
Secondary Schooling: Swiss educational system

Stephanie Clark, MRW, MCRS • New Leaf Resumes • www.newleafresumes.ca

Javier Rodriguez

Atlanta Metro Region

404-654-3210 • javier.rodriguez@att.net • LinkedIn

Regional Sales Manager – International Business
Bilingual Spanish / English

Sales Leader and Army Veteran with 20+ years of sales results, business management experience, and expertise in forecasting customer, business, and industry trends.

Performance Highlights

- Delivered double-digit sales increases year after year in intensely competitive markets.
- Successfully introduced products into Latin America, Europe, and Hispanic markets in the US.
- Led region to $4M growth by adding 100+ new distributors over 5 years.
- Formulated a market-entry strategy for Latin America and negotiated exclusive agreements in 3 countries.

Skills

- Sales Management
- Solution Selling
- International Expansion
- National-Level Profit & Loss
- Training & Development
- Financial Management
- Sales Reporting & Analysis
- Deal Negotiation
- Customer Relationship Management

PROFESSIONAL EXPERIENCE

Daisy Foods USA – Atlanta, GA

National Food Service Sales Manager   2017–Present

Craft and execute strategic roadmap for the food service and retail markets, establishing new products and enhancing current product sales. Collaborate with customers – top retailers and major restaurant chains – on product marketing, promotions, and advertising. Lead a team of 7 Regional Managers.

- Grew year-over-year (YOY) sales **18%** despite intense market competition; projecting **40%** growth in 2019.
- Led corporate initiative to penetrate food service and retail markets with new premium ice cream products. Introduced **2** new brands to distributors and **10** new SKUs to large grocery store chains. Generated **$2.6M** in new product sales in less than a year.
- Developed plan for unified and consistent messaging for all marketing and advertising materials.

Summer Edibles, Inc. – Roswell, GA

Food Services Sales Manager / Regional Sales Manager   2013–2017

Developed and directed sales in food service sector, creating sales and marketing strategies to drive brand growth. Led and coached sales team and oversaw a network of food brokers, distributors, and supermarket chains. Negotiated and implemented marketing programs. Created budgets, forecasts, and financial projections.

- Drove **25%** increase in YOY sales by promoting both brand and product quality to customers.
- Managed **35%** of the company's annual revenue and increased Southeast region's revenue by **15%**.
- Propelled **11%** sales expansion by focusing on incremental sales of new core products.
- Gained **9%** in sales in the Southeast region by adding core brand with a Hispanic distributor.

Dynamic Marketing – Atlanta, GA

Director of Sales & Marketing   2008–2013

Brought on board to lead sales and marketing for young imported foods company poised for growth. Implemented direct and indirect sales plans, established product pricing policies, and trained and mentored business partners and distributors. Added staff to support growth, ultimately supervising 5 sales and marketing employees.

- Focused on distributor channel to drive rapid growth. Quickly added 100+ new distributors, leading to **$4M** sales growth in 5 years.

- Expanded international footprint and increased total sales **15%** by recruiting 12 new affiliates in 7 nations.

- Increased revenue **9%** through an innovative private-label program for dessert manufacturing company.

Globe Corporation – Atlanta, GA

International Sales Manager   2001–2005

Directed worldwide promotion of military footwear. Facilitated sales distribution, advised representatives and distributors, and devised marketing strategies.

- Grew annual sales revenue by **$2M** in 3.5 years.

- Created a brand image program that resulted in international recognition built around the company's reputation as the main provider of military footwear to the US Department of Defense.

- Formulated and led market entry strategy for Latin America. Negotiated exclusive agreements in 3 countries and established the company's entire Latin American presence.

- Discovered and pursued a new product channel in Europe in response to an emerging fashion trend, an innovative approach and strategic repositioning that led to a **10%** increase in overall sales.

EDUCATION

BS Business Administration (International Business specialization), 2003

Emory University, Atlanta, GA

MILITARY

US Army, 1992–2001

Honorable Discharge

COMMUNITY ENGAGEMENT

Wounded Warrior Project

Boys & Girls Clubs of Metro Atlanta

Today's Job Search Reality

As you view all of the resume samples in this book, you will notice that many do not strictly follow the ATS guidelines we've just described. That's because we wanted to showcase a wide variety of options for resume content, format, and design to spark your creativity and show you what's possible.

Quite likely, all of the job seekers with highly designed and graphic resumes also have a second, plainer version that they use when uploading.

But even more importantly, those job seekers are not relying on passing a keyword scan as their primary strategy for finding their next job. They understand the reality of today's job search—where keyword-scanning systems are everywhere but are *not* the only or the best method for you to find a job!

If that surprises you, you're not alone. After all, you keep hearing how important it is for you to write and design your resume to make it through the scanning systems. Yes, it's important—and we've just told you how to do that. But even more important is understanding how most people find jobs and how most jobs get filled.

Consider this:

- When you apply to jobs online, you are one of many. The average number of resumes per job has been reported to be anywhere from 115 to 240.

- Your uploaded resume must rise to the very top based on keyword match, specific qualifications, and other factors. Only 2% to 3% of those 115+ resumes are selected from all of the uploads, and only those candidates—the top handful—are invited to interview.

How, then, do most people find jobs? For the majority, the most effective method is to get a referral to the hiring company or hiring manager. When you become a referred candidate (e.g., John refers you to a contact of his who is looking to hire a new staff accountant), rather than a faceless resume in a crowded databank, you instantly become a favored candidate!

> **PRO TIP: 100% of referred candidates who have the qualifications will get an interview,** according to one of our most reliable sources, Gerry Crispin of CareerXRoads.

Based on these job search truths, we don't want you to obsess about keyword matching and ATS scanning.

Yes, you should have a version of your resume that is suitable for uploading and scanning. Yes, you should peruse job postings and apply when appropriate. But don't think of that as your *only* avenue or your *best* method for finding a job. It is quick and easy, but for many people it is not very effective.

Clearly, you will get the best results if you spend most of your time seeking referrals to hiring managers at your target companies instead of simply uploading resumes in response to job postings. A targeted search, with networking as its core component, is the time-tested and effective job search method that produces the most leads, interviews, and job offers.

PART IV:

Modernize Your Resume Design

The 6 Principles of Modern Resume Design

- Capture Attention in a Flash
- Follow the Practices of Good Page Design
- Match Design Elements to Your Industry & Profession
- Match Design Elements to Your Career Story
- Be Distinctive
- Embrace Color & Graphics

What design elements will add visual punch to your resume? How can you create an engaging visual presentation that is closely aligned with your profession and industry—and will instantly attract the right people and hiring decision makers?

Here are some of our favorite design elements.

Charts, Graphs, Call-outs, and Tables

Visuals that communicate specific messages add powerful and immediate impact to your resume. A chart (shown left) instantly conveys growth and success. A call-out (shown right) draws attention to impressive achievements that can be explained more fully in a bullet point.

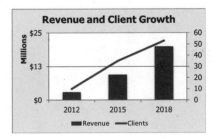

Lines, Borders & Boxes

Here's a small sampling of the variety of lines you can apply using MS Word's Borders feature—the easiest and most reliable method for adding lines to your resume. Alternatively, borders and boxes can be added as graphic files if you prefer that method.

Boxes—either text boxes or table cells—are another great option.

Shading draws attention to boxed content.

Images, Graphics & Illustrations

As you've already seen in the resumes we've shared earlier in this book, visual enhancements like these get noticed.

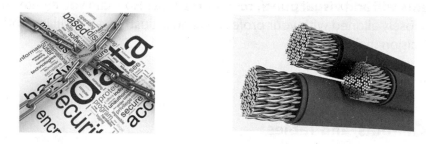

In the following 6 chapters, we'll demonstrate and discuss how to use the above design elements, when color is a great addition, and what other visuals can enhance your resume's appeal. Use these techniques wisely and you'll be able to apply the perfect finishing polish to your new and more modern resume.

CHAPTER 14:
Capture Attention in a Flash

The visual presentation of your resume matters … a lot! Before ever reading a single word, people see your resume, notice its visual cues, and form an immediate impression. Make that impression positive and make it count.

A huge part of getting your resume noticed is to stand out and capture attention instantly. If your resume doesn't do that, readers move on to the next candidate. Seconds matter!

Ask yourself these all-important questions for creating attention-grabbing resumes:

- **Is capturing attention all about using bold designs?** Maybe … for the right candidates in the right industries and professions.

- **Are images, illustrations, and other graphics an important addition to your resume?** Possibly … If you're in an industry or profession where those design elements amp up your presentation.

- **Do tables, graphs, and charts add value to resume design?** Maybe … if you're in an industry or profession where you can measure and quantify your performance.

- **Should you use company and product logos and images?** Perhaps … if those elements add value in terms of positioning you for your next career move.

- **Does every resume have to be filled with design elements?** Of course not! A minimally designed resume will serve you better than one that's so over-designed it creates a negative impression.

- **Does color make your resume stand out?** The answer to that question is a resounding yes! In today's world of job search, where color printers are commonplace and many people will be viewing your resume online or on screen, color adds a rich enhancement and punch.

Because this book is in black and white, you can't see the wide range of colors that have been used on many of the sample resumes. Of course, even in black and white they look sharp and they engage the reader. But color adds distinction and, when used well, is appropriate for just about any job seeker.

Use Design Elements Appropriately

Design should be used judiciously with an emphasis on including elements that boost your credibility, visibility, and professional brand.

If you're a 62-year-old finance executive with a steady career in the IT industry, you're likely not going to have a resume filled with multiple design elements. It's inappropriate and off-brand. Anything more than a few tasteful design additions would not be right for you, your industry, or your profession.

Conversely, if you're a 28-year-old graphic artist, your resume is your canvas! You can use color, images, icons, illustrations, and original art to create a resume that actually shows what you can do. The flexibility of modern resumes provides you with a wealth of opportunities to visually demonstrate what you know.

Online Job Search Considerations

Technology has had a far-reaching impact on how people look for jobs and how recruiters and hiring managers find candidates. You'll need to keep these realities in mind as you design your resume.

If your resume is filled with design elements, you'll want to save it as a PDF file and share it that way whenever possible. That's easy when you're emailing your resume to humans! But the design that makes your resume so attractive to people may cause problems when scanned by Applicant Tracking Systems (ATS)—even if the job board or career site accepts PDF files for upload.

Our recommendation is to prepare a second, simplified Word version of your resume. (See Chapter 13 for specific guidelines to make your resume ATS-compatible.) Use the highly designed PDF whenever you can, but have the less-designed Word version ready to go when you need it.

Techniques for Capturing Attention in a Flash

Following are 5 of our favorite methods for capturing attention quickly. They are illustrated—very effectively—in the 2 resumes that follow.

Jason Herrigan Resume—pages 111–12
Aiden Wells Resume—page 113

- **Add a design element at the very top of your resume.** A good example is the simple yet distinctive "JH" monogram that sits to the left of Jason's name.

- **Use a branding statement.** Aiden doesn't want you to miss the fact that he has "14 straight years of exceeding goals in a multimillion-dollar territory." He positions this powerful statement immediately beneath the headline in his Summary.

- **Introduce colorful and appropriate graphics.** See the logos on both pages of Jason's resume and the intersecting circles on Aiden's. They're attractive, distinctive, and, most importantly, appropriate.

- **Enhance with links.** In addition to the traditional links to email and LinkedIn, notice how Jason incorporates video links—and accompanying snapshots—at the bottom of the page.

- **Highlight achievements.** This technique applies to both the *content* of your resume and the *design*. Of course, you should include all of your relevant achievements, quantified if possible, as discussed throughout Part II—Modernize Your Resume Content. To capture attention in a flash, don't hide those achievements in small type or dense text; rather, let them shine with the right design.

JASON HERRIGAN

jason.herrigan@gmail.com | Northbrook, IL 60062
773-847-5555 | www.jhstudio.com

Multimedia Director | Digital Media Strategist

Tenacious problem solver who brings innovative digital communication solutions to lead organizations in creating stronger brands

Create high-performing teams: Built 3 departments at 3 different companies from inception to content production.

Anticipate trends: Increased web traffic 500% by introducing new techniques to improve viewer interactivity.

Streamline processes: Cut production time 50% by improving back-end content management workflow.

PROFESSIONAL EXPERIENCE

Chicago Tribune, Chicago, IL   2013–Present

MULTIMEDIA PRODUCER & MANAGER

Elevate organization's communications in a way that effectively immerses audience to gain a deeper connection with the brand.
Reports: *15 (max)* • **Projects:** *400+ annually*

SITUATION:

Challenged with creating digital communications strategies that increase web presence and grow brand visibility.

STRATEGIES:

Collaboration – Led cross-functional teams to take raw content and translate it into effective digital communications.

Innovation – Introduced new ways to present media and implemented processes to improve production time.

Production – Orchestrated construction and design of 2 $600K studios to support 5 different publications.

Editing Workflow – Developed editorial processes to capture most compelling story elements.

Team Leadership – Grew team from 1 to 7; managed up to 10 freelance photographers, videographers, and designers; mentored 10+ interns.

RESULTS:

- Increased page views 500% for flagship product.
- Gained 3M+ views on YouTube for Transformers 3 Filming video as part of social media strategy.
- Optimized budget by outsourcing specialized multimedia talent.
- Expanded advertising opportunities by strategizing with sales team on promotion to sell space on videos.

PORTFOLIO HIGHLIGHTS:

| Shedd Aquarium | 40 Under 40 | Transformers 3 |

CAREER SNAPSHOT

AWARDS

ILLINOIS PRESS PHOTOGRAPHERS ASSOCIATION
2018: 2nd Place for Best of Multimedia

NATIONAL PRESS PHOTOGRAPHER'S ASSOCIATION
2017: 1st Place - Video

THE NEAL AWARDS
2016: Best use of video

PETER LISAGOR AWARDS
2016: Best use of online video

THE SOCIETY OF AMERICAN BUSINESS EDITORS AND WRITERS AWARDS
2016: Best use of video
2014: Best in Business Online Audio/Video
2012: Best in Business Online Audio/Video

THE ALLIANCE OF AREA BUSINESS PUBLICATIONS AWARDS
2017: Gold: Best Multimedia Story/Feature
2016: Online Gold: Best Multimedia Story
2014: Gold: Best Multimedia Story/Feature

HUGO AWARDS
2013: Commitment to Excellence Award

EMMY NOMINATION
2012: Best Documentary – Inside 9/11

NY FESTIVAL
2012: Best Documentary – Inside 9/11

See full details of awards at
www.linkedin.com/in/jasonherrigan

ADVISORY BOARDS

Chicago Media Arts Academy
Improve film and broadcast curriculum.

Columbia College
Provide professional insight on curriculum, new trends in multimedia, and new teaching methodologies.

JASON HERRIGAN jason.herrigan@gmail.com | 773-847-5555 | 2 of 2

TriCom Media Inc., Chicago, IL   2010–2013

FINISHING EDITOR | OFFLINE EDITOR

Promoted within 1 year to Finishing Editor for exceeding expectations and learning new skills quickly.

Projects: 50+ shows

- Implemented first detailed training manual to onboard new associate editors faster and more efficiently.
- Earned an Emmy nomination for work on Inside 9/11 documentary.

CLIENT SNAPSHOT:

National Geographic, A&E Network, The History Channel, PBS, NBC

J.H. Studio, Chicago, IL   2008–2010

PHOTOGRAPHER | VIDEO EDITOR | DESIGNER | FOUNDER

Directed creative teams in producing digital and multimedia content.

- Improved website production efficiencies 20% by hiring up to 7-person teams that included developers, designers, and writers.
- Established reputation through grassroots marketing efforts and built business from 0 to 20 clients in 2 years.

CLIENT SNAPSHOT:

Boeing, Starbucks, Dreyer's Ice Cream, Holland America, Windstar Cruises

Travel Channel, San Francisco, CA   2005–2008

MULTIMEDIA & DESIGN MANAGER

Established first-ever 17-person web design and multimedia department.

- Streamlined and built new infrastructure to support everything from shooting videos and photos to publishing them on the website.
- Grew sales 15% by authoring and developing multimedia-viewing module with e-commerce capabilities.
- Increased website views 30% and doubled ticket sales through strategic partnership alliances and customized content.

CNN, Atlanta, GA   2002–2005

MULTIMEDIA PRODUCER

Pioneered role of multimedia producer to integrate photos, videos, 360° images, and audio clips to create immersive experience for viewers.

- Led multimedia production of all worldwide news events and major headline stories.
- Developed new processes to produce multimedia and trained others.

CLIENT SNAPSHOT

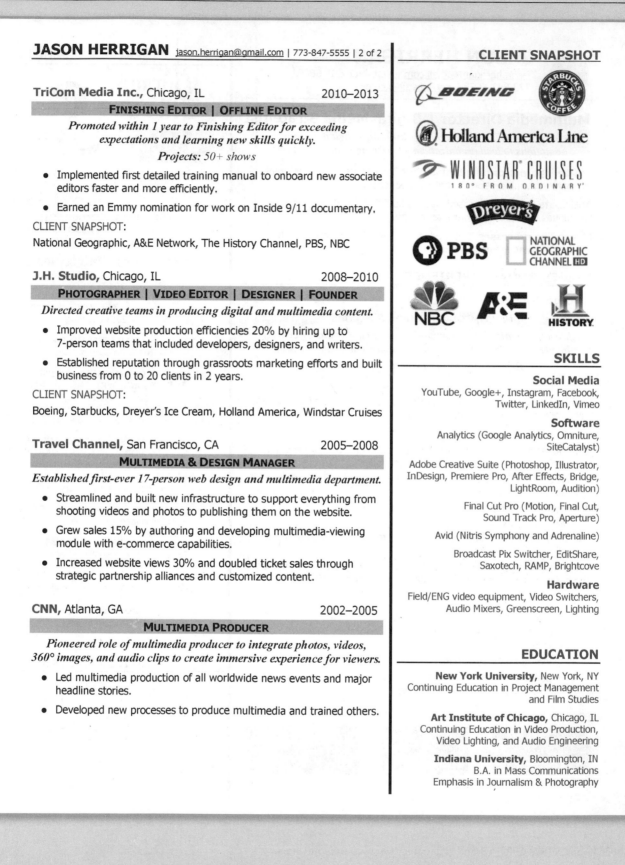

SKILLS

Social Media
YouTube, Google+, Instagram, Facebook, Twitter, LinkedIn, Vimeo

Software
Analytics (Google Analytics, Omniture, SiteCatalyst)

Adobe Creative Suite (Photoshop, Illustrator, InDesign, Premiere Pro, After Effects, Bridge, LightRoom, Audition)

Final Cut Pro (Motion, Final Cut, Sound Track Pro, Aperture)

Avid (Nitris Symphony and Adrenaline)

Broadcast Pix Switcher, EditShare, Saxotech, RAMP, Brightcove

Hardware
Field/ENG video equipment, Video Switchers, Audio Mixers, Greenscreen, Lighting

EDUCATION

New York University, New York, NY
Continuing Education in Project Management and Film Studies

Art Institute of Chicago, Chicago, IL
Continuing Education in Video Production, Video Lighting, and Audio Engineering

Indiana University, Bloomington, IN
B.A. in Mass Communications
Emphasis in Journalism & Photography

AIDEN WELLS

Birmingham, AL
(205) 555-1212
aidenwells1992@imax.com

SALES REPRESENTATIVE

14 straight years of exceeding goals in a multimillion-dollar territory

New Business Development – Profit Margin Optimization – Creative Solutions
Corporate Relationship Prospecting – New Sales Closing – Client Needs Assessment

☐ **Business Development:** Added 6 figures to monthly revenue with a single new-account win.

☐ **Crisis Management:** Preserved business by rapidly resolving costly equipment malfunction for key customer.

☐ **Connecting with People:** Consistently become a trusted member of customers' teams by understanding their business goals and providing solutions to their needs.

SIGNATURE SALES SKILLS

Business Partnerships	Values & Integrity
Customer Service Focus	Current Product & Market Knowledge
Internal & External Communication	Budgeting & Sales Projections
Persistence & Reliability	Innate Work Ethic

PROFESSIONAL EXPERIENCE

SALES REPRESENTATIVE   2004 to present
Infinite Paper, Birmingham, AL
A top wholesale distributor in the Southeastern U.S.; 32 distribution centers and 22 stores in 12 states

Sell fine printing papers and press-room supplies and equipment in a 70-account multimillion-dollar territory. Apply supply chain logistics knowledge to build relationships with key stakeholders and expand business opportunities within customer accounts.

☐ Tackled a challenging North Alabama territory, successfully penetrating large accounts such as the University of Alabama at Birmingham (UAB) and UnderArmour.

☐ Outperformed quota *every year* and averaged 112% of margin goal for 14 consecutive years.

☐ Acknowledged as "Outstanding Salesperson" in multiple divisions of the Infinite Paper Professional Sales Club.

☐ Became known as a problem solver, cementing strong business relationships with customers.

EDUCATION

Bachelor's Degree in Business Administration
Auburn University, Auburn, AL

COMMUNITY INVOLVEMENT

Advisory Boards, Birmingham Metro Chamber of Commerce and Liberty Park Golf and Country Club
President, Birmingham Kiwanis

CHAPTER 15:

Follow the Practices of Good Page Design

Good page design is important no matter what the page—resume, cover letter, business correspondence, project proposal, advertisement, marketing flyer, book, or magazine. But before you can begin to design great pages, you must understand the practical basics and structural fundamentals of what makes a page look great.

> **PRO TIP: Good design practices are relevant to *all* job seekers, not just those in creative industries and professions.** They are the underlying foundation—the infrastructure—upon which your own resume will be built.

Focal Point

Remember that readers have many competing demands for their attention. When they open your resume file or glance at your printed resume, make sure that their eyes fall first on something important!

Good options for focal point include:

- Your name—personalizing your resume instantly.
- A headline—announcing who you are (your job target). This is important because it immediately causes readers to start thinking about you in the framework of that profession or industry.
- A chart, graphic, or other image that sends a quick message about you and your capabilities.
- Subheadings that introduce bullet points—reinforcing your primary keywords and giving readers clues about what's in the bullet points.
- One or a few impressive accomplishments—just the highlights, for a quick jolt of positive information.

Even as you strive to draw your readers' attention to the important things, work just as hard to draw their attention away from things that aren't that important (e.g., job duties, locations). Or, if you're changing industries, do not draw special attention to or include lots of information about your current employer and industry focus, because they don't align with where you're headed.

Use design to showcase what's relevant to your current objectives while visually downplaying what's not.

Balance

Your resume should be well balanced on the page and on the screen. You don't want it to be top-heavy or pushed to the right or otherwise create an image that will diminish the visual presentation. Use these tips to create a balanced page:

- Set equal margins all around. We recommend a minimum of .5 inch and a maximum of 1 inch. Adjust as needed to fit your content.
- Adjust line spacing and blank lines so that your resume fills the page nicely, with no big gaps at the top or bottom.
- Be certain that the spacing is consistent between sections, between job titles and job descriptions, between sections of bullet points … consistency everywhere.
- If your resume is 2 pages long, you do *not* need to fill page 2 completely to the bottom. Don't add in lots of blank lines and extra space just to fill the page. If it's a half page, that's fine. If it's a third of a page or less, edit or redesign to see if you can fit onto 1 page without compromising readability.

Proportion

When elements are in proportion, the most significant are the most prominent. Proportion might refer to:

- Size—*larger* draws more attention.
- Emphasis—**bolder** is eye-catching.
- Contrast—anything *different* gets noticed.

Use this principle wisely so that you are calling attention to what you want readers to see.

For example, in many resumes the employer names are larger and bolder than job titles. That's great *if* the employer name is what you want your readers to notice first. More often than not, however, your job titles are more important—and therefore should be more prominent—because they tell your career story and quickly identify your professional expertise. Design your resume accordingly!

White Space

White space is not simply blank space on the page. To the contrary, it performs several important functions:

- Indicates the end/beginning of different items and sections in the resume.
- Sets off discrete items such as headings and subheadings so they can be scanned quickly.
- Allows readers to pause and absorb information before moving on to learn more.
- Adds readability to text-rich documents such as a resume.

You can finitely adjust the white space in your resume to promote balance, improve readability, and increase visual appeal. Add blank lines or use the Paragraph feature in MS Word for precise spacing control. Above all, be sure that you are breaking up any large clumps of text that readers are very likely to just skip over.

Consistency

Why does it matter that similar elements in your resume are designed in the same way? Quite simply, consistency aids in reader understanding.

When readers see a job title formatted a certain way, for example, they expect to see *all* job titles formatted that same way. If they don't, there's a disconnect that causes them to pause and shift focus from what they're reading to a "what's wrong with this picture" distraction.

Consistency gives readers clues about the kinds of information they are processing. And consistency gives your resume a polished and professional look.

MS Word has 2 features that will help you create consistent documents:

- Use Styles to build and apply specific formats for different parts of your resume—from the basic paragraph style to headings, subheadings, tables, hyperlinks, and any other design elements. Styles can be challenging to use because Word often applies them automatically, so be careful if you choose to use this tool.

- Our favorite, the Format Painter tool, allows you to quickly copy the format of any one word or paragraph to any other in your resume. We find this to be one of the most useful tools in Word because you can zip through the document and format or reformat in a flash.

Placement

Where will you place each element of your resume—your name and contact information, headlines and headings, design elements, graphics, and all of the text?

Placement is related to several of the design principles we've already discussed—Focal Point, Balance, White Space. But the more design elements you introduce, the more choices you have regarding what goes where and why.

As you are placing elements on the page, keep these points in mind:

- The top third of page 1 of your resume is prime real estate. Whatever you place there should be of paramount importance. This should include your name and contact information, summary, and notable achievements; it may also include your headline, branding statement, and a graphic.

- Because readers typically read top to bottom, left to right, it makes sense to left-justify your section headings, such as Professional Experience and Education. That is most typical and what we recommend. However, you can try centered headings (a classic presentation), or even right-justified headings, to see how that affects readability and overall appearance of your resume.

- If you are using graphics or charts, you will need to place them so that they support the appropriate text but don't interfere with its readability.

- Think about economy and efficiency in placing different elements on the page. For example, do you need multiple lines for job titles and company names, or for college degrees and universities, or can you fit that information on 1 line? When appropriate, that can be a huge space saver.

- Where will you place your employment dates? The knee-jerk reaction would be, "at the right margin, of course!" Indeed that's where you'll find the dates on most resumes. That placement certainly makes it easy for employers to scan your employment history, and it's the right choice for many.

  But you do *not* want a spotlight on dates if you have gaps in employment, many short-term jobs, are currently unemployed, or are trying to bring older experience to the forefront to support a career change. In those situations, move your dates elsewhere so that they are not a visual focal point.

Images, Graphics, Tables, Charts & Other Visuals

We live in a visual world, and print material in all forms—from traditional newspapers to advertisements, brochures, billboards, and even books—now includes more images and fewer large blocks of text.

Studies have shown that online content with images draws many more viewers and keeps them on the page longer, as compared to content only. We think this is true for printed pages as well.

If you choose to use images in your resume, keep these rules in mind:

- Choose an image that supports the content of your resume and relates to either your industry or your profession. A random graphic is not going to add value.

- Be sure the image reproduces well in black and white, because you can't be sure that everyone who receives your resume will have a color printer.

- Do not use copyrighted images unless you have permission to do so. An exception would be corporate logos—it's fine to use those images in your resume because they are explicitly linked to the company.

- Don't allow images to overshadow the all-important content. An exception would be an infographic resume, where the image *is* the message. See Chapter 17 for additional discussion and an example of an infographic resume.

Now, let's see all of these design principles at work!

Andrea North Resume—pages 119–20

The most notable design elements you'll find in Andrea's resume are:
- Attractive black, gray, and white color scheme.
- Use of shaded boxes to segment and call attention to important information—creating multiple focal points for her name, summary, core skills, and a great endorsement.
- Nicely balanced pages with centered headings.
- Ample white space between bullets.
- Consistent treatment of employer names, job titles, dates, and other fundamental details.
- Interesting and attractive bullet shapes.

Ellen Colbert Resume—pages 121–22

When you review Ellen's resume, the standout design features that you'll immediately note are:

- Two eye-catching charts that instantly convey a career punctuated by growth and success.
- A headline that clearly states her expertise, followed by a subheading that further identifies her most valuable strengths.
- Four 1-line bullet points in the summary section that capture her most impressive performance results.
- Consistent presentation of company names, company information, and job titles.
- Succinct text, with most bullet points 1 or 2 lines and paragraphs no longer than 4 lines.
- Sufficient white space to ensure readability.

ANDREA NORTH

Boston, MA 02134 | 617-553-1234 | andreanorth@mac.com

COMMUNICATION SPECIALIST

Influencing the hearts and minds of target audiences through …

Clear, precise storytelling and reporting, applying AP style
Exceptional speechwriting, integrating each presenter's natural speaking style
Passionate communication of a brand's story, as an in-person host/media spokesperson

CORE SKILLS

Public Relations
Communication Management
Writing & Editing
Presentations & Speechwriting
Research & News Reporting
Media Relations / Press Releases
Multimedia Communication
Brand Communication
Marketing Collateral
Relationship Building

- Charismatic and creative communication director, PR strategist, and journalist with a track record of delivering messages that make a positive impact.
- Forward-thinking strategist who formulates targeted communication plans to support internal organizational programs and external PR efforts.
- Well-traveled reporter who has journeyed to nearly all continents, including Africa, Asia, and Europe, to pursue journalistic opportunities.
- Passionate executive speechwriter who designs cogent discourse that engages audiences and gives presenters a competitive edge.

"Andrea is such a breath of fresh air! Her creativity and natural writing talents shine in everything she does. City Charity has seen a massive increase in public donations over the past few years, and Andrea has been a big reason why." – Simon Smith, VP, City Charity

SPOTLIGHTED SUCCESSES

PR/COMMUNICATION IMPROVEMENT
Elevated the quantity and quality of content produced by City Charity's communication department through a presentation to the Board of Directors, encouraging the engagement of highly qualified PR specialists and journalists to design compelling messages rather than relying on inexperienced volunteers.

PERSUASIVE WRITING
Secured national press coverage for City Charity on NPR, brought attention to the charity's international efforts to combat childhood hunger, and boosted donations 150% in just 3 months by researching and developing a detailed case for a 3-part news series showcasing the charity's Children First program.

PROFESSIONAL EXPERIENCE

CITY CHARITY, Boston, MA ✧ 2013 – Present
ASSISTANT COMMUNICATION DIRECTOR FOR NEWS

Author, edit, and produce persuasive, high-quality content for City Charity Network (CCN). Oversee editorial team of writers and photographers covering global programs. Coordinate news releases and serve as media spokesperson. Orchestrate media events, researching and developing scripts for speakers.

- Improved the quality of internal writing and editing by overhauling the CCN style guide.
- Transformed CCN into a world-class charitable news service by introducing op-eds, leading the creation of a weekly email news bulletin, and facilitating hands-on training for communication department staff.
- Recruited, mentored, and directed a talented team of reporters, photographers, and volunteers for the charity's annual Giving Back Gala, a 7-day conference attended by 2,000 officials from other charities nationwide.

Andrew Pearl, CPRW, CEIP, CERM • Precision Resumes, Inc. • www.precision-resumes.com

ANDREA NORTH

Page 2 of 2
617-553-1234 | andreanorth@mac.com

ASSISTANT COMMUNICATION DIRECTOR FOR NEWS (CONTINUED)

◇ Promoted financial transparency, strengthening member and public confidence in the organization, by initiating an annual budget news feature to apprise readers of key financial matters.

◇ Gained 500,000 readers by authoring amusing feature stories about the world travels of volunteers working within the charity's 3 main global programs: Children First, Operation Education, and Heal the Earth. Earned the attention of, and special features in, the *Boston Globe.*

RECOGNITION FROM COLLEAGUES AND PROGRAM LEADERS

NEWS SERVICE TRANSFORMATION: "You have certainly made us proud, Andrea! What a fantastic accomplishment to gain attention for City Charity in the *Globe*. Your creative writing is really grabbing the interest of the public and giving us a lot of momentum to move forward with our programs around the world. Thank you!" – Allan Smith, Program Director

GIVING BACK GALA PR TEAM LEADERSHIP: "We just wanted to thank you for giving us the guidance—and freedom—needed to succeed during the gala. It's clear you know how to manage PR, and you've proven that you can bring diverse talent together to support an organization's communication goals." – Jill Smith, Senior Vice President of Special Events

SUBURBAN TIMES, Waltham, MA ◇ 2011 – 2013

STAFF REPORTER

Engaged to produce news features for this growing suburb with a population of 300,000 (at that time). Attended and covered city government meetings. Authored and edited reports on municipal organizations and city personalities.

COMMUNITY CHARITY, Boston, MA ◇ 2007 – 2011

EDITORIAL ASSISTANT (2008 – 2011) ◇ **COMMUNICATIONS INTERN** (2007 – 2008)

Hired immediately following internship for responsible role writing and editing news and feature stories for Community Charity publications. Assisted editor with projects and copyedited all materials, including television scripts, news stories, and marketing brochures.

◇ Created a streamlined, straightforward concept for a full-page ad that was selected by Community Charity leadership for placement in the *Boston Globe* to apprise the American public of a major health crisis in Africa.

◇ Authored and revised features for Community Charity's website, traveling to report on stories and representing the organization at trade shows. Developed creative fundraising letters and coordinated a fundraising concert.

EDUCATION

Master of Arts in Journalism & Mass Communication, 2009
University of Massachusetts, Boston, MA

Bachelor of Arts in Communication, 2007
Boston University, Boston, MA

AFFILIATIONS

Public Relations Society of America | American Society of Journalists

Ellen Colbert

ellen.colbert@gmail.com   **617-555-1710**   linkedin.com/in/ellencolbert

Business Development Executive: Technology & Telecommunications

Revenue Growth Driver • Fortune 50 & SMB Relationship Builder • Deal Closer & Negotiator

Proven leader who has spent the last 12 years identifying, defining, and penetrating nascent markets while leading exponential revenue growth across diverse industries. *Career highlights:*

- Expanded customer base 12-fold in 1 year for TechStars.com.
- Generated $10M+ recurring annual revenue to elevate Cranford Group to one of America's fastest-growing firms.
- Averaged 134% of annual sales goal for Whiz Business Services.
- Rose to #1 in region, #7 nationwide in sales for XTeam.

Professional Experience

TechStars.com   Cambridge, MA • 2017–2019

Privately held technology and services firm with a proprietary platform (MyMortgageDocs) and a national network of industry-compliant notaries and signing agents who facilitate loan closings for clients.

VP BUSINESS DEVELOPMENT

Recruited to lead turnaround and expansion for niche player in the mortgage refinance market. Brought on originally as a consultant and quickly hired as chief operations and business development officer for company dealing with multiple challenges: aging technology, inefficient operations, and a single anchor client in an industry sharply affected by changing conditions in the mortgage refinance market. Directed 15 staff.

- Recruited talented CTO and worked closely to plan and launch new technology platform in first 6 months.
- Grew client base from 1 account to 15, reducing anchor client's share of revenue from >95% to <50%.
- Automated processes and delivered operational improvements – e.g., slashed A/R reconciliation from 4 days/4 departments to half a day.
- Identified untapped opportunity for newly developed technology with large potential in expanding industries.

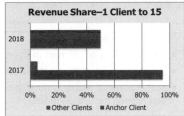

Cranford Group   Boston, MA • 2010–2017

Privately held market niche leader providing technology/communications solutions to large financial institutions.

VP SALES, 2012–2015 • **DIRECTOR OF SALES**, 2011–2012 • **SENIOR SALES CONSULTANT,** 2010–2011

Spurred >5X growth in total company revenue and personally delivered more than 50% of new business. Brought on board to rapidly grow sales for outsourcing division that had stalled in its first year. Transformed sales approach from high-level concept discussions to practical solutions delivery and built division to $20M+ annual revenue.

Promoted 2X in 3 years to lead sales and business development for the expanding business. Generated and managed $10M+ personal book of business and maintained relationships with all key accounts while developing overall sales strategy and directing 5-member project team.

- Invigorated and expanded division from a handful of clients to 50+ of the nation's leading foreclosure attorneys.
- Negotiated and sold long-term multimillion-dollar contracts to marquee clients: GMAC, Citigroup, Fidelity, Chase/Washington Mutual, and others.
- Drove record revenue growth, earning status as one of the country's fastest-growing private firms, as recognized by multiple benchmarking organizations (Inc. 500, Deloitte Technology Fast 500, Software 500).

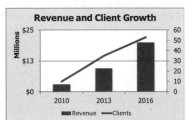

Louise Kursmark, MRW, CPRW, JCTC, CEIP, CCM • Best Impression Career Services • www.louisekursmark.com

Ellen Colbert • Page 2   ellen.colbert@gmail.com • 617-555-1710

Whiz Business Services   Burlington, MA • 2009–2010
Provider of advanced voice, data, and video products.

SENIOR SALES CONSULTANT

Consistently outperformed goals, selling integrated solutions to Fortune 1000. Performed full range of sales prospecting, qualifying, needs assessment, data gathering, and presentation to director and C-level executives. Developed proposals and negotiated pricing, multi-year contract terms, and SLAs for an eclectic range of WAN, IP, disaster recovery, managed security services, VoIP, MPLS, equipment, and hosting solutions.

	2009	2010
Performance to Goal	118%	150%

- Landed 60% of new business through referrals from existing clients.
- Developed methodical processes for consistent follow-up with clients both during and after the sale.
- Steadily expanded business contacts through active involvement in regional networking events and trade shows.

XTeam Communications   Boston, MA • 2006–2009
$150M B2B provider of integrated broadband data and voice communication services.

MAJOR ACCOUNT MANAGER, 2007–2009

One of 10 hand-picked from 130 account managers to lead strategic, intensified focus on major accounts. Exceeded all sales goals and landed 2 of the company's top 5 accounts. Hunted new business every month, identifying needs and selling comprehensive communications solutions to targeted businesses.

	2007	2008
Performance to Goal	122%	107%

- Ranked #7 out of 130 reps in the company, #1 in Boston office, 2008.
- Landed company's #1 client ($100K/month) and a second top-5 account at 30X company average.
- Built a powerful network, developing and maintaining relationships with business owners, controllers, VPs, vendors, and networking groups throughout Northeast US.

ACCOUNT MANAGER, 2006–2007

In 3 months, learned technology-based product/service line and ramped up to 100% of quota performance. Developed new business month after month, targeting small to medium-sized businesses and proposing integrated solutions to meet their telecommunications needs.

- Developed exceptional customer relationships built on integrity, trust, and solutions focus.
- More than doubled revenue ($6K to $14.5K monthly) at 1 account without adding services.

Education

MBA, Northeastern University – D'Amore-McKim School of Business	2016
BS, University of Hartford – Barnard School of Business – Business Administration/Marketing	2005

CHAPTER 16:

Match Design Elements to Your Industry & Profession

Does your resume design communicate an enticing message to the industry and profession that you are targeting? From the design elements you've used, can readers instantly recognize that you're a web designer, business leader, sales producer, or theater stage manager?

Choose your design elements to create that much-needed alignment so that, with just a glance, people can see that you belong in the industry or profession that you're targeting. Start by thinking about what matters most for the companies and positions to which you are applying.

Here are a few examples:

- **Sales.** In sales professions, what matters most is delivering the numbers: exceeding sales quotas, capturing new clients, closing deals, and growing sales revenues. Charts with rising columns and upward arrows are a great design match.

- **Hospitality and Retail.** Major brands in these industries are instantly recognizable and impressive, so adding corporate logos can both dress up your resume and quickly communicate the right industry message.

- **Health and Wellness.** Depending on your niche within this industry, you might choose to include images identified with fields that are traditional, such as medicine or pharmacy, or nontraditional, such as massage or yoga.

- **Business and Executive Leadership.** Business leaders have specific goals: typically to grow the business and increase profits. Charts, tables, and graphs can quickly illustrate your success in doing just that, again with rising columns and other visual indicators of upward performance. If appropriate, you can also add in the logos of blue-chip companies where you've worked.

- **Nonprofit.** You might enhance your resume with images that align with the mission of the organizations where you've worked or your specific niche within the industry. For example, if you work to improve literacy, a book graphic could be appropriate.

As you'll see in the following 2 resumes, design elements that align with the individual's industry and profession create just the *right* impression and instantly distinguish that resume from all others.

Amy Black Resume—page 125

Amy's resume could not possibly be confused with anyone else's: It includes images of her own work—projects she's managed and products she's designed. The 2-column format is unusual and allows her to include a long listing of technical skills without detracting from the core text of the resume. The overall design is clean and clear, giving the reader further evidence of her design expertise.

Lawrence McMaster Resume—pages 126–27

Lawrence is a business leader who has taken nonprofit organizations to new heights. We can see that instantly from his resume, from the chart on page 1 to the upward-pointing arrow on page 2. Despite its many design elements, Lawrence's resume still projects an executive image. Notice his personal brand statement—Building Socially Responsive Organizations Through Innovation, Operational Excellence, and Leadership—used as a footer on both pages of his resume. There is no doubt as to who Lawrence is and what he does so very well.

ENGINEER – PROJECT LEADER

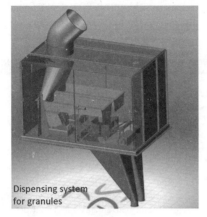

Dispensing system
for granules

EDUCATION
BS Mechanical Engineering, 2010
Concentration in Machine Construction
University of Washington, Seattle, WA

TECHNICAL SKILLS
▪ Software
Microsoft Project – SolidWorks –
Solid Edge – Dynamic Designer

▪ Mathematics Programs
Mathcad – Matlab – Mathematica

▪ Programming Tools
GX Developer – GS Works – IX Developer

▪ Construction
Ansys

LANGUAGES
English & **Norwegian** – bilingual
German – conversational

Z conveyor, maintenance free for 10 years

AMY BLACK
206-270-8857 ▪ amyblack@gmail.com ▪ LinkedIn ▪ Seattle, WA

DESIGN ENGINEER: Innovator, troubleshooter, skilled programmer, and machine constructor with a reputation for paying great attention to detail and always exceeding expectations.

- Designed innovative conveyor that has performed flawlessly—without maintenance or repair—for 8 years.
- Developed pioneering concept turned high-profile research project at University of Washington. Received industry-wide praise. Invited to lecture at research conference in 2019.

ENGINEERING CONSULTANT / MACHINE CONSTRUCTOR
RF Technology, 2012–Present

Perform consulting assignments for a variety of clients, including the company's #1 customer, DFG Mills.

Core Skills: Production Flow Analysis – Investment Documentation – Procurement – Machine Programming – Process Programming – Project Management – Installation – Hydraulics – Pneumatics – Process Engineering – Special Tool Construction

Key Projects:

- **Dispensing system for granules** with special hygiene and flexibility request. *Concept design, procurement, monitoring, installation, programming, and deployment.*
- **Belt conveyor** for bread traveling through 2 floors, from bakery to packing. *Design, project management, programming, and installation.*
- **Packing lines** for 2 mill sites. *Design, project management.*
- **Z conveyor** (food-approved) with special requirements for cleaning access. *Design, project management, deployment.* **8 years of 100% maintenance-free operations**.

  "Amy's ingenuity and problem-solving skills are exceptional."
  (President, RF Technology)

MECHANIC, T. H. Workshops, 2010–2012

Created prototypes and manufactured test samples for production runs of instruments, wooden toys, and furniture for customers that included renowned Thomas Mosier Cabinetmakers. Customized products for clients and designed tools to streamline production.

Key Projects:

- **Mechanical control system** for external profile milling. *Installation of circuit diagrams and deployment.*
- **New PLC control system** for 5 machines filling and closing bags of pellets. *Installation of circuit diagrams and deployment.*
- **Development of new, fully automated packing machine.** *Design, manufacturing, and deployment.*

  "Amy is smart, resourceful, and a natural problem solver."
  (Production Supervisor, T. H. Workshops)

Birgitta Moller, ACRW • www.cvhjalpen.nu

LAWRENCE MCMASTER

Montreal, PQ H3C 1V2 Canada

lmcmaster@hotmail.com • 514.222.1111

SERVANT LEADER | PRESIDENT & CEO | BUSINESS TURNAROUND EXPERT

Award-Winning Association Executive driving organizational change and fiscal accountability in highly competitive environments. Change driver for socially responsive organizations requiring **sustainable business transformation.**

Critical Competencies

- Strategic Planning
- Fund Development
- Change Management
- Program Development & Delivery

- Media & Government Relations
- National Health Policy Development
- Volunteer Recognition & Rewards
- Donor Relationship Strategies

- Capital Development & Project Planning
- Zero-Based Budgeting & Cash Flow
- Community Relations & Advertising
- Corporate Governance | Risk Control

Professional Experience

PRESIDENT AND CEO Lung Association of Canada 2010 – Present
Non-profit dedicated to preventing and managing lung disease through research, advocacy, patient services, and education.

Reorganized underperforming association to a sustainable, results-oriented charity business.

CEO with full planning, operating, marketing, financial, legislative, regulatory, and administrative responsibility for programs, services, and business affairs. Reporting to Board of Directors, lead staff of 10 and $1.2M operating budget.

Organizational & Industry Leadership

- **Reversed 7-year decline in net revenue** by redesigning direct-mail program and annual Christmas Seals campaign.

- Co-Chaired Canadian National Health Strategy Committee and **secured $300K** disbursement to guide the delivery of lung health services across Canada.

- Negotiated purchase and renovation of 11,000 sq. ft. commercial property to serve as association headquarters and provide lucrative tenant revenue stream—resulting in **zero rent expense** for the association.

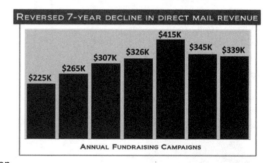

REVERSED 7-YEAR DECLINE IN DIRECT MAIL REVENUE

$225K $265K $307K $326K $415K $345K $339K

ANNUAL FUNDRAISING CAMPAIGNS

- **Generated $200K** from Public Health Agency of Canada to create "Asthma Aware," an evidence-based program to educate community leaders with children in their care.

Fundraising & Community Programs

- Exceeded $800K goal for planned-giving program with a **$1M planned gift.**

- Increased participation in Credit Union "Lung Run" from **280 to 850** and revenues from **$17K to $116K** in 5 years.

- Grew "Airway Run" revenues from **$32K to $65K,** partnering with Montreal International Airport Authority.

- Orchestrated and created "**Learn to Run for Smokers**" program—now delivered in 3 provinces.

BUILDING SOCIALLY RESPONSIVE ORGANIZATIONS THROUGH INNOVATION, OPERATIONAL EXCELLENCE, AND LEADERSHIP.

Maureen Farmer, CHRP, CCMC, CRS, CCS • Word Right Career • www.wordrightcareer.com

PRESIDENT AND CEO	Special Olympics of Canada	1997 – 2010

Created the most successful athlete recruitment program in Canadian Special Olympics history ...
invited to present program to Special Olympics International Congress in Washington, DC.

Initially hired as the Provincial Program Director; led the creation of the athlete/coach development programs and the current competitive structure. Named nationwide General Manager in 2000 and the first President and CEO in 2003.

Organizational & Industry Leadership

- In partnership with core leadership team, recruited, motivated, and engaged a high-profile Board of Directors featuring numerous corporate and community leaders.

- Implemented sustainable system of volunteer and staff professional development and established a leadership structure within each of the **15 Special Olympic regions,** building future sustainable growth.

- Attended as Chef de Mission at 5 National Games and **directed 23 provincial multisport games** featuring 4–7 sports and approximately 1000 coaches and athletes.

- Served on the initial Special Olympics Canada Site Visit Team along with Dr. Frank Hayden—**world founder** of Special Olympics—evaluating programs and structure of Special Olympics British Columbia.

- **Elected by colleagues** to National Sport Program Committee, Special Olympics Canada, and Sport Manager Team Canada at World Special Olympics Summer Games in New Haven, CT.

Fundraising & Community Programs

- Grew revenues from **$250K to $450K and** diversified the fundraising program.

- Increased sustainable public funding from **$6K to $42K** annually as a result of a successful provincial government assessment. Result: Special Olympics of Canada ranked 7th of 60 national sport organizations.

- In partnership with National Tire, created the "National Tire Asthma Awareness School Program," presented to **12,000+ school children** and 350 teachers in inaugural year.

Fueled $200K in private + $36K public funding

Education and Professional Development

Bachelor of Arts in Economics and Marketing | University of New Brunswick, Fredericton, NB | 1995
Successfully Leading and Selling Change | Dalhousie University | Halifax | 2011
Strategic Planning to Lower Fundraising Costs and Boost Revenues | Ottawa University | Ottawa | 2011
Certificate in Leading Innovation | Saint Mary's University | Halifax | 2010
Governor General's Canadian Leadership Conference | 2010 and 2017

Awards and Accolades

- Awarded **Queen Elizabeth II Diamond Jubilee Medal** by Special Olympics of Canada in 2014 in recognition of exemplary past contributions.

- Earned Stamp of Excellence for transforming Special Olympics of Canada from an unrecognized sport organization to *NATIONAL SPORT ORGANIZATION OF THE YEAR in 2007* — awarded by Sport Canada.

BUILDING SOCIALLY RESPONSIVE ORGANIZATIONS THROUGH INNOVATION, OPERATIONAL EXCELLENCE, AND LEADERSHIP.

CHAPTER 17:

Match Design Elements to Your Career Story

Your career story is unique to you, so make it the focus of your resume design. To achieve that, you must send a powerful message of *who* you are, *what* you do, and *how* well you do it by choosing design elements that help readers understand:

- Where you've been—your prior jobs and employers—and how all of that leads to your next role.
- Your greatest career successes—related to the trajectory of your career.
- Why you have been successful—the intangible qualities you've illustrated throughout your career that will be instrumental in your next position.

As you'll see in the samples that follow, creative presentations are not confined to creative fields. A nurse can very effectively and professionally include graphics, while a technology sales manager can use unusual fonts and eye-catching design elements to capture attention.

The key is to keep your target audience in mind and create something that expresses *you* while simultaneously appealing to *them*—because, ultimately, your resume is—and should be—all about what you can do for your next employer.

Infographic Resumes

With regard to career story designs, we would be remiss if we did not mention the trend of infographic resumes. An infographic ("information graphic") is a translation of data into a graphic format, and an infographic resume is a pictorial representation of someone's career.

We do not recommend infographic resumes for most job seekers for 2 specific reasons:

- Because they are primarily graphics rather than text, these resumes include a very limited amount of information. They do not allow job seekers to share all that they know and all that they have done to position themselves for appropriate opportunities. Yes, we want you to *write tight, lean, and clean*, but we do want you to write powerful, informative, and achievement-driven content.

- They don't work well in today's world of online job search. Infographic resumes cannot be scanned by digital readers, they typically include few keywords, and many of the fundamentals—job titles, employers, degrees—are either excluded or presented in such a manner that they are overlooked.

As with everything related to resume writing, there are no rules, and infographic resumes can work for some job seekers in some professions. Review Noah Birnbaum's infographic resume on page 130 and then determine whether this type of presentation is right for you.

PRO TIP: An infographic resume can be a great supplement to your traditional resume. As mentioned, it's tough to tell your whole career story in a few words and graphics, and we do not recommend infographics as a *primary* resume for most. But as an adjunct, a well-done infographic can be a great attention-getter and conversation piece.

Add a link at the top of your resume to a website where you have posted your infographic resume, share it on LinkedIn, and send it before or after interviews. It will help you stand out!

In the 2 resumes that follow the Infographic resume, notice how all of the design elements work together harmoniously to tell an effective career story.

Ida Davis Resume—pages 131–32

Ida's resume emphasizes her profession via the heart-shaped stethoscope that adorns the top of her resume. Additionally, she has highlighted several impressive rewards with star-shaped bullets that call out this evidence of her nursing skill and compassionate manner.

Denise Reynolds Resume—pages 133–34

Denise uses shading, tables, charts, and other graphics to provide a cohesive story of her success in sales. Notice that the actual text of this resume is quite slim—there is a lot of white space and great use of graphics to balance the lean, clean content. The logo is distinctive, and isn't sales all about getting noticed in the crowd?

Infographic Resume

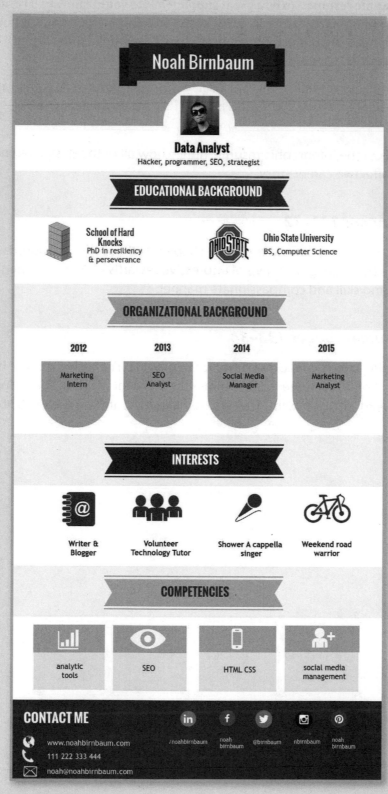

Hannah Morgan • Job Search Strategist • http://careersherpa.net

IDA DAVIS, RN, BSN

25 Easter Street ▪ Melville, NY 11747 ▪ 631.555.7777 ▪ IDRN@gmail.com

CAREER TARGET: DIRECTOR OF NURSING—ELDER CARE
ASSISTANT DIRECTOR | NURSE MANAGER | WELLNESS NURSE

Confident and compassionate healthcare provider with proven hands-on experience and a genuine passion for geriatrics.

Maintain an excellent balance of empathy and authority to ease resident and family stressors. Easily establish positive and productive rapport with geriatric population; sensitive and responsive to meeting diverse needs in varied situations. Remain calm and professional throughout critical incidents.

EDUCATION AND PROFESSIONAL CERTIFICATION

Bachelor of Science in Nursing, Adelphi University of Nursing, Garden City, NY
Associate of Science in Nursing, Nassau Community College, Hempstead, NY

State of New York Registered Professional Nurse
State of New Jersey Registered Professional Nurse

New York Department of Health and Senior Services, RN Instructor – Certified Medication Aide
BLS Certification ▪ IV Certification ▪ Telemetry Certification

KEY SKILLS / AREAS OF EXPERTISE

Cardiac ▪ Care Planning ▪ Client Relations ▪ Customer Service ▪ Dementia ▪ Geriatric & Assisted Living ▪ HIPPA ▪ Leadership & Management ▪ Needs Assessment ▪ Patient Advocacy ▪ Patient Education ▪ Quality Improvement ▪ Problem Solving ▪ Rapport Building ▪ Social Service ▪ Staff Education ▪ Team Building ▪ Team Supervision & Mentoring ▪ Workforce Planning

CAREER HISTORY

First Care Senior Services, Port Washington, NY   **2017 to Present**
Provider of private-pay home care services.

REGISTERED NURSE CARE MANAGER

★ Recipient, Key Contributor Award, 2018 ★

Hired to develop an education program for direct-care staff and to ensure compliance with state regulations. Assist with corporate mission to become a preferred provider for the State of New York.

- Assumed newly created role of staff liaison; respond to employee issues and concerns.

- Serve as Clinical Coordinator for clients and families. Perform home visits to address and re-assess needs. Recommend/assist calling physicians as needed. Gain and maintain positive rapport to work with clients and families for determining best level of care.

- Educate and supervise direct-care staff (Home Companions and Certified Home Health Aides). Ensure caregivers are properly prepared and educated on best practices for on-boarding new clients and have full understanding of expectations and responsibilities.

- Assess/re-assess nursing needs for clients and families, develop individualized care plans for each client, and educate caregivers on plans.

Michelle Riklan, ACRW, CPRW, CEIC, CJSS • Riklan Resources • www.riklanresources.com

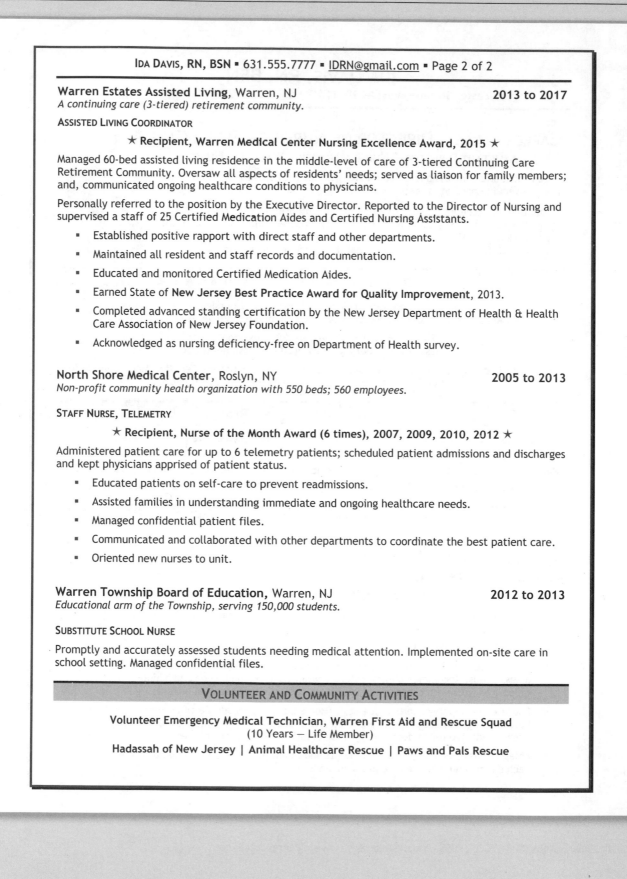

Warren Estates Assisted Living, Warren, NJ   2013 to 2017
A continuing care (3-tiered) retirement community.

ASSISTED LIVING COORDINATOR

★ Recipient, Warren Medical Center Nursing Excellence Award, 2015 ★

Managed 60-bed assisted living residence in the middle-level of care of 3-tiered Continuing Care Retirement Community. Oversaw all aspects of residents' needs; served as liaison for family members; and, communicated ongoing healthcare conditions to physicians.

Personally referred to the position by the Executive Director. Reported to the Director of Nursing and supervised a staff of 25 Certified Medication Aides and Certified Nursing Assistants.

- Established positive rapport with direct staff and other departments.

- Maintained all resident and staff records and documentation.

- Educated and monitored Certified Medication Aides.

- Earned State of **New Jersey Best Practice Award for Quality Improvement**, 2013.

- Completed advanced standing certification by the New Jersey Department of Health & Health Care Association of New Jersey Foundation.

- Acknowledged as nursing deficiency-free on Department of Health survey.

North Shore Medical Center, Roslyn, NY   2005 to 2013
Non-profit community health organization with 550 beds; 560 employees.

STAFF NURSE, TELEMETRY

★ Recipient, Nurse of the Month Award (6 times), 2007, 2009, 2010, 2012 ★

Administered patient care for up to 6 telemetry patients; scheduled patient admissions and discharges and kept physicians apprised of patient status.

- Educated patients on self-care to prevent readmissions.

- Assisted families in understanding immediate and ongoing healthcare needs.

- Managed confidential patient files.

- Communicated and collaborated with other departments to coordinate the best patient care.

- Oriented new nurses to unit.

Warren Township Board of Education, Warren, NJ   2012 to 2013
Educational arm of the Township, serving 150,000 students.

SUBSTITUTE SCHOOL NURSE

Promptly and accurately assessed students needing medical attention. Implemented on-site care in school setting. Managed confidential files.

VOLUNTEER AND COMMUNITY ACTIVITIES

Volunteer Emergency Medical Technician, Warren First Aid and Rescue Squad
(10 Years — Life Member)
Hadassah of New Jersey | Animal Healthcare Rescue | Paws and Pals Rescue

denise reynolds

SENIOR TECHNOLOGY SALES MANAGER

ACHIEVED 16 STRAIGHT YEARS OF DOUBLE-DIGIT YOY SALES

LEADERSHIP STYLE:

↗ Drove unprecedented triple-percentage sales gains, catapulting US sales from 28% to 76% of HP's business. Fueled above-and-beyond team performance by harnessing talent and empowering emerging leaders.

BEST-IN-CLASS MARKETING:

↗ Capitalized on new marketing initiatives to drive +12% profits, +13% market share, and +24% consumer awareness.

↗ Pioneered social blogging outreach recognized by *Computing Magazine* for boosting brand visibility 53%.

SALES & MARKETING RESULTS:

↗ Strengthened cash flow by slashing advertising budget $143M (44%) and lowering company inventory 52%.

↗ Restructured divisional field structure to trim headcount 23% and lowered promotional spending from $212M.

OUT-PACED SALES GOALS UP TO 130%

YEAR	TARGET	SALES	% TO PLAN
2018	$184M	$214M	130%
2017	$172M	$201M	128%
2016	$156M	$198M	125%
2015	$76M	$97M	123%
2014	$58M	$69M	120%
2013	$22M	$27M	118%

CORE COMPETENCIES:

- ATTAINING BREAKTHROUGH SALES
- DOMINATING RETAIL CHANNELS
- MAXIMIZING VERTICAL SALES
- SUSTAINING MARKET SHARE
- TURNING AROUND PROFITABILITY
- REBUILDING SALES TEAMS
- OVER-PRODUCING REVENUE TARGETS
- INCREASING DIGITAL LEADS
- REVAMPING SALES COMP PLANS

SENIOR SALES LEADERSHIP EXPERIENCE

HEWLETT PACKARD   2000 – Present
NORTH AMERICAN VP OF SALES [2012 – Present]

Promoted to reverse declining national sales growth, rebuild product development, and regain market dominance. Direct $46M divisional P&L with 325 staff, 300 agency personnel, and 4.2K US channel partners. Lead $27M in domestic advertising.

TURNED AROUND US SALES:

↗ Halted hemorrhaging sales, regained growth, and pushed revenue from $28M to $46M. Revamped national sales team and compensation strategies around rebranded products.

↗ Improved printer revenue 28% ($21M) by deepening brand-level margins. Cut costs $14M and decreased spending 19%.

$21M SINGLE-YEAR SALES GAIN

REVITALIZED PRODUCT DEVELOPMENT:

↗ Championed "test-and-learn" strategy to reinvigorate innovation, restructured talent development, and revamped product line leadership. Streamlined new product rollout cycle from 18 to 3 months.

↗ Transformed product positioning through realignment of brands with profit targets. Consolidated 12 product lines to 3 and rewrote web marketing playbook while strengthening channel partner training and product knowledge.

AUSTIN, TX · 490.528.7033 · DREYNOLDS7@GMAIL.COM

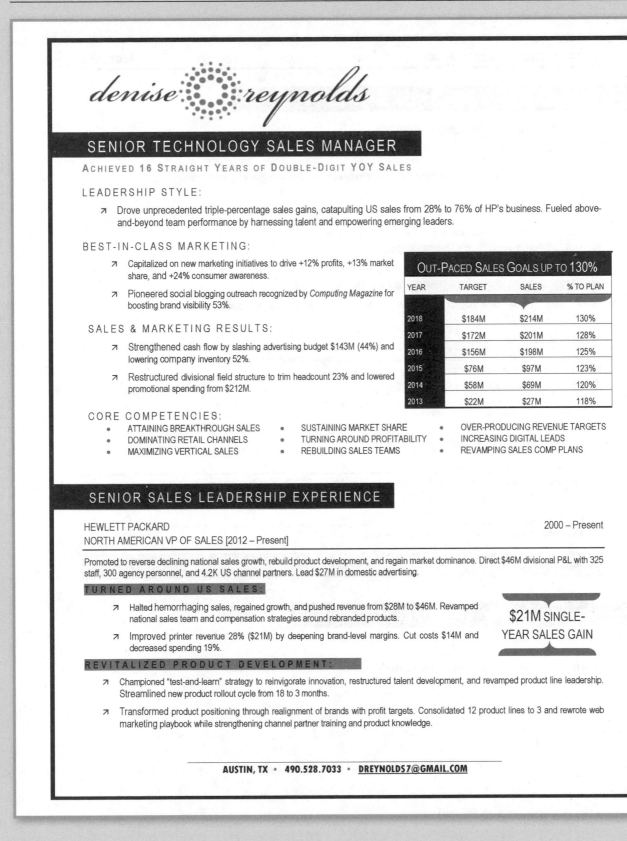

Cheryl Simpson, CMRW, ACRW, COPNS • Executive Resume Rescue • www.executiveresumerescue.com

SENIOR SALES LEADERSHIP EXPERIENCE CONTINUE

RECAPTURED MARKET DOMINANCE:

↗ Propelled market share from 7.2% to 20.2%, the largest netbook industry boost, employing aggressive advertising benchmarked against key competitor strengths.

↗ Fueled 3-place industry ranking rise from #5 to #2 in 2 years by earning #1 Consumer Reports product accolades.

DIVISION GM [2009 – 2011]

Tapped to spearhead market share recapture Initiative for a division producing 55% of sales revenue and contribution margin for HP's US business. Directed a team of 227 and 1.4K matrixed personnel with $38M P&L accountability.

DOMINATED RETAIL SALES MARKET:

↗ Guided retail sales up 98% over 2010 by designing and steering a 3-phase marketing blitz for the all-new LaserJet brand.

CAPTURED CONSUMER SOCIAL MEDIA FEEDBACK:

↗ Upgraded market positioning for new product launches, integrating social media into consumer research. Increased social media participation >74%.

NORTHEAST REGIONAL GM [2006 – 2008]

Positioned region for next-level sales performance, strategizing and leading organizational realignment impacting 373 employees and 1.7K channel partners in 14 states. Enhanced marketing and incentives; managed $26M P&L.

SALES & PARTNER TURNAROUNDS:

↗ Surpassed sales contribution margin $70M above forecast. Gained 1.5 market share points in ultra-competitive market.

↗ Reorganized field sales force into 4-region structure while boosting pre-owned sales from 73% to 141% – the highest level industry-wide.

SET NEW INDUSTRY
SALES BENCHMARK

VP OF SALES – HP PRINTERS [2003 – 2006]

Produced the highest US annual sales in 53 years and propelled profit margin 32%. Drove national sales operations, from partner management and distribution to sales training and incentives, with a 278-member team and a $17M P&L.

NORTHEAST REGIONAL SALES MANAGER [2000 – 2003]

Improved partner development 34% in 28 Northeastern markets.

ADDITIONAL HP EXPERIENCE: Promoted rapidly through 7 territory and district management promotions spanning sales and business development in NJ, OH, MI, IL, and NY.

EDUCATIONAL CREDENTIALS

Executive Development Program • WHARTON SCHOOL OF BUSINESS
MBA in Sales & Marketing • COLUMBIA UNIVERSITY
BA in Economics with a Minor in Business Administration • UNIVERSITY OF SOUTHERN CALIFORNIA

AUSTIN, TX • 490.528.7033 • DREYNOLDS7@GMAIL.COM

CHAPTER 18:
Be Distinctive

How can you stand out when a recruiter or hiring manager has an in-box full of 200+ resumes to review? His goal is to eliminate as many as possible and reduce the stack to a manageable pile of potential candidates whose resumes he will review more closely.

That is why first impressions—particularly visual impressions—are so vital to your success in the job search process. Your goal is to make certain that your resume gets at least a second look—every time—based on the strength of its visual presentation. You can accomplish that by giving it a unique, memorable, and distinctive *look and feel* that lets you stand out from the crowd.

Here are some practical steps to make that happen:

- **Introduce yourself boldly.** Position your name so that it pops off the page, using a font that is large and clear. Don't be overly creative in the placement of your name. People expect to see your name at the top of your resume and that's where it should go, whether flush left, centered, or flush right.

- **Don't be afraid to stand out.** You want to be different … instantaneously noticeable … distinctive from the crowd of other candidates. Don't go over the top or get too carried away, as your resume is *not* an art project. However, there are so many things that you can do to stand out—from simple font enhancements to major design elements and many things in between.

  Just be wise and appropriate about your decisions, always considering who your audience is and what matters most to them.

- **Don't look like everyone else.** If you use a resume template or simply follow the crowd, you'll create a resume that is very difficult to distinguish from anyone else's. Even a single element—such as your name in a very large font, or a colored page border, or a tasteful graphic—will make a difference and keep your resume (and you) from blending into the background.

- **Exude professionalism.** You've invested a lot of time and effort in creating your resume. Employers know that, and they expect it to be an example of your very best work. Make sure that your resume doesn't disappoint!

  From the content to the format to the final design, every element must be done well—correctly, professionally, neatly, and with attention to detail and care for the finished product. Not every job seeker is as meticulous as you'll be, and that gives you a great advantage—a resume that stands out simply because of its polished presentation.

- **Brand yourself.** In Chapter 1 we discussed the importance of expressing your personal brand in your resume. One element of branding is consistency across all online and offline search platforms.

  When you choose design elements for your resume, use those same themes, fonts, colors, and graphics for your personal website, business card, professional bio, and any other marketing materials that you create. Every message and every image that a recruiter or employer sees will continuously reinforce your brand.

Following are 2 particularly great examples of resumes filled with distinctive design elements that give these job seekers instant recognition and a solid competitive edge.

Jane Howard Resume—page 137

Jane's resume employs a font (Corbel) that is a bit unusual—just enough to be distinctive while still projecting a very professional image. She uses square bullets as a design element in her headings, and of course the powerful chart is a real attention-getter.

Anthony Tanner Resume—pages 138–39

One of Anthony's key assets as a health care administrator is his ability to generate revenue. The money graphic in the top left corner instantly makes that point. His resume also includes 2 well-designed charts that illustrate his success in several distinct areas that will interest prospective employers. The font choice (Gill Sans), large drop-cap in the summary, and dark-shaded boxes are further distinguishing touches.

JANE HOWARD

(213) 875-5555 | jhoward@gmail.com | www.linkedin.com/in/jhoward | Los Angeles, CA

SENIOR SALES PROFESSIONAL
B2B SALES ■ B2C SALES ■ TEAM LEADERSHIP ■ STRATEGIC MARKETING

- Personally closed deals with 4700+ clients, generating $4.7M and regularly ranking in the top 5% companywide.
- Led team to a 125% increase in new corporate memberships in first 2 years as Sales Manager.

"I would bet on you for any problem-solving, strategy, or sales management competitions." —GM, All Star Athletic Clubs

■ SALES EXPERIENCE ■

All Star Athletic Clubs   Pacific Palisades, CA | 2009 – Present
An upscale health club with 11 locations and 40,000 members
Sales Manager | 2016 – Present • **Senior Sales Representative** | 2013 – 2016 • **Sales Representative** | 2009 – 2013

Market and manage B2B and B2C membership sales, renewals, and personal training. Heighten company brand awareness through innovative corporate initiatives such as outreach programs and promotional events.

Cultivate and maintain an extensive network of contacts/clients through prospect lead generation, cold-calling, lead tracking, marketing campaigns, and print advertising. Recruit, train, and lead sales representatives.

B2B SALES

- Led Santa Monica sales team that increased total corporate revenue 59% and new corporate memberships **125%** over past 2 years by mining, targeted cold-calling, cultivating and developing C-level relationships, and offering exclusive programming for businesses.

- Closed **8** new corporate accounts; maintained and grew 12 existing accounts.

B2C SALES

- Regularly ranked in top **5%** among **60–80** sales reps.
- Achieved a consistent average of **114%** of quota.
- Averaged **60%** success rate in cross-selling personal training packages, exceeding corporate average of **41%**.
- Generated **48%** of sales from referrals.

TEAM LEADERSHIP

- Led sales team to generate **$2.8M** in sales and close deals with 2700 clients. Met or exceeded median club performance **19** out of **22** months, despite increasing local competition.
- Personally produced **$1.2M** with **1400+** clients while leading sales team during past 2 years.
- Surpassed goals for new membership units, with a team average of **111%** over quota in first year as Sales Manager.
- Achieved highest team renewal rate companywide, with **6%** increase from prior year.

TECHNOLOGY ACCOMPLISHMENTS

- Created a robust Excel customer tracking system to supplement outdated CRM.
- Selected as company beta-tester for Salesforce.com and Motionsoft.

■ EDUCATION ■

PEPPERDINE UNIVERSITY | Bachelor of Arts in Psychology, With Highest Honors | Malibu, CA | 2009

ANTHONY J. TANNER

Richmond, VA 22932 | 434.555.2623
tony.tanner@gmail.com | linkedin.com/in/tonytannerhealthcare

HEALTH CARE ADMINISTRATOR

Clinical operations leader who articulates vision for the organization, drives strategic execution, and engages direct reports in delivering high-quality results.

Progressive thinker committed to advancing the capacity and capability of a progressive health care system. Socratic, collaborative approach: define objectives, welcome input, and factor in data and insights.

Innovator who's impacted clinical operations, ambulatory care services, freestanding radiation therapy facilities, and partner-based radiation oncology programs to the benefit of the institution and all patients.

"EXCELLENT ADMINISTRATIVE LEADER & EXPERT ..."

"Tony has no comparison in this field when it comes to establishing and growing clinical operations. He is an excellent administrative leader and expert whose unique talent is engaging clinicians so they understand the critical impact of the services they deliver."

LEADERSHIP COMPETENCIES

Health Care Administration	Patient Services	Performance Optimization
Clinical Operations Management	Physical Relations	EMR & Technology Implementation
Clinical Program Development	Partner Engagement	Data Management, Analysis & Intelligence
Ambulatory Services Operations	Staff Recruitment & Leadership	Quality & Standardization Initiatives
Fiscal & Budget Management	Employee Engagement	Outcomes Measurement

PROFESSIONAL EXPERIENCE & SIGNATURE ACHIEVEMENTS

SOUTHERN VIRGINIA HEALTH SYSTEM, Norcross, VA   **2008 to Present**

570-bed hospital comprising NCI-designated Cancer Center, Outpatient Surgery, Children's Medical, and Long-Term Care Centers.

Senior Administrator (2016 to Present): Advanced to this role to strategically direct operations and service delivery for 50 outpatient clinics.

Declared vision of change and transformation to eliminate siloed culture and promote cross-departmental relationships. Rightsized organizational infrastructure. Leveraged and paired managers of clinics providing complementary services. Recruited and installed dynamic team after evaluating candidates for fit with the new culture. Conducted research and delivered national presentations.

- **Led critical initiative** to raise appointment availability. Evaluated utilization data and identified openings to assign patients to providers.
  - Invested $2K in telemedicine technology to schedule appointments previously blocked for grand rounds.

- **Drove year-over-year employee engagement** to 75th percentile. Critical factor was realigning salaries with area market.

- **Built financial snapshot** for medical directors and executive leadership indicating budget, volume, and utilization for 3-year cost reduction and budget-rebalancing initiatives.

- **First of 4 family medicine clinics to gain approval** to operate as officially sanctioned patient-centered medical home.

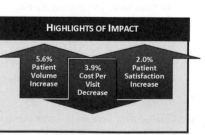

HIGHLIGHTS OF IMPACT

5.6% Patient Volume Increase | 3.9% Cost Per Visit Decrease | 2.0% Patient Satisfaction Increase

Professional Experience & Signature Achievements Continued On Page 2

Jewel Bracy DeMaio, CPRW, MRW, ACRW, CEIP • Perfect 10 Resumes • www.perfect10resumes.com

ANTHONY J. TANNER

434.555.2623 | tony.tanner@gmail.com | linkedin.com/in/tonytannerhealthcare | Page 2

SOUTHERN VIRGINIA HEALTH SYSTEM (CONTINUED)

<u>Medical Center Director</u> (2010 to 2016): Guided operations of radiation oncology and focused ultrasound. Scope encompassed financials and budgeting, clinical care delivery, and patient satisfaction. Promoted change management in the form of telemedicine adoption and technology implementation.

- **Principally directed series of initiatives** key to increasing gross hospital revenue from $18M to $31M.

  - Markedly increased awareness of clinical trial program and raised trial enrollment 25%, directly leading to $15.1M in new revenue in a single year.

  - Orchestrated opening of focused ultrasound facility, which exceeded projections and generated $10.5M the 1st year.

  - Captured $5.4M annually in highly competitive radiation oncology service and raised patient satisfaction 4.4%.

- **Promoted medical records virtualization** by using Mosaic to capture all manual data and by defining EMR workflow process. Launched chartless environment with Mosiac several years prior to implementing EPIC.

$18M TO $31M REVENUE GROWTH

Radiation Oncology $5.4M · Focused Ultrasound $10.5M · Clinical Trials $15.1M

<u>Chief Medical Dosimetrist</u> (2008 to 2010): Recruited to newly created role to provide change management as center capitalized on series of technological advancements and transitioned from 100% paper environment.

Promoted technology adoption and leveraged technology to advance radiation oncology research capabilities. Led QA, data compilation, and process and procedure development regarding IMRT implementation. Oversaw dosimetrists at 3 radiation facilities. Assisted in providing radiation therapy didactic and clinical education.

LOUISVILLE RADIATION ONCOLOGY, Louisville, KY   2004 to 2007

Start-up radiation oncology service that progressed to leading status in Louisville metropolitan market.

<u>Administrator</u>: Merited advancement to this role following 4 years as *Medical Dosimetrist*. Directed daily operations and led formulation of calculations to maximize radiation dose to tumor cells while sparing healthy tissue.

EDUCATION

MASTER OF HEALTH SCIENCE ADMINISTRATION
Virginia State University, Petersburg, VA   2016

BACHELOR OF SCIENCE, OCCUPATIONAL TRAINING & DEVELOPMENT
University of Kentucky, Lexington, KY   2005

CERTIFICATE IN MEDICAL DOSIMETRY
Boston Medical Center, Boston, MA   2003

PRESENTATIONS

U.S. Society of Therapeutic Radiation Oncological Practice
"Can Holding Your Breath Be That Important?" (2018)

34th Annual National Panel of Medical Dosimetry Practitioners
"Quest for a Chartless Department in an Academic Medical Center: Lessons Learned" (2017)

CHAPTER 19:
Embrace Color and Graphics

Resumes and job search have changed dramatically in recent years. Yet, at its core, the resume is still a business document, and those receiving it expect to see a fairly traditional presentation of career information. A wild and crazy design is not always appropriate and can, at times, be counterproductive.

This is especially true for people in traditional and conservative professions. It is rare that a boldly creative resume for an accountant, manufacturing manager, actuary, attorney, or insurance claims adjuster would be appropriate, because it sends mixed messages … like the infamous mullet haircut that was "business in the front and party in the back"!

That certainly doesn't mean resumes for traditional professions have to be staid, boring, or cookie-cutter. Tasteful and appropriate images, charts and graphs and a professional touch of color can be added to just about any resume to give it a distinctive appearance while still remaining professionally conservative.

We encourage you to embrace the use of color and graphics in your resume. Consider these possibilities for adding visual impact, along with ideas for when and how to use them:

- **Tables, Charts, and Graphs.** As we've demonstrated in several resumes in prior chapters, tables and charts (also known as graphs) communicate an instant message and add a great deal of pizzazz to a text-rich resume.

  Tables are a standard feature of Microsoft Word and other word-processing programs. Charts and graphs can be created in Word or in a spreadsheet program and imported into the Word document (resume).

  Tables are useful for presenting several specific pieces of information—perhaps a list of technical competencies or core skills—in a way that keeps each item separate for easy skimming. Tables can also be used to display relevant numbers and can incorporate color across rows, down columns, or in headings.

  More visually exciting than a table, a **chart or graph** can quickly show upward or downward movement. It's perfect for illustrating growth in sales or revenue, reduction in costs or errors, increases in productivity or efficiency, and other points of measurement and comparison.

  When creating a chart, be certain that the visual display sends the right message. For example, if you've had a lot of up-and-down sales years, you would probably be better off highlighting total sales growth over a period of years rather than showing a graph with numbers that veer wildly from good (up) to bad (down).

Experiment to see if a colorful, eye-catching table, chart, or graph will help to tell your story while increasing the visual appeal of your resume.

- **Boxes.** A simple box—shaded and colored or not—is an easy technique for setting off important information in your resume. We recommend that you use Word's "Borders and Shading" feature to create a box, rather using the "Insert Text Box" feature. As mentioned in Chapter 13 (Prepare for the Complexities of Online Search), the contents of a text box cannot be read by Applicant Tracking Systems and that has the potential to negatively impact your search results.

  Try different styles and widths of borders and different colors of fill and shading to find the right combination that emphasizes important information in your resume while keeping the look entirely professional.

- **Borders and Lines.** Horizontal borders are one of the easiest techniques to master and use in your resume. Use Word's "Borders and Shading" tool to create lines across the page, above or below headings, and in other places to create a visual break and to separate sections of your resume. When you look at the resume samples in this book, you will see dozens of border and line treatments that you can imitate and use for your own resume.

  Border lines are also an ideal place to add a dash of color to your resume without compromising readability or going overboard with too many design elements.

- **Logos.** Logos are not commonly used in resumes, but when they are, they can be extremely effective in communicating key points about your experience. Take a look through the sample resumes and you'll find examples where a logo creates instant identification with a company, product, or school.

- **Images.** It's possible to add photographs, drawings, and clip art to your Word document. Examples in this book include a stethoscope for a medical professional, a bulldozer for a construction manager, a pile of money for a finance executive, and—most unusually!—a martini glass for a cocktail waitress. Be certain that any image you add to your resume strengthens the message, is relevant to your current career goals, and is appropriate for your profession and level.

- **Shapes.** Microsoft Word's "Smart Art" feature is a great source of interesting shapes that you can insert into your resume, adding color and distinctiveness while highlighting brief bits of relevant career information. As with any graphic insertion, take care that what you're adding is going to enhance and not distract from the key messages in your resume.

- **Color.** Color helps your resume stand out, sends a more modern message than the traditional black-and-white resume, and garners longer looks from readers—it's been proven in several studies. While it's never necessary to add color, it can be beneficial, and we recommend that you give it a try—remaining appropriate, professional, and tasteful, of course!

> **PRO TIP:** Because this book is printed in black-and-white, you can't see the glorious colors that were used to create many of the resume samples. We encourage you to check out the winners of our quarterly "Modernize Your Resume Contest," for which professional writers submit their finest work. Several of the winners are featured in this book, and you can find them all online (in color) at:
> **www.emeraldcareerpublishing.com.**

The following 2 examples illustrate the value of embracing color and graphics in your resume.

Lucy Simpson Resume—page 143

Notable graphic elements of Lucy's resume include:

- A colorful "gear" graphic at the top that conveys a technical message for this newly graduated computer engineer and highlights the 3 most important things she brings to any employer: Technical Aptitude, Educational Preparation, and an Inquisitive Nature.
- A headline ("Computer Engineer") in reverse type inside a darkly shaded box.
- A well-organized table that efficiently presents her many technical competencies—one of the key qualifications for every job she is pursuing.
- A full border around the edges of the page that neatly encloses all of the contents and gives a very polished look to her resume.

Anthony Charles Resume—page 144–45

Anthony's 2-page resume is rich with graphical elements that create a unique look and a positive impression. Specifically:

- A graphic to the left of his name that emphasizes his expertise: Business, Growth, and Success.
- A reverse-type box, directly beneath his name, that conveys his personal brand as a "Masterful Relationship Builder" and his professional expertise as a "B2B Sales Leader."
- Boxes and shading throughout the resume that highlight headings, areas of expertise, and banners announcing his top sales results.
- Tables on page 1 and page 2 that are used to distinguish his most notable achievements in each position.

LUCY SIMPSON

lucysimpson@nu.edu | **617.555.2345** | linkedin.com/in/lucysimpson
https://www.lucysimpson.com/portfolio

COMPUTER ENGINEER

High-achieving Northeastern University graduate seeking computer engineering opportunity in the Greater Boston area.

Results-driven, self-motivated, and appreciative of team environments where members share ideas, promote industry best practices, and learn from each other.

"I'm ready to get to work!"

Software Development | Team Leadership | Collaborative Work Style | Multi-Project Management

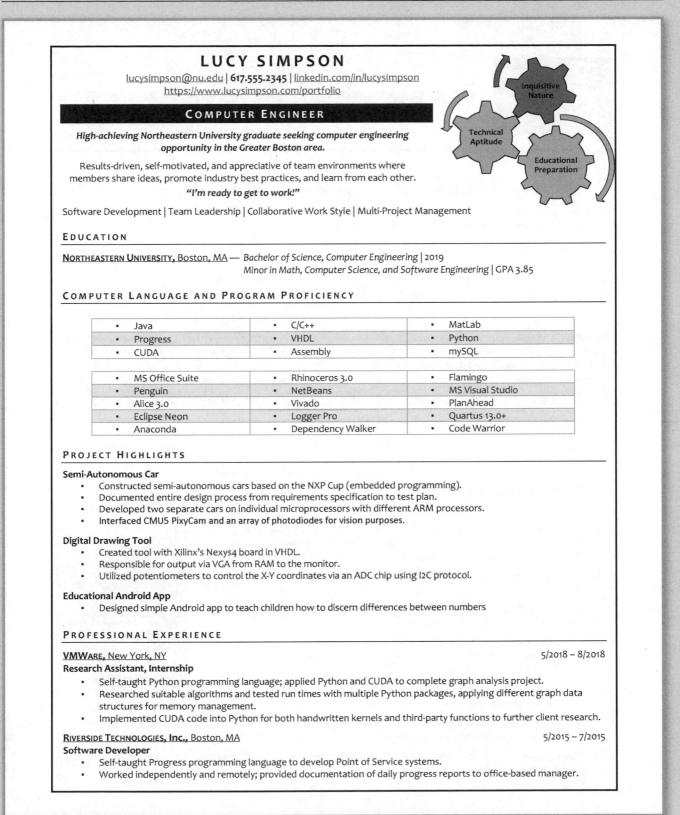

EDUCATION

NORTHEASTERN UNIVERSITY, Boston, MA — *Bachelor of Science, Computer Engineering | 2019*
Minor in Math, Computer Science, and Software Engineering | GPA 3.85

COMPUTER LANGUAGE AND PROGRAM PROFICIENCY

Java	C/C++	MatLab
Progress	VHDL	Python
CUDA	Assembly	mySQL

MS Office Suite	Rhinoceros 3.0	Flamingo
Penguin	NetBeans	MS Visual Studio
Alice 3.0	Vivado	PlanAhead
Eclipse Neon	Logger Pro	Quartus 13.0+
Anaconda	Dependency Walker	Code Warrior

PROJECT HIGHLIGHTS

Semi-Autonomous Car
- Constructed semi-autonomous cars based on the NXP Cup (embedded programming).
- Documented entire design process from requirements specification to test plan.
- Developed two separate cars on individual microprocessors with different ARM processors.
- Interfaced CMU5 PixyCam and an array of photodiodes for vision purposes.

Digital Drawing Tool
- Created tool with Xilinx's Nexys4 board in VHDL.
- Responsible for output via VGA from RAM to the monitor.
- Utilized potentiometers to control the X-Y coordinates via an ADC chip using I2C protocol.

Educational Android App
- Designed simple Android app to teach children how to discern differences between numbers

PROFESSIONAL EXPERIENCE

VMWARE, New York, NY   5/2018 – 8/2018
Research Assistant, Internship
- Self-taught Python programming language; applied Python and CUDA to complete graph analysis project.
- Researched suitable algorithms and tested run times with multiple Python packages, applying different graph data structures for memory management.
- Implemented CUDA code into Python for both handwritten kernels and third-party functions to further client research.

RIVERSIDE TECHNOLOGIES, Inc., Boston, MA   5/2015 – 7/2015
Software Developer
- Self-taught Progress programming language to develop Point of Service systems.
- Worked independently and remotely; provided documentation of daily progress reports to office-based manager.

Cathy Lanzalaco, CPRW, CPCC, MBA, SPHR, SHRM-SCP, RN • Write-Resume-For-The-Job • www.write-resume-for-the-job.com

ANTHONY CHARLES

BUSINESS-TO-BUSINESS (B2B) SALES LEADER | MASTERFUL RELATIONSHIP BUILDER

206-255-8736 ◆ anthony.charles@gmail.com
Seattle, WA 98136 ◆ LinkedIn.com/in/anthony.charles

SALES MANAGEMENT EXECUTIVE

COMMERCIAL AEROSPACE ◆ ELECTRONICS ◆ DEFENSE ◆ HEALTHCARE ◆ PHARMA/BIOTECH

Champion multimillion-dollar growth in international and domestic market segments, driving sales strategy, key market expansion, channel partner development, and program management.

Deliver consistent year-over-year (YOY) growth. Provide organizational leadership in matrix environments. Inspire teamwork, develop exceptional talent, and achieve sustainable sales results.

PROFESSIONAL EXPERIENCE

Safety Detection Systems, Inc., Tacoma, WA [2013–Present]

Lead efforts to expand market presence in critical infrastructure and emergency response markets for global safety and security technologies, advanced threat detection solutions that safeguard society (civil and military) from chemical, biological, radiological, and nuclear materials (CBRNE) and explosives.

DIRECTOR OF US SALES 2016–Present	DIVISIONAL SALES MANAGER – EAST 2015–2016	REGIONAL SALES MANAGER 2013–2015
130% of Quota >$28M Business Revenue +4% Market Share Gain	#1 Sales Performer 101% of Quota #1 Company Account	↑92% Regional Sales +$10M Exclusive Contract #1 of 16 Sales Representatives

DIRECTOR OF UNITED STATES (US) SALES (2016-Present)

**Lead Development of Scalable Business Strategy and Commercial Plans to Drive National Performance
Outperformed Sales Goals Annually: +28%, 2016 | +30%, 2017 | +31%, 2018**

Sales Leadership – Plan and execute sales strategies for diverse clients (private and governmental agencies, including Department of Defense and Department of Homeland Security) with critical infrastructure. Manage $300K department budget, 12 direct reports.

Manage Programs
Align Organization Goals
Conduct Market Research
Perform SWOT Analysis
Expand Market Presence
Engage Clients
Attract Business Partners
Convert Prospects
Improve Market Share
Deliver Net Revenue/Profit
Exceed Growth Targets

- Develop sales objectives, analyze key metrics, and evaluate performance of business/product lines.

- Interface with stakeholders across the US, Mexico, Latin America, the Caribbean, Canada, Finland, Germany, and the United Kingdom.

- Exercise profit and loss (P&L) responsibility for achieving revenue and profit targets. Ensure efficiency and effectiveness of US Sales go-to-market activities; manage field sales activities; develop sustainable pipelines.

- Guide strategic development of a comprehensive US Commercial Distributor Program, spanning internationally across key market segments.

- Provide corporate representation within global areas of operation; liaise with key leadership/stakeholders of charitable and civic institutions and professional associations.

Talent Management – Collaborate with sales leadership across divisions. Establish sales force training plans, forecast funnel activity, and reinforce critical sales competencies.

– Continued on Page 2 –

ANTHONY CHARLES

DIRECTOR OF UNITED STATES (US) SALES (continued)

Business Development – Develop and implement long-range business plans for the Americas. Manage and grow company revenue, margin, and market share across business segments. Develop strategic partnerships and executive-level networks to support a lucrative client base.

Organizational Leadership – Lead a geographically dispersed sales organization (4 continents); build, cultivate, and empower high-performance teams across a multichannel go-to-market strategy.

Quality Systems Management – Safeguard standardization across functional areas; monitor import/export controls, international procurement, brand management, marketing, professional development, and worldwide security regulations.

EASTERN DIVISION SALES MANAGER (2015–2016)
REGIONAL SALES MANAGER (2013–2015)

Ranked #1 Sales Performer of the Year | Achieved 101% of Annual Quota | Landed Company's #1 New Account

Sales– Consistently exceeded sales goals and earned recognition for sales results: revenue growth, customer relationship management, contract negotiations, business expansion.

- As DSM, captured the company's largest account, negotiating a multiyear, exclusive supplier agreement with a major global transport company. Contract value exceeded $10M. Ranked #1 company-wide in sales.

- Over a 2-year period, grew regional sales by 92% (from $1.3M to >$2.5M). Ranked #1 of 16 in sales.

Capture Planning – Identified business opportunities, analyzed advances in technology, and created pursuit strategies. Led brainstorming sessions to drive key initiatives.

Customer Relationship Management (CRM) – Exceeded customer expectations while promoting sales growth and facilitating product line expansion.

MediSurge Pharma, Seattle, WA [2009–2013]

Presided over sales of neuroscience products, medicines designed to promote health equity and improve health outcomes for patients with depressive disorders, schizophrenia, and bipolar management.

TERRITORY BUSINESS MANAGER

RANKINGS	GROWTH STRATEGIES	ORGANIZATION DEVELOPMENT
#7 – Southeast Region Top 15% of 365 Nationally #7 – Race for President's Club	Customized Roadmaps (30, 60, 90 Sales Plans) Proactive Customer Needs Assessment Solution-Oriented Selling	Sales Meeting Leadership Team Training and Mentoring Introduction of Sales Analytics

RECENT TRAINING

Leadership Edge Training, Pinon Group *[2017]* | Mastering the Six Levels of Leadership, Sales Concepts *[2017]*
Sales and Leadership Academy, Safety Detection Systems *[2017]* | Key Account Management, ASLAN *[2017]*
Certified in Radiation Safety, Amboy & Associates *[2016]*

ACADEMIC EDUCATION

Master of Business Administration (MBA)
University of Washington, Seattle, WA [2018]

Bachelor of Business Administration (BBA), Major in Marketing
Oregon State University, Corvallis, OR [2005]

PART V:
Resumes for Challenging Situations

Many job seekers are faced with particularly challenging job search situations, the most common of which are:

- Changing careers
- Making a military-to-civilian career transition
- Returning to work after an extended absence

If you fall into one of these categories, pay special attention to the information and resume samples in Chapters 20, 21, and 22 on the following pages. You'll find clear and concise explanations of each of the 3 categories along with specific resume writing strategies to position yourself for the career opportunities you are pursuing today.

> **PRO TIP: The most important thing to remember about writing a resume in a challenging situation** is to focus on the things that matter most to your current objectives and downplay the items that are less relevant.

For some job seekers facing challenging circumstances, past work experience will be the most relevant information in their resume. For others, educational credentials will be primary. And for the vast majority, at the forefront will be "transferable skills"—expertise that you gained in one field but now want to use in another.

Let's consider the concept of "transferable skills" for a moment. The idea is great—you can transfer skills that you already have from one profession to another! However, we recommend that you avoid using that term—"transferable skills"—because it sends a message that you are not familiar with your new field and will have to adapt your skills and knowledge rather than being productive immediately.

In our view, once you have a skill—no matter where you developed it—you own that skill and can prominently position it in your resume as one of your key qualifications. Don't minimize it by referring to it as "transferable" just because you learned it or used it in a different environment. Don't shortchange yourself or your value!

If you are changing careers, transitioning from military service to a civilian career, or returning to work after an extended absence, use the resumes in this section to guide your resume writing decisions. However, feel free to use other samples from this book to give you even more ideas on how to present your experience, educational credentials, skills, and all of the other information that makes you a uniquely qualified candidate.

CHAPTER 20:
Resumes for People Changing Careers

This chapter will be relevant to you if you are making a big change in your career and moving from one profession to another. That's what we consider a true career change and the types of resumes that we showcase in this chapter.

Of course, a "career change" is not always a dramatic transition. People make career changes all the time. They get promoted, they switch industries but retain similar career paths, they move through numerous similar positions with multiple companies, and they transition from for-profit to non-profit.

These are just a few examples and, of course, all involve change. For those types of career changes, you'll uncover valuable tidbits of information in this chapter but would be better served by using the sample resumes in the other chapters and the Resume Portfolio in Part VI.

When writing a true career-change resume, the focus should be on showcasing the skills and knowledge you have that are most relevant to your new career objective. Often this means separating your skills from the environment (jobs or industries) in which those skills were acquired.

> **PRO TIP: Begin your resume writing process by identifying the skills, knowledge, and expertise you possess that will be valuable in your new career.** Never belittle those skills or their relevance by thinking of them as "transferable." Of course, you'll be using them in a new environment, but you own those skills and they're genuine and strong, no matter the job, company, or industry where acquired.

As you've read earlier in this book, it is our general recommendation that resumes be written in a combination-chronological style—beginning with a summary section, then showcasing your employment history and career achievements, and ending with your education and any other important information.

However, that is generally *not* the case with career-change resumes. More often than not, career-change resumes are functional in style, beginning with a detailed summary of skills, qualifications, experiences, educational credentials, projects, achievements, and other details from your career that align with your current career goals. How you organize that summary section (or multiple sections) can vary dramatically from resume to resume, as you'll see in the samples in this chapter and in the Resume Portfolio later in this book.

Following the detailed summary portion, most functional resumes include a brief listing of work experience (to communicate that you do have work history and to share important details *if* they are relevant or impressive), an education section, and other information—such as technical skills, languages, testimonials, affiliations, public speaking, and the like—that could be of value.

> **PRO TIP: When writing a functional resume, be certain to follow the content, format, and design rules described in detail throughout this book**—the identical guidelines that we recommend for the modern combination (chronological) resume. You'll be arranging the material differently, but you still must create highly readable, powerful, and relevant content to position yourself for your new career.

The very best way to explain how to write a career-change resume is to demonstrate—in detail—how and why the following 2 resumes were written.

Rolf Hoel Resume—page 151

Rolf's entire career has been in Security, and his objective now is a position as a Java Developer. His resume must present him as a qualified Java Developer so that prospective employers can easily understand his value.

Let's explore each component of his 1-page resume—an excellent example of how effective the *right* functional writing strategy can be.

- **Headline—Java Developer**—does 2 things at once. First, it tells you who he is, and second, it communicates the position he is targeting.
- **Bullets at Top**—Each addresses an important skill or attribute for success in his chosen field.
- **IT Skills**—This section succinctly communicates all of the specific technical qualifications that are critical for the jobs he is seeking.
- **Education**—First, Rolf's recent Java Developer training is included with some detail. Then, notice that his prior education is listed as a "BSc Program" (and not a "BSc Degree"). This is a very effective and 100% honest way to present the education for someone who has attended a school or university but not completed a degree.
- **Professional Skills**—This section highlights Rolf's achievements and areas of responsibility from his previous professional experience that are relevant to his current job goals, directly and indirectly.
- **Experience**—Now, after reading all of the above and perceiving that Rolf is a techie, you realize that any technical experience he has was just a part of his job as a Security Officer. However, he's positioned himself as a viable candidate for Java Developer positions by demonstrating all of the right skills and qualifications for his new profession.
- **Languages and Kudos**—Languages add another great skill and dimension to this job seeker, and third-party testimonials are a powerful addition.

END RESULT: A resume that positions Rolf as a qualified Java Developer with an advantage over other recent graduates. Not only does he have the educational credentials, he has real-life work experience, a definite plus.

ROLF HOEL

▶ **0710-497 67 61** ▶ rolf.hoel@gmail.com ▶ linkedin.com/in/rolf-hoel

JAVA DEVELOPER

- **Trained group leader.** Always calm in critical situations. Meticulous, analytical, and persistent.
- **Trusted problem solver.** Handpicked for complex technical solutions requiring security clearance.
- **Company representative,** working directly with customers either on own assignments or in teams/on projects.
- **Reliable partner.** Known for meeting deadlines and understanding customer and production requirements.

IT SKILLS

Languages/Technologies:	Java, UML, SQL (MySQL, phpMyadmin, MS SQL), Java for Android app development, HTML/CSS, JEE, JavaScript, XML, XLS, PHP, Struts, Apache Ant
Development Environments:	Eclipse, NetBeans, Android Studio, Visual Paradigm
Server Environments:	Tomcat, Apache, Orion

EDUCATION

Java Developer, BD Education AS   2016–2018
- Java: Programming, network programming, advanced interface development, and mobile development
- Advanced object orientation with UML ▪ Data structures and algorithms
- Web application development

BSc Program in Data Technology, University of Oslo (UiO), Norway   2006–2008

PROFESSIONAL SKILLS

Troubleshooting/Communication
- Executed all school projects within set timeframes and scored "high pass" or "with honors."
- Contend with daily vacancies and motivate co-workers to carry out assignments. Oversee 6 departments of ≈300 armed security guards and close protection officers.
- Support group leader with technical skills.

Project Management/Teamwork
- Collaborate daily with 8- to 10-member teams. Coach staff on assignments.
- Met 100% of deadlines in all UiO courses by leading work process, setting goals, allocating tasks, and motivating 4–5 team members with diverse backgrounds. Won "high pass" for 90% of projects.

EXPERIENCE

ARMED SECURITY GUARD / TEAM LEADER, Securitas Norway AS   2009–Present
ARMED SECURITY GUARD & SECURITY OFFICER, Royal Security AS   1998–2009

Protect objects with very complex alarm systems, such as buildings, airports, military security shelters, luxury hotels, and high-profile people. Selected to attend numerous industry-specific trainings.

LANGUAGES

English (fluent, completed 1 year at high school in USA), **Norwegian** (native), **Spanish** (conversational)

KUDOS

"You are easily one of the most talented students I have had … you do more than expected!" —*BD Education AS*
"Rolf has demonstrated discretion, responsiveness, customer care, loyalty & professionalism." —*Royal Security AS*

Birgitta Moller, ACRW • www.cvhjalpe.nu

Aminah Sarhadi Resume—pages 153–54

Aminah's 2-page resume paints the picture of an accomplished "Multi-Lingual Healthcare Professional"— and she is. To truly understand her, however, look at the second page of her resume and you'll see that her entire professional career has been in television news and media (except for a 3-month project with a non-profit organization).

So how do you make a journalist appear as a healthcare professional? For Aminah, the answer is her education, which became the foundation for her new resume. Let's look at each component:

- **Headline—Multi-Lingual Healthcare Professional**—accomplishes the same 2 things as Rolf's headline—it identifies "who" this job seeker is and "what" she wants to do. (Note that this will only work if you have related experience, education, skills, or other qualifications so that the "who" is accurate.)

- **Branding Statement**—The sentence immediately below the headline that starts with "High-performing …" is most frequently referred to as a branding statement—someone's unique value proposition. Aminah's brand very effectively merges her healthcare, media, and related expertise into one statement that positions her as both qualified and with a distinctive skill set.

- **Boxed Section**—Each of these 3 statements focuses on a different skill—organizational leadership, communications, operations/program management—all of which are important to her current career goals as a Healthcare Administrator (not a care provider).

- **Strengths and Competencies**—This section demonstrates an effective technique for integrating a number of essential keywords into a resume to create a strong match with job descriptions and electronic resume scanning requirements.

- **Languages and Awards**—These unique bits of information add dimension, interest, and third-party validation of Aminah's success, even if they were from the television industry. (Who doesn't want to meet someone who's had 5 Emmy nominations?) It can often be the unusual things—related to nothing about your job target—that most entice people to reach out to you.

- **Education**—It's perfect that Aminah's recent Master of Health Administration (MHA) degree is prominently listed, along with her other degrees from Columbia and Yale. Even though her majors are unrelated to her current goals, those Ivy League names are impressive and communicate a positive message themselves.

- **Healthcare Fieldwork and Research Experience**—Highlighting 2 major projects she did while pursuing her MHA degree, Aminah's experience section looks like "real" jobs. They were "real" experiences and are presented in a typical job format to give them maximum impact.

- **Professional Experience**—Readers don't even know about Aminah's extensive career path in media until they reach page 2. Although not related to healthcare, the few items mentioned for each job are interesting, unique, adventuresome, and worldly, all of which add value to her job search and help to position her as a uniquely qualified Healthcare Professional who brings much more than just educational credentials.

END RESULT: A dynamic Healthcare Professional resume that can stand alone with just page 1. When you add page 2, you create an even more intriguing picture of that same qualified job seeker with a wealth of other, valuable experience.

AMINAH SARHADI

(585) 689-7837 ◆ aminah@georgetown.edu ◆ www.linkedin.com/in/aminahsarhadi ◆ Washington, DC 21789

MULTI-LINGUAL HEALTHCARE PROFESSIONAL

High-performing, collaborative leader committed to leveraging over a decade of success in global media, PR, program management, and client relations to advance healthcare system viability and patient outcomes.

➢ Thrive in dynamic, deadline-driven, multi-cultural environments; engage stakeholders at all levels; and build relations with health leaders, agencies, donors, physicians, and patients to achieve common goals.

➢ Exercise sophisticated editorial judgement, global perspective, and media savvy to deliver impactful, enterprise-wide communication strategies and compelling, consistent messaging across media platforms.

➢ Drive efficiency across complex operations through strategic program management, competitive benchmarking, and technical innovation while continuing to deliver demanding daily results.

~ Strengths and Competencies ~

Communication Strategy • Media Relations • Press Releases • Public Relations • Research • Public Health
Writing • Editing • Client Relations • Community Advocacy • Program Management • Disaster Preparedness
Benchmarking • Healthcare Marketing • Community Advocacy • Budgeting • Program Management

Languages – English, French, Hindi, Urdu, Dari, and Farsi *Traveled to 30+ Countries*

Awards – Earned **2 Peabody Awards** and **5 Emmy Nominations**

EDUCATION

MHA – Master of Health Administration – GEORGETOWN UNIVERSITY – Washington, DC *(Expected May 2019)*
MS in Broadcast Journalism – COLUMBIA UNIVERSITY – New York, NY
BA in International Relations, Peace and Justice Studies – Magna Cum Laude – YALE UNIVERSITY – New Haven, CT

HEALTHCARE FIELDWORK AND RESEARCH EXPERIENCE

GEORGETOWN UNIVERSITY MASTER OF HEALTH ADMINISTRATION PROGRAM   Aug 2018 – Dec 2018
Healthcare Marketing Simulation, Insurance Expansion Team Leader – New York, NY
Led 6 healthcare professionals in designing a marketing plan to expand insurance coverage across Colorado.
- Established a cohesive brand and compelling multi-cultural marketing message by creating a memorable tag line and color scheme, developing a website, launching a social media campaign, and writing a blog.
- Developed a targeted advertising campaign in English and Spanish through TV, print, and online ads, direct mail, community outreach partnerships, and marketing collateral for hospitals and healthcare providers.

GEORGE WASHINGTON UNIVERSITY HOSPITAL METHADONE TREATMENT CLINIC   Feb 2017 – May 2018
Fieldwork Consultant, Georgetown University Master of Health Administration Program – Washington, DC
Partnered with COO to transform substance abuse clinic serving 6,000 patients across 16 locations from an insolvent entity into an integrated care provider with restored profitability and enhanced patient outcomes.
- Collaborated with 6 MHA students and faculty advisor to develop new business model and org structure.
- Led needs assessment by conducting site visits, staff and patient surveys, and external benchmarking.
- Reduced prescription costs and turnaround time by upgrading health records management system.
- Expanded program reach and comorbidity treatment by bolstering cooperation with healthcare partners.

Julie Wyckoff, M.Ed., CPRW • Custom Career Solutions • www.customcareersolutions.com

AMINAH SARHADI

(585) 689-7837 ◆ Page Two

PROFESSIONAL EXPERIENCE

ABC NEWS   Aug 2010 – Present

International Desk Editor and Acting Supervisor – New York, NY

Lead 6 editors in delivering award-winning news on air, print, and the web for world's leading news network.

- Gain a decisive edge in reporting high-stakes breaking news by using social media and in-depth knowledge of world cultures, geography, and political landscapes to secure timely eyewitness accounts and videos.
- Earned 2 **Emmy Nominations** for Syria and Israel-Gaza coverage and won **Peabody Award** for Gulf Oil Spill.
- Coordinate editing, logistics, technical details, and visuals to deliver robust, multi-dimensional stories.
- Prioritize daily global news stories in partnership with the London, Hong Kong, and Abu Dhabi bureaus.
- Provide editorial oversight to the field, research trends, and recommend stories to senior management.

Healthcare and Humanitarian Coverage

- Covered Ebola, H1N1, MERS, Avian Flu, Haiti Earthquake, Japanese Tsunami, and Philippines Typhoon.
- Developed healthcare networks with stakeholders in the WHO, CDC, health ministries, and hospitals to cover infectious disease outbreaks and the health implications of natural disasters, war, and refugee crises.
- Earned an **Emmy Nomination** for extensive coverage of the international Ebola crisis.

ABC International Newsource Affiliate Editor – New York, NY   Jun 2008 – Aug 2010

Managed global video, print, and editorial content platform, 25 international affiliate partners, and daily news gathering and transmission supporting ABC's largest expansion, connecting the resources of 200+ affiliate stations.

- Developed extensive client relations to acquire 12 new global affiliates and extend existing contracts.
- Delivered 24x7 client support and integrated new technology to meet evolving needs while reducing costs.
- Provided field news story editorial oversight and coordinated recruiting and training of affiliate journalists.
- Earned a **Peabody Award** for outstanding coverage of the 2008 United States Presidential Election.

HORIZON NEWS TELEVISION   Jun 2007 – Dec 2007

Writer, News Anchor – Karachi, Pakistan

Wrote, produced, and anchored daily foreign affairs program for Pakistan's first English-language news channel.

- Conducted web research and community outreach to secure interviews and create video news stories.

HOPE HUMANITARIAN ASSISTANCE   Jun 2006 – Aug 2006

Project Officer – Khorog, Tajikistan

Secured funding and managed disaster preparedness projects for developing areas at risk for natural disasters.

- Improved resource utilization via thorough work plans, financial models, cost-benefit analyses, and training.
- Wrote 3 grant proposals and tracked and presented performance status reports to key donor stakeholders.

EARLY CAREER IN PR COMMUNICATIONS AND MEDIA RELATIONS

- **Writer and Editor, The News International Newspaper**: Composed and edited interviews, editorials, and in-house packages on foreign affairs as a 2005 Summer Editor in Karachi for Pakistan's first English newspaper.

- **PR and Media Relations Specialist, Afghanistan Ministry of Foreign Affairs:** Led PR and media relations in 2003, handling media inquiries, releases, and packages for new Minister of Foreign Affairs in Afghanistan.

CHAPTER 21:
Resumes for Military-to-Civilian Career Transitions

The most important question to ask yourself when writing a military-to-civilian transition resume is, who is your target audience? In general, you could target 2 distinct groups of companies, agencies, or organizations:

- Option 1: Military, Government, NGO, and Defense Contractors
- Option 2: General Corporations and Organizations (not affiliated with the military, government, or defense)

If you are targeting Option 1, your resume writing process will be easier because much of what you've done in your military career will be relevant—to some degree—to your new targeted positions. Common military jargon, abbreviations, acronyms, technologies, ranks, operations, and more will most likely mean something when your resume lands in the hands of a government agency or a company such as Lockheed Martin.

Even more important, these agencies, companies, and organizations often prefer to hire separating military personnel because of their specific expertise, experience, training, security clearances, and record of performance. You want to prominently and proudly display your record of service and be confident that most readers will understand all that you share.

To the contrary, that same information probably won't make much sense if you're writing to a general corporation that manufactures tires, consumer products, rugs, industrial HVAC units, and the like. It also won't be relevant to organizations that sell financial services, pet supplies, apparel, home improvement products, and more.

Yet, even in those circumstances, you can uncover common denominators—things that you did in the military that can be related to your current objectives. In this situation, you are often writing a resume similar in structure and strategy to career changers who work to separate skills and qualifications from the environment in which they were acquired. If you fall into this category, be certain to carefully read Chapter 20 (Resumes for People Changing Careers) and follow the principles we've outlined there.

To best understand the differing approaches to these distinct audiences, let's look carefully at 2 resumes, one written for a "military-friendly" audience and the other written for a general company.

Montell Wardner Resume—page 157–58

Montell Wardner had a long and prestigious career with the US Air Force. His goal is to transition his senior-level program management skills into a military, government, or defense-related organization, where his career positions him perfectly for an opportunity.

- **Minor Headline**—Under Montell's name, at the top of his resume, are 3 very important words— Senior Program Manager. You instantly know who he is and what he does.

- **Summary Section**—The 2 short paragraphs in this section give a great overview of his experience with the USAF, along with his strong academic credentials, security clearance, and other distinguishing qualifications. The Skill Sets section lists the 5 most important functions of the jobs he has performed—which are precisely the same skills needed for the jobs he Is targeting. Finally, in that same section are 4 achievement statements to further solidify his qualifications and track record of performance.

- **United States Air Force**—Although you could add the section heading "Professional Experience" or "Military Experience," it's not mandatory. We can quickly see that Montell's entire career has been with the USAF. The job descriptions share his overall scope of responsibility and then focus on his most notable achievements, just as you would write for any civilian resume. The strategy is … "Tell me what you did and how well you did it." And, because he is targeting positions in Program/ Project Management, he uses those words to introduce his achievements and activities in each of the job descriptions. With this technique he reinforces his strongest skills, which align 100% with his objectives.

- **Education & Training**—This section includes his collegiate degrees and summarizes his extensive military training experience in just 2 short lines. There is no need to mention every training course at this point in the job search process. A prospective employer who wants to know will ask for all of the details.

END RESULT: This resume is a perfect presentation for a similar Program Manager position with a company that is closely aligned with the military. Manhours, money, missions, aircraft, and other essential information is showcased throughout, demonstrating Montell's success in the USAF and the exceptional talents he brings to a new organization.

MONTELL SHANE WARDNER
Senior Program Manager

moward1@gmail.com | 816-562-7572

High-achieving, analytically minded Senior Program Manager with MS in Engineering Management plus 8 years of program development and leadership while serving as a top-ranked pilot instructor and officer for the U.S. Air Force.

Ideally suited for process-focused role in Engineering, Production, Logistics, or Technology, having led multimillion-dollar projects in this arena and always found ways to cut costs through Lean Systems Thinking and Six Sigma methods. Top Secret Security Clearance.

SKILL SETS

Program Management
Project Management
Change Management
Operations Improvement
Process Engineering
Team Coordination

⇒ Reputation for building world-class training, compliance, and evaluation programs while concurrently inspiring teams of 15–200 staff to exceed their own expectations.

⇒ Talent for finding and eliminating the root cause of inefficient systems and processes and building solutions with positive cross-functional impact.

⇒ History of impressing high-ranking officials with metric-driven change-management initiatives; record of challenging and winning support from the Pentagon.

⇒ Multi-award-winning instructor pilot held in esteem by supervisors and peers alike.

UNITED STATES AIR FORCE | 1997-PRESENT

Senior Program Director, Aircrew Training (Edwards AFB) .... May 2015 – Present
Recruited by past supervisor to plan and lead pilot training at the highest level of authority, on a $250M budget. Managed 3 program supervisors and 25 military and non-military staff driving the training of 1,500 personnel.

Program Management – Training
- Oversee all 8 flight training programs, comprising 59,000 hours of flying time. Maintain 1,300 records and authorize $4.5M in instructor salaries.
- Initiate and lead quarterly and annual training program evaluations, chairing a 17-person review board.
- Coordinate scheduling, training, and compliance documentation of 950 aircrew, completing 9,000 mandatory air and classroom training events in 1 year.

Project Management – Technology Upgrades
- Directed upgrade of $23M simulation system, including requirements/contract approvals and oversight of private-sector consultants.
- Managed implementation of $48M worth of instrumentation in KC-10 aircraft. Benchmarked with federal agencies and orchestrated RFP process with vendors.

> **Process Improvements**
>
> *—Saved $20M/year, integrating 30% of airfield training into flight simulator system.*
>
> *—Revamped task delegation protocol: set up software and defined approval hierarchy.*
>
> *—Introduced cross-training to maintain productivity through 40% RIFs.*

Assistant Operations Officer (Edwards AFB) .... Nov 2010 – May 2015
Developed and supervised aircrews in executing short-notice cargo and air refueling missions all over the world. Supported allied and multiservice agencies as directed by the President and Secretary of Defense. Served as Interim Operations Officer.

Program Management – Training
- Created, organized, and managed more than 20,000 flight and ground training activities for 160 crew.
- Minimized required flights 20% and completed training 33% ahead of schedule by developing a streamlined requalification program that enabled trainees to retain their office positions.

Program Management – Divisional Compliance
- Championed audit process across 18 departments to preempt official inspection. Developed 42-point checklist encompassing 1,100 points of evaluation, ultimately identifying and resolving 27 infractions.
- Attained 100% compliance across Records, Safety, Scheduling, Quality Control, and Logistics units.

Chief of Flight Training (Lemoore Naval Air Station) .... Oct 2007 – Oct 2010
Formalized $400M "weed-out" combat system officer training program, enrolling 350 students per year with a <20% pass rate.

Program Management – Training
- Established and finalized all aspects of training program, from strategic planning through program development, collateral creation, implementation, and evaluation.
- Boosted trainee productivity 25% by innovating the training program evaluation model.

Cliff Flamer, NCRW, CPRW, NCC, MS Counseling • BrightSide Resumes • www.brightsideresumes.com

Montell Shane Wardner
moward1@gmail.com

UNITED STATES AIR FORCE | CONTINUED

Flight Commander / Instructor (Lemoore Naval Air Station)..Oct 2004 – Oct 2007
Turned around a failing combat systems officer training program in Florida, Colorado, and Texas that was riddled with non-compliance issues. Passed inspection and earned Flight Commander of the Year Award for the entire naval station.

Program Management – Training
- Pinpointed every single point of non-compliance for a 4-phase training program, developed remediation strategy, and advised supervisor operations officer and 41 instructors on implementing adjustments.
- Developed metric-driven report showcasing 2 months of data to challenge the Pentagon's proposed timeline for matriculating pilots. Quantified the need for 20% more planes and 33% more pilots to work on existing timeline, resulting in a 3-day extension per class – eliminating trend of late graduation.
- Designed criteria for the inspection team to evaluate this new training program.

Executive Officer / Instructor (Edwards AFB)..............................Jul 2001 – Jul 2004
Won nominations and awards for efficiency, reliability, and commitment to working beyond the job description. Oversaw personnel activities and career development for 175 unit members.

Project Management – Records
- Dedicated 42 hours to processing a backlog of 35 reports that had been outstanding for 6 months. Digitized and catalogued all documentation.

Program Management – Transport Missions
- Planned 5,000 sorties to 50 airfields, transporting 108,000 passengers and 18 million pounds of cargo. Directed crew members in using $88M aircraft.
- Spearheaded high-visibility missions such as humanitarian relief and airlifts for the Secretary of Defense and the President of Afghanistan.

Operations Manager, Mobility Dept (Edwards AFB)................Jul 1998 – Jul 2001
Ensured travel readiness of 200 unit members by keeping meticulous, updated documentation. Served as interim chief for 2 months.

Program Management – Compliance
- Monitored well over 100 qualifying items for each team member, including visas, passports, medical records, firearm knowledge, combat training and credentials, and airport security clearance.
- Designed a Microsoft Access database with "smart" filter that intelligently auto-populated the correct fields on a suite of forms – cutting out hours in the day per person in data entry.

Program Manager, Awards Dept (Edwards AFB)......................Jul 1997 – Jul 1998
Tracked awards for 180 staff, plus flew a mission to clear airspace for the space shuttle launch.

Program Management – Awards & Decorations
- Wrote 200+ award citations and monitored the approval process across 6 levels of leadership.
- Cut outsourcing costs 300% by developing an in-house lithograph production method (used to design awards).

Pilot Instructor Experience

Concurrent with program management work, flew 100+ missions as a pilot.

Earned the highest-level instructor credential – an FTU Instructor Pilot, taking responsibility for teaching unqualified pilots to fly.

Instructed senior aircraft commanders on strategy, effective decision-making, and task management in high-pressure situations.

USAF Leadership Awards

Gold Leader Award
1 of 17 finalists out of 1,000+ nominated leaders

National Noble Airmen
Outstanding leadership at work and in the community

Instructor Pilot of Year
Ranked #1 out of 42 pilots

Commander of Year
Ranked #1 out of 58 CCs

Distinguished Graduate
Ranked in top 10% of class of 311 students.

EDUCATION & TRAINING

MS Engineering Management: Johns Hopkins University, Baltimore, 2013
BS Astronautical Engineering, Minor in Mathematics: U.S. Air Force Academy, Colorado Springs, 1997

Completed numerous leadership and flight training courses in team management, decision-making, strategic planning, pilot instruction, water survival, parachuting/freefalling, combat, and instrumentation.

Jacob Davidson Resume—pages 160–61

In contrast to Montell Wardner, Jacob Davidson is not looking to work for a company that has any connection to the military—so his resume takes an entirely different approach.

Jacob is targeting a position where he can use his extensive experience as an electrician and mechanic, most likely with a builder, manufacturer, or industrial company. The most important thing his resume accomplishes is to eliminate as many references to the military as possible. It's obvious that's been his career, but the strategy here is to downplay the military while showcasing the actual work he performed.

You'll note that the approach to writing and formatting this resume is very similar to that for career-change resumes, as discussed in Chapter 20. Let's explore how it was done.

- **Wire Graphic**—This little graphic instantly communicates electrical, industrial, and other related functions/operations. It's a subtle but effective message.

- **Headline**—As repeated throughout these special chapters and the entire book, a headline is a great way to start a resume. With one quick glance, the reader knows who you are and what you want to do. There's no wasted time trying to figure it out.

- **Summary Section**—The introductory paragraph, in bold print, gives a quick overview of Jacob's knowledge and capabilities without ever mentioning his military service. This is an excellent example of separating skills from the environment in which they were acquired. For additional value, the 4 bulleted statements that follow focus more on the important personal attributes he brings to the workplace.

- **Core Competencies**—This easy-to-skim section presents a host of relevant skills and qualifications for quick review by any reader—human or electronic. These all-important keywords must be integrated somewhere in the resume, whether in a separate section like this or interspersed throughout the document.

- **Certifications & Licenses**—By sharing this vital information in the top section of his resume, Jacob instantly communicates that he is exceptionally well qualified.

- **Professional Career Experience**—Notice that your eye focuses on the job titles and not the military installation or unit. A brief paragraph of overall responsibility introduces each job, and Key Results showcase his achievements and project highlights. Virtually all of this information is applicable to any company he might approach, so the resume is successful in separating and showcasing his skills and not restricting him to a military-related role or organization.

- **Professional Training**—Although Jacob does not have a college degree, he has a wealth training that is important to include. Instead of readers instantly thinking "no degree," we want them to think "lots and lots of training."

- **Awards & Honors**—No matter the profession, industry, or situation, earning honors and awards is impressive and validates everything else that's been written in the resume.

END RESULT: This professional resume clearly demonstrates that Jacob is a talented electrician and mechanic with a wealth of certifications, licenses, and training that are applicable in just about any industrial environment. In turn, he has opened himself to countless potential opportunities across numerous different industries. His military career laid the foundation; now, he's ready for a corporate career.

JACOB DAVIDSON

Seattle, WA | 206-555-1009 | jd2001@gmail.com

ELECTRICIAN | MECHANIC PROFILE

Credentialed and skilled Electrician and Mechanic with 10 years' experience maintaining and repairing generators, HVAC, mechanical equipment, and vehicles for diverse organizations supporting global operations.

- Train and manage skilled technicians in high-stress, fast-paced environments.
- Deliver strategic solutions through effective problem solving.
- Quickly assess, identify, and mitigate risk.
- Support teams and staff as an advisor, mentor, and technical expert.

CORE COMPETENCIES

Leadership & Supervision	Generators & HVAC Equipment	Quality Assurance/Quality Control
Logistics/Strategic Planning	Automotive Mechanics	Regulatory & Safety Compliance
Change Management/Crisis Management	Heavy Vehicle Maintenance	Inspections/Troubleshooting
Personnel Management	Engines & Fuel Systems	Instruction/Training/Briefings
	Utilities Equipment Repair	

CERTIFICATIONS & LICENSES

- ☑ Certified Electrician
- ☑ Certified Mechanic
- ☑ Certified Fuel Specialist
- ☑ Certified Refrigerant: Recovery, Recycling, Reclamation
- ☑ Certified Heavy Vehicle Operator
- ☑ Air Conditioning Specialist
- ☑ Certified MVAC Technician
- ☑ Certified Forklift Operator
- ☑ Licensed Skid Operator
- ☑ HAZMAT Trained
- ☑ Sanitation Knowledge

PROFESSIONAL CAREER EXPERIENCE

SENIOR POWER GENERATION TECHNICIAN   Dec 2016 to Present
Combat Support Hospital (CSH) – Joint Base Fort Lewis-McChord, WA

Senior Power Generation Equipment Repairer for 375-bed hospital. Manage staff of 10 technicians.

Supervise operations and direct personnel performing scheduled and unscheduled maintenance, repair, or service of the generators, air conditioning systems, and heaters. Hold 100% accountability for the serviceability and accountability of $1M in essential equipment.

Selected for superior technical knowledge to serve as Senior Manager in a high-volume, fast-paced maintenance section. Provide quality control of 300+ critical parts.

Key Results:

- Steered first ever *power distribution set-up* of a "concept 40-bed hospital" – *not attempted before* – during critical preparation exercise for deployment.
- Coordinated/supervised 6000 successfully executed job orders – 350 services distributed across 6 units.
- Trained 100 staff on proper installation, monitoring, and maintenance of power generation equipment. Instructed 12 staff on generators and power distribution boxes.
- Ensured 94% operational readiness rate – exceeded expectations.

JACOB DAVIDSON

POWER GENERATION TECHNICIAN   Nov 2013 to Dec 2016
South Korea

Power Generation Equipment Repairer for an organization providing direct support maintenance to 5 companies. Supervised and directed 11 staff. Managed and performed maintenance repairs for all power generation equipment, internal combustion engines, and associated equipment.

Key Results:

- Ensured 98% readiness rate by implementing quality control processes for equipment standards.
- Maintained 100% accountability of special tools, test sets, and supplies worth more than $2M.
- Incorporated comprehensive management and safety procedures – resulted in zero accidents/injuries.
- Trained new staff on power generation repair, working during personal time to ensure appropriate skill levels.
- Earned Army Award for Maintenance Excellence.

GENERATOR MECHANIC   Jun 2008 to Oct 2013
Fort Hood, TX

Generator Mechanic on largest US Army base with short/no-notice worldwide requirements missions. Expertly performed maintenance and repair services for generators and heavy-wheel vehicles. Conducted scheduled/unscheduled maintenance on more than 90 pieces of rolling stock. Directed 2 staff.

Expert Inspector, performing quality control and assurance inspections. Troubleshot, identified issues, requisitioned repair parts, and resolved problems. Oversaw equipment worth $25K.

Key Results:

- Reduced safety incidents 75% by emphasizing risk management and safety procedures.
- Crossed-trained wheeled vehicle mechanics on generators; increased operational proficiency.

PROFESSIONAL TRAINING

☑ Generator Operations Course	☑ Advanced Leadership Course
☑ Emergency Operations Communications	☑ Leadership Development
☑ HP UNIX System Administration	☑ HAZMAT / Safety

AWARDS & HONORS

Army Commendation Medal (5) ■ Army Achievement Medal (4) ■ Army Good Conduct Medal (4)

CHAPTER 22:
Resumes for People Returning to Work

The most important thing to consider when writing resumes for people who are returning to work after extended absences is how to mask that they haven't worked in 6 months, a year, 5 years, or 15 years. The reasons for unemployment might include:

- Staying at home to raise children
- Supporting a spouse's military or corporate career with continual relocation
- Returning to work after injury or illness
- Caring for someone else through injury or illness
- Returning to work after retirement
- Reentering after incarceration
- Taking an extended sabbatical to travel the world or pursue educational opportunities

Many of the same career-change strategies presented in Chapter 20 can also be quite effective for return-to-work resumes, so be certain to review that chapter and all of those recommendations.

One question to consider when writing is whether a combination-chronological or modern functional format will be best to showcase you, your skills, and your experience. We've found that combination-chronological formats tend to work the best for people who do have experience that is related to their current objective. Conversely, if the experience is not related at all, then follow the guidelines for creating a functional resume just as you would do for any other career change.

Perhaps the greatest challenge when writing a return-to-work resume is whether or not to include dates for experience and education, and how to include them. There is no single recommendation regarding dates since there are so many variables to consider. Here are a few ideas to help you determine how best to manage dates on your own return-to-work resume.

- You'll notice that both of the sample resumes in this chapter have dates. On the first, the dates are visually minimized by their location on the resume. Although this job seeker has been out of work for a while, it's not a remarkably long period of time, so it's best to include the dates so that readers will not think that she is significantly older. Often, without dates, readers assume that job seekers are older candidates who are trying to mask their age. On the second sample resume, the dates are positioned in their "normal" location (flush right on the page), but the sections have been reorganized to showcase relevant experience.

- A unique solution for someone who has been out of work for a relatively long period of time is to use number of years at each position rather than specific dates. Instead of writing "1990 to 1999," you would state "9 years." Although not always the best solution, this technique can work favorably if the actual dates will communicate long-term unemployment (hasn't worked since 1999) and/or older age.

- The final recommendation is to delete dates entirely. While we don't use this strategy often, it might be the best for someone with lengthy and frequent unemployment.

Bottom line: Consider the message you're sending with dates and their placement on your resume. Many employers are understanding of short gaps and recent unemployment, so don't be unduly concerned if your resume reflects those circumstances. But if your career history reflects lengthy gaps, multiple periods of unemployment, or long-time unemployed status, employers may be leery—so it's best not to give them detailed information that may cause them to reject your candidacy before ever meeting you.

As with all of our suggestions, put your best foot forward when writing and formatting your resume; save the less-than-favorable specifics for the interview, after your future employers have already met you and are impressed. Then, those items aren't quite as significant.

PRO TIP: Do you include the reason you've been out of work on your resume? Almost never! That's a conversation better had during an interview. However, there are no absolutes in resume writing. If you spent the last year climbing the tallest mountain peaks in Asia, it might be worth a 1-line mention on your resume so that you're easily accounting for the time you weren't employed.

Let's explore the resume samples in this chapter, starting with Samantha Baker, who fits into the largest group of people returning to work—moms and dads.

Samantha Baker Resume—page 165

- **Headline—Event Planner | Hospitality Professional**—Samantha has held these jobs before and it's what she is targeting now, so it's the perfect introduction.
- **Summary Paragraph and Bullet Points**—One short paragraph combines important achievements and Samantha's most notable skills as they relate to her targeted positions. This information is specific, yet broad enough to allow her to apply for a host of different types of hospitality-related jobs, from banquet manager to front desk manager to special events planner and more.
- **Signature Skills**—As mentioned for other resumes, a separate keyword section is an effective way to integrate a large number of relevant terms into your resume without taking up too much space. Keywords are essential because they are the backbone for online resume scanning and applications. They are the words that will get your resume noticed and selected; the words that often lead to an interview.
- **Professional Work History**—Samantha does have relevant experience from 3 different positions, all jobs she held before becoming a stay-at-home parent. These job descriptions are well written, highlight her most notable contribution to each organization, and proudly showcase major projects and achievements. Most important, the dates of employment are visually downplayed and not put at the right margin as is the norm on most resumes. In this resume, the dates are so non-visually prominent that they almost disappear, and that's precisely the point.

- **Education**—Her degree and university are included with no frills—just the facts, which are more than sufficient.
- **Community Involvement**—This brief section adds more dimension to the resume and communicates that she's been busy contributing to her family, her neighborhood, and her community while not working outside the home. Plus, these volunteer experiences have given her new skills to add to her qualifications and make her a more well-rounded candidate.

END RESULT: A resume that showcases a talented Event Planner & Hospitality Professional with the right skills, qualifications, and experiences, with barely a notice that she hasn't worked in years.

Lucas Adams Resume—page 166

Another interesting return-to-work story is that of Lucas Adams, who was a long-time Shipping and Receiving Manager until a workplace injury left him out of work for a year. At that point he had some significant physical limitations and could no longer work in an industrial environment, so he took a desk job. Now he's 100% healthy and ready to return to the work that he loves most. How does he handle the fact that he left his related profession for almost 10 years?

- **Forklift Graphic**—This instantly communicates a message of warehouse work and is perfect for the jobs that Lucas is targeting.
- **Paragraph Summary**—In just 4 lines, this section clearly summarizes the years of experience that this job seeker has in his targeted industry and includes some personal attributes that are vital to top performance in those types of jobs. This instantly focuses the reader on his 14 years of experience as one of the first things they learn about him, rather than focusing on his specific dates of related employment.
- **Core Competencies**—Lucas showcases his most relevant skills with just enough detail to demonstrate that he's well qualified.
- **Related Experience**—The "Related Experience" heading is one of the techniques that professional resume writers use quite often for people returning to work and, sometimes, for career changers. Why does this work? Because it allows you to move your relevant experience to the forefront rather than sticking with a traditional chronological style that would have put this job—his related experience—after his current, unrelated, job.
- **Current Experience**—As mentioned, by reversing the order of presentation of his work experience, the most relevant comes first. However, this job is also important because it showcases that he has been working full time, albeit in a different profession.
- **Training**—Just a brief mention of his relevant training experience is all that matters. Although he is a high school graduate, that information is not included because he does have relevant professional training.

END RESULT: A resume that clearly communicates Lucas' skills, qualifications, and 14 years of experience that relate to his current objective. Because of the style of presentation, it's almost an afterthought that the relevant experience is not current. And that's precisely the point of using this resume format and structure.

SAMANTHA BAKER

Lakewood, WA | 253-475-5678 | SBaker@gmail.com

EVENT PLANNER | HOSPITALITY PROFESSIONAL

ENERGETIC and **CLIENT-CENTRIC** professional with diverse background across guest services, event management, program management, client relations, and office administration. Proven track record of turning around underperforming programs/departments, tripling revenue, and implementing process improvements that enhance bottom-line results. Calm under pressure. Dependable and highly organized.

SIGNATURE SKILLS

☑ Event Planning / Management	☑ Business / Office Management	☑ Marketing & Advertising
☑ Program Oversight	☑ Strategic Planning / Scheduling	☑ Process Improvements
☑ Quality Control/ Quality Assurance	☑ Staff & Personnel Development	☑ Emotional Intelligence
☑ Sales / Influential Selling	☑ Client Relations / Public Relations	☑ Clear Communication

PROFESSIONAL WORK HISTORY

GUEST SERVICE ASSOCIATE | 2004–2012 | **Olympia Country Club,** Olympia, WA

Delivered exceptional customer service as "first point of contact" to a premier and semi-private full-service country club. Controlled inventory; monitored equipment and supplies.

- As the "face of organization," worked with clients directly to accommodate and schedule their requested sports, activities, or services. Quickly responded to and resolved client issues.
- Managed men's and women's tennis leagues.
  - ✓ **Increased court use 5% and reduced complaints 60%** by implementing a new, highly efficient appointment system that optimized staff's efforts with each client.
- Increased public relations and drove brand awareness. Answered questions and provided education and information about services, events, and activities.

DIRECTOR | 2002–2004 | **Fabricon Labs,** Portland, OR

Managed departmental operations for company developing and producing Nutraceutical products.

- Inherited inefficient, poorly managed department. Rapidly identified process deficiencies and developed procedures to improve workflow, timeliness, and productivity.
  - ✓ **Tripled business in 5 months** by improving service and implementing new pricing structure.
  - ✓ **Saved company $30,000 per year** through process and efficiency improvements.
- Initiated and fostered professional relationships with physicians and medical field professionals.

DEVELOPMENT OFFICER | 2000–2002 | **Cystic Fibrosis Foundation,** Portland, OR

Steered fundraising efforts for national nonprofit organization.

- Led key events that included nationwide walks and silent auctions in collaboration with local businesses.
  - ✓ **Exceeded fundraising goals by 10%** in 2000, **16%** in 2001.

EDUCATION

Bachelor of Science Degree in Biology | 1999 | University of Portland, Portland, OR

COMMUNITY INVOLVEMENT

- Spearheaded successful fundraising activities at J.C. Green Elementary and Lakewood Middle School.
- Served as Girl Scout Leader and initiated community outreach to local food pantry and homeless shelter.

Lucas Adams

WAREHOUSE SUPERVISOR

Wayne, NJ | 973-555-1111 | ljadams@ymail.com

Offering 14 years of experience in all aspects of material handling and storage; 8 years in management. Unique ability for 3-dimensional thinking with quick recall of numerous and complex material locations within a huge warehouse. Seeking to return to former career where there is a need for a conscientious and well-organized leader willing to go the extra mile to ensure efficient operations.

CORE COMPETENCIES

- ✓ **Operating and/or repairing:** electrical/mechanical forklifts … hand trucks … pallet jacks … cherry pickers … various automated equipment
- ✓ **Driving:** box trucks and delivery vans (commercial driver's license)
- ✓ **Managing inventory:** daily record keeping … monthly cycle counts … yearly audits
- ✓ **Leading teams:** shipping/receiving … picking/packing … staging … loading/unloading trucks
- ✓ **Assisting in production area:** setting up machinery for specialized projects

RELATED EXPERIENCE

SHIPPING & RECEIVING MANAGER, 1995–2009   Holstead Fabricators, Inc., Paterson, NJ
Custom molding and stamping facility using metals and plastics to make products for the medical, automotive, and electronics industries.

- Started as assembler and rapidly advanced through 4 promotions. In 2001 advanced to comanage a 10,000-sq.-ft. warehouse, formerly operating out of 3 locations. **Impressed superiors with knowledge** of where all pieces were stored.
- Adapted to frequent management changes. Provided department input in bi-weekly meetings and **enforced any new directives to enhance operations.**
- Trained, scheduled, and led team of 5–7 warehouse workers. **Ensured accuracy and timeliness of picking and packing parts** ranging from minuscule clips to assemblies weighing up to 90 lbs.
- Maintained accurate shipment and inventory records in an automated system monitoring 30,000 parts in different locations for easy access when needed. **Researched reasons for over or short quantities** to bring physical inventory in line with books.
- Expedited urgent materials needed before next FedEx pick-up. **Saved truck rental costs** by personally making local deliveries using a 28-foot box truck.

CURRENT EXPERIENCE

DATA CENTER TECHNICIAN, 2010–Present   BioData Systems, Dover, NJ
Provider of outsourced sleep diagnostic services.

- As sole operator on my shift, process sleep study files received from 30 sites in the Northeast. **Handle an average of 200 transmissions daily** at peak of operations.
- Organize data consisting of 7–12 pages per file to prepare for scoring by doctors. **Achieved 97% accuracy** in typing, formatting, scanning, and manipulating pages in required order.
- Address minor computer problems. **Avoided IT service calls, repeatedly saving half-day system downtime.**
- Overcame challenges in receiving data from some locations to meet strict turnaround deadlines. **Prevented loss of revenue due to late submissions.**

TRAINING

Bergen County Vo-Tech Institute, 1993 | CNC Machining Technology

Melanie Noonan • Peripheral Pro • peripro1@aol.com

PART VI:
Resume Portfolio

We've already shared more than 45 samples in Parts I through IV ... now, here are 45 more!

There's no doubt that the sample resumes in this book are a very valuable resource. Every resume you'll see was written by a professional resume writer for a unique client with a precise set of circumstances that dictated the content, format, and design.

We provide these resumes not to give you a template or model, but to give you *inspiration* and *ideas* for how to handle your own specific challenges; best present your information; write about your profession and your industry; and overall create a modern resume that is sharp, powerful, and effective so that you can *get noticed and get hired!*

As well, we are delighted to share the contact information of all of the resume writers who contributed their work. You'll find the writer's name, credentials, and website (or email address) at the bottom of each resume.

While our goal is to give you everything you need to write your own resume, we know that some of you will find the process challenging. Others will lack sufficient time. Still others will simply decide to hire the best to help them with this important job. We know that our contributors *are* the best, so we hope you will call on them for expert assistance should you have the need.

In the meantime, enjoy the samples and be motivated to produce a resume masterpiece of your own!

NADINE KIM

303.771.2830
NKim23@Oregon.edu

ARCHITECT INTERN

Motivated problem solver with architectural design experience. Effective collaborator with diverse customers and teams, ensuring accurate project scope and high-quality results.

EDUCATION

UNIVERSITY OF OREGON
Bachelor of Arts, Architecture
Class of 2019

Honors & Affiliations
National Honor Society
2016–2019

Technical Society
2016–2019

Design Scholarship
2015–2017

Member, American Institute of Architecture Students
2015–2019

KNOWLEDGE AND SKILLS

Physical Modeling: building, modeling, and designing

Software: AutoCAD, Revit, Illustrator, Photoshop, InDesign, Microsoft Office Suite, Google SketchUP

Drawings: hardline, freehand, renderings in color pencil, ink, and watercolor

EXPERIENCE

SUPERINTENDENT INTERN, McWhinney Partners, 2018–2019

Assisted with $4 construction project. Coordinated on-site construction activities, ensured safety practices were used, and assisted with driving project completion on schedule and within budget.

Participated in meetings. Organized and maintained records on project activities. Updated RFI and ASI reports. Developed designs built from redline drawings. Gathered, organized, and delivered various documents to city offices for construction compliance.

STUDY ABROAD, Prague Institute, Czech Republic, 2017

Contributed to hospital master plan, with rehabilitation addition and sustainability emphasis, while under supervision of Hedrick Schmidt, VP of AIA Europe and owner of Schmidt Architects.

Increased knowledge of European government funding for sustainability building and design projects.

MAINTENANCE REPRESENTATIVE, Columbine Company, 2016

Provided property maintenance and repairs for offices and commercial locations. Led projects, including landscaping and lawn care. Coordinated special events setup and cleanup.

PROJECT VOLUNTEER, National Center for Craftsmanship, 2015

Supported building renovation, debris containment, recycling, and construction cleanup efforts. Worked with teams coordinating efforts during demolition and building processes.

Ruth Pankratz, NCRW, CPRW, MBA • Gabby Communications • www.gabbycommunications.com

Note: Dual-column format displays equal emphasis on education, knowledge, and skills as well as practical experience. Graphic immediately communicates the target industry of this graduating student.

Charles F. Williams

Cherry Hill, NJ 16026 | cfwilliams@mail.com | 483-685-5215

CAREER OBJECTIVE:
Sales Leadership | Marketing | Business Development

Motivated, collaborative, and driven business professional with outstanding interpersonal and communication skills and a strong entrepreneurial spirit. Adept at successfully managing a full-time career with full-time undergraduate work. Looking for a challenging opportunity in the life sciences industry where I can apply my professional experience, educational background, and passion for health and wellness. Core competencies:

Customer Service | Customer Relationship Management | Customer Outreach
New Business Development | Strategic Alliances | Product Merchandising

RELEVANT EXPERIENCE

Customer Advocate – PK Laboratories Inc. (Collingswood, NJ)   Oct 2017–present
Pharmacogenetic testing laboratory specializing in personalized medicine in psychiatry and neurology.

Managed clinician registration, order fulfillment, service support, data gathering, data entry, and reporting.

- **Promoted twice during first 2 months** of employment – from part-time to full-time internship, then to full-time employment in the business department. Each role was newly created and customized.
- Identified and capitalized on strategic expansion opportunities into **$35B substance abuse treatment industry** via partnership with private facilities. Orchestrated sales meetings with executive teams.

Administrative Assistant – Treatment Trends of America (Denver, CO)   Mar 2017–Jul 2017
Private, not-for-profit 501(c)3 corporation providing mental wellness and substance abuse treatment; 13 locations, including the only psychiatric hospital between Aspen and Park City.

Registered clients, scheduled medical tests, maintained records, and interfaced with client families.

EDUCATION

Bachelor of Arts, English – Drexel University (Philadelphia, PA)   *May 2019 (candidate)*
- Relevant Coursework: *Microeconomics, Macroeconomics, Financial Accounting, Statistics, Essentials of Organizational Behavior, Principles of Marketing, Finite Math Application in Business*
- Minor: Business Administration

High School Diploma – Saint Michael's Preparatory (Philadelphia, PA)
- Service: *Operation Swim* (student officer); *Gesu School* (tutor); *International Volunteer Headquarters*

TECHNICAL PROFICIENCIES

Microsoft Office (Excel, PowerPoint, Word), SharePoint, Salesforce.com, PK Lab Portal, Lab Information System (LIS), Apple Products

OTHER WORK HISTORY

Sales Associate	**Colorado Skiing Company** (Denver, CO)	Dec 2016–Mar 2017
Real Estate Clerk	**Shore Real Estate Agency** (Atlantic City, NJ)	Summers 2014, 2015, 2016

Kate Madden, CPRW, MBA • Fresh Start Resumes • www.freshstartresumes.com

Note: Strategic use of an objective clarifies career targets for this full-time employee and full-time student preparing to graduate. High school diploma from exclusive prep school is valuable for networking during job search.

LUCAS MATTHEWS
312-555-1234
lucasmatthews3@notredame.edu

INDUSTRIAL & OPERATIONS ENGINEER
Project Management | Technical Design & Implementation | Process Improvement

Senior college student with respected engineering education enhanced by real-word experience with **2 of the top 10 Fortune 100 companies.**

Mature interpersonal and communication skills serve as foundation for success. Reputation as focused, analytical, and professional with high ethical and quality standards. Possess initiative to drive independent and team projects.

Technology:
- CAD
- Phrogram
- C++
- Alice
- Minitab
- MS Office

Education

THE UNIVERSITY OF NOTRE DAME
College of Engineering | Notre Dame, IN

Bachelor of Science in Engineering (May 2019)
Major: **Industrial & Operations Engineering**, *Honors:* **Dean's List**, *GPA:* **3.9**

- National Society of Leadership and Success
- National Society of Collegiate Scholars
- Sigma Alpha Lambda [Leadership & Honors]
- Phi Gamma Delta – Pledge Educator, Social Chair

Professional Experience

CHEVRON (Summer 2018)
Americas Products | San Ramon, CA

Project Analyst

Autonomously conducted study to evaluate efficacy and measure actual use of sales process tool across the enterprise. Developed questionnaire and conducted interviews with sales force and affiliated stakeholders worldwide. Compiled, interpreted, and refined data; identified key factors hindering use.

➲ Presented executive team with recommendations (subsequently implemented) to sustain existing users and facilitate greater adoption of the tool.

FORD MOTOR COMPANY (Summer 2017)
Louisville Assembly Plant | Louisville, KY

Intern — Operations

Singlehandedly managed project and performed engineering to introduce new robotic technology into production process. Designed, built, installed, and programmed tooling. Conducted extensive testing and troubleshooting during development and implementation of technology projected to save $300K annually.

➲ Challenged to install robot on assembly line and ensure its functionality during intense 1-week plant shut-down. Met deadlines and achieved all metrics.

Related Experience

Intern — Mesirow Financial Services | Chicago, IL (Summer 2016)
Mentored by financial planner to gain foundation in investing. Reviewed client portfolios to gain insight into philosophies, strategies, and results.

STEM Camp Leader — University of Notre Dame | Notre Dame, IN (Summers 2015–2016)
Recruited by professor to mentor, teach, and lead 30+ gifted and underserved high school students in engineering, mathematics, and computer programming as part of 4-week enrichment programs.

Janet Beckstrom, MRW, ACRW, CPRW • Word Crafter • www.wordcrafter.com

Note: Formatted to draw immediate visual attention to prestigious academic institution and experience with 2 top-10 Fortune 500 companies. Tech skills perfectly positioned—using minimal space with maximum impact.

Daniel K. Holland

dkholland@gmail.com • 269-294-2570
http://www.linkedin.com/in/danielkholland

ECONOMIC ANALYST
RESEARCH, ANALYSIS & CONSULTING

Project & Team Leadership Skills • Business & Statistical Software (MS Excel, SAS, SPSS, Statistix) Proficiency

EDUCATION

Master of Arts, Applied Economics   2019
UNIVERSITY OF WASHINGTON, Seattle, WA

- GPA: 3.7 / 4.0. University Graduate Scholarship and Assistantship.
- Relevant Coursework: Econometrics, Microeconomics, Macroeconomics, Regional Economics, Cost-Benefit Analysis, International Trade, Quantitative Analysis.

Bachelor of Arts, Economics   2017
SEATTLE PACIFIC UNIVERSITY, Seattle, WA

- GPA: 3.2 / 4.0.
- Studied at Regents College, London, for 4 months and traveled extensively throughout Europe.
- Varsity soccer player, 4 years. Volunteer Service Award, Washington Special Olympics, 2015.

EXPERIENCE

Co-Founder and Principal Investigator   2017–2019
APPLIED ECONOMICS RESEARCH GROUP, University of Washington Department of Economics

Played a key role in launching consulting practice providing economic analysis for local businesses and institutions. Group grew from initial 4 founders in 2017 to 15 investigators in 2 years.

- Developed consulting proposals and led teams in research, analysis, and report preparation. Delivered presentations to clients' Board of Directors and management teams.
- Completed economic analysis for major national retailer exploring entry into the Seattle market.
- Performed employment analysis for economic-development organization studying immigrant labor issues.
- Established scholarship fund to channel consulting proceeds to graduate-level economics students.

Research Assistant, DEPARTMENT OF ECONOMICS, University of Washington   2017–2018

Performed research for professor who is an expert consultant and published writer on economic ramifications of tax schemes and financial policies. Read and summarized relevant articles; assisted in paper preparation (credited on 4 published papers); brainstormed to develop new research topics.

Teaching Assistant, DEPARTMENT OF ECONOMICS, University of Washington   2017–2018

Assisted 3 professors in managing their course load; taught, guided, and advised economics students in undergraduate Macro- and Microeconomics courses. Held weekly office hours for students needing assistance.

Graduate Team Project: REGIONAL SHIFT-SHARE ANALYSIS   2018

Performed shift-share analysis of several Metropolitan Statistical Areas. Located economic data sources and performed quantitative analysis to determine industry mix, location quotients, and regional share index. Prepared comprehensive report that is currently used as reference material by an economics consultant.

Available for relocation.

Louise Kursmark, MRW, CPRW, JCTC, CEIP, CCM • Best Impression Career Services, Inc. • www.louisekursmark.com

Note: Concise summary showcasing just the right amount of information is followed by an expansive education section for both undergraduate and graduate degrees. Job descriptions add excitement to what could be a dry subject.

CAROL PETERSON

✉ Boston, MA 02210 | 🖥 carol.peterson@email.com| ☎ 857-345-1211

ELEMENTARY SCHOOL TEACHER

Dedicated teacher and facilitator of learning through a positive environment that encourages student exploration and builds a strong foundation of reading skills.

Areas of Expertise

- Classroom Management
- Curriculum Development
- Differentiated Instruction
- Classroom Technology

- Creative, Well-rounded Lesson Planning
- Teaching in Alignment with Common Core
- Assessment Tools and Strategies
- Off-Site Learning Opportunities

- Integrated Reading Instruction
- Balanced Literacy Program
- State Standardized Testing
- Parent-Teacher Relations

Professional Experience

Teaching / Curriculum Development
- Instructed students individually and in groups, using various teaching methods such as guided practice, discussions, and field trips to curriculum-relevant locations.
- Established clear objectives for all lessons, units, and projects and communicated expectations to students.
- Provided a variety of materials and resources for children to use both in learning activities and imaginative play.
- Implemented and monitored ongoing formal and informal student learning assessments.
- Administered standardized ability and achievement tests to kindergarten and elementary students.
- Worked with teachers and administrators to develop, evaluate, and revise kindergarten and elementary curriculum.

Student Management / Family Relations
- Used behavior management and conflict mediation strategies to keep order and create a positive learning environment.
- Met with parents and guardians to discuss their children's progress, set priorities, and determine resource needs.
- Conferred with parents, administrators, and testing specialists to resolve students' behavioral or academic problems.

JOSIAH QUINCY ELEMENTARY SCHOOL, Boston, MA   2010–present
2nd Grade Teacher
- All students reached proficient reading level at the end of the school year as measured by the DIBELS reading test.
- Designed a literacy program with guided reading, small groups, phonetic awareness, and literacy activity centers that were fully integrated with math and science studies.
- Introduced a number of multicultural lessons using music, dance, art, and field trips in conjunction with class curriculum.
- Utilized "Reading Raps" as a unique way to instruct reading and reinforce learning in a fun and creative method.

BAY STATE LEARNING CENTER, South Boston, MA   2007–2010
Kindergarten Teacher

SUNRISE LEARNING ACADEMY, Quincy, MA   2005–2007
1st Grade Teacher

CHELSEA COMMUNITY PRESCHOOL, Chelsea, MA   2001–2005
Preschool Teacher

Education and Credentials

UNIVERSITY OF MASSACHUSETTS, Boston, MA
Master of Education

SALEM STATE UNIVERSITY, Salem, MA
Bachelor of Arts with a Minor in Early Childhood Education
Cum Laude

+ Massachusetts Teacher Certification +

Madelyn Mackie, CCMC • Madelyn Mackie & Associates • www.activateyourcareerdreams.com

Note: Consolidating experience into 1 description avoids repetition for jobs that have essentially the same responsibilities. Date of college graduation is deliberately omitted to disguise her age.

MARK BARNES

315.961.3252
TeachPE@ymail.com
www.linkedin.com/pub/mark-barnes/5/98/cc6

NYS LAST Certified
NYS ATS-W Certified
Lifeguard and WSI Certified

PHYSICAL EDUCATION TEACHER AND COACH

Versed in K–12 programming. Experienced leading Varsity and JV teams in track & field, tennis, and soccer.
Specialized training in behavior modification, adaptive learning, and total-body conditioning strategies.

EDUCATION:			
	MLA – Coaching Concentration	SUNY Oneonta	2010
	BSED – Physical Education, ADPE Concentration	SUNY Plattsburgh	2005
	Varsity Swimmer – State record holder for 100-yd Free and 1650-yd Fly		

TEACHING

Potsdam Central School District, Potsdam, NY
Physical Education Teacher, Sept 2018 – Present
(temporary hire – maternity leave coverage)

- Demonstrated flexibility and leadership by serving in all schools and at all grades, often being the only Phys. Ed. Teacher in the building for all programs and curriculum.

Multiple Adirondack Region Districts, NY State
Substitute Teacher, 2015–2018

West Babylon Schools, West Babylon, NY
AEHS Physical Education Teacher, 2013–2015

- Provided Physical Education for students in Alternative Evening High School.

Smithson Alternative School, Smithson, NY
K–6 Physical Education & Health Teacher, 2007-2013

- Created a Physical Education and Health curriculum in a unique environment.
- Behavior Specialist for SFA reading group.

Herrick's Middle School, Albertson, NY
Searingtown Elementary School, Albertson, NY
Student Teacher (K–8), 2005

- Taught Archery, Indoor Soccer, Apparatus, Quidditch, Project Adventure & 50s Games.

COMPUTER SKILLS

iPad, Windows, MS Word, Excel, Power Point

COACHING

Potsdam Central School District, 2015–2018

- **Assistant Soccer Coach** (Varsity)
- **Assistant Tennis Coach** (Grades 7–8)
- **Assistant Track & Field Coach** (JV & Varsity)

West Babylon Middle School, Babylon, NY, 2013–2015

- **Head Tennis Coach** (Grades 7–8)

Smithson Alternative School, Smithson, NY, 2007–2013

- **Tennis & Soccer Coach** (7th and 8th grade)

MEMBERSHIPS/CERTIFICATIONS/AWARDS

NYSAHPERD Member (Current)

CPR/AED/First Aid Certified (Current)

Jaime Escalante Student Teacher Award (2010 & 2014)

Self-Defense Instructor Certified (2013)

Volunteer at Project Adventure Clinic (2005 & 2008)

Lab Assistant for Adapted Physical Education (2004)

Although he is early in his career, Mark engages students in a way that few educators do. His energy and enthusiasm are contagious. I give him the highest recommendation.

Josh Michael
Athletic Director – Smithson Alternative School

Andrea Howard • New York State Department of Labor • www.labor.ny.gov

Note: Showcasing dual career paths as both teacher and coach, the 2-column format is efficient and easy to skim. Placement of essential credentials at the top of the page makes sure they won't be overlooked.

Anaya Singh

Winnipeg, MB ▪ 702.555.1111 ▪ asingh@email.com

HUMAN RESOURCES PROFESSIONAL ▪ RECRUITER
▪▪▪ Finding the Right People Using the Best Channels to Deliver Results ▪▪▪

Seasoned HR and recruiting professional with diverse international experience. Partner with business leaders to identify and fulfill staffing needs in technical and non-technical environments.

RECRUITING	HUMAN RESOURCES	BUSINESS AND OPERATIONS
Talent Sourcing	Administration	Trade Shows
Social Media	HR and Administrative Budgets	Media Relations
Recruitment Matrix	Pre- and Post-Employment	Online Marketing
Employer Branding	On-boarding and Training	Project Management
Job Descriptions	Benefits Coordination	Shipping and Logistics

Qualifications and Achievements

- ✓ **Lowered "time to hire" from 16 weeks to only 8 weeks** by revising method for writing job descriptions, adapting keywords, and partnering with managers to determine ideal skills and qualifications.

- ✓ **Secured trade show registrations at 25% below market value** and consulted with trade publications to earn 20% discount on services and free press releases.

- ✓ **Lowered monthly health insurance premiums 62%** by sourcing and negotiating with 7 health benefit consultants to redesign benefit plan and adjust contribution program.

- ✓ **Directed HR representatives across 21 regional offices and at more than 450 corporate branches** in recruiting and on-boarding more than 2,000 full-time and seasonal employees.

Professional Experience

Insight Wireless Ltd. – Winnipeg, MB   2015 – 2019
Provider of data analytics solutions for mining, utility, and hydro operations across Central and Western Canada.

RECRUITER

Partnered with external consultants to design recruiting tools and establish budgets. Matched candidate strengths and skills with requirements through screening and interviewing. Conducted staff orientations, developed policies, administered compensation and benefits, and completed pre-employment items, including reference checks.

- Optimized job titles in accordance with Manitoba wage requirements, hiring developers, data scientists, field application engineers, and other technical professionals based on knowledge of local hiring market.

- Coordinated office move from shared services site to dedicated office, saving thousands on furniture, equipment, and utilities.

- Improved components of health benefit plans, including reimbursements, couple/family rates, and contributions, avoiding price increases of more than 23% annually.

"Anaya is a self starter and did a phenomenal job as the head of our HR group. She executes on her promises and delivers results."
CEO, X-10 Technology Corporation

Jennifer Miller, CPRW, CRS, CARW • Professional Edge Resumes • www.professionaledgeresumes.com
Note: Key features include a clear headline and on-point branding statement, 3 boxes segmenting specific areas of expertise and essential keywords, and wow achievements from a 15-year career.

River Rock Business Services – Mumbai, India   2013 – 2014
Multi-business conglomerate with investments in real estate, hotels, healthcare, travel, and education.

HEAD OF HUMAN RESOURCES

Acquired talent for 21 regional offices and 450 branches, selecting vendors, negotiating contracts, and monitoring HR activities for 5 corporate branches. Supervised 24 staff serving 11,500 employees.

- Aligned recruitment and selection policies with overall business objectives, reducing recruiting budget and lowering sourcing delays.
- Initiated use of LinkedIn's Recruiter sourcing platform, incorporating executive search capabilities and improving employer branding and social media recruiting programs.
- Created HR manual and employee handbook for non-unionized employees.
- Audited and revised HR systems and processes, improving efficiency and access to information for recruiting, on-boarding, employee changes, and departures

X-10 TECHNOLOGY CORPORATION – Mumbai, India   2012 – 2013
US-based software company catering to financial services companies, providing outsourcing of IT and business processes.

HEAD OF HUMAN RESOURCES DEVELOPMENT

Liaised with project managers and clients for recruitment, selection, and project implementation. Created recruitment and selection policies as well as recruiting budget. Reviewed and updated HR policies to improve functioning between staff in India and USA. Tracked employee performance and implemented retention program.

PRIOR

ASSISTANT HUMAN RESOURCES MANAGER – Launch Tech – Mumbai, India   2011 – 2012
HUMAN RESOURCES MANAGER – Telecommunications Ltd. – Mumbai, India   2008 – 2010
BRANCH ADMINISTRATOR – British Financial – Cornwall, England   2006 – 2008

Education, Certifications, and Training

Master of Global Management – University of Toronto, Toronto, ON

Master of Arts, Human Resources Management and Employment Relations – University of Falmouth, UK

Bachelor of Commerce, Accounting – University of Mumbai, India

Certified Human Resources Professional (2016 Completion)

Human Resource Management Association Round Tables ▪ BCIT Events ▪ TechVibes – Tech Fest
Light House Labs – Demo Days ▪ CASCADIA ▪ IURPA / NURPA ▪ University of Toronto Career Fair
NASCOM ▪ Chartered Institute of Personnel and Development: HRD, CIPD Annual Conference

Volunteer Involvement

Mentor & Career Coach – YWCA – Winnipeg, MB (2016 – Current)
Mentor – University of Manitoba, Winnipeg, MB (2015 – Current)

MS. RANDY SMITH

NY/NJ Metro • 914-555-8209 • randysmith2244@gmail.com

SENIOR STAFFING EXECUTIVE

Talent Strategy, Acquisition & Leadership: Dyson Medical, KDF, Stanworth Pharma, Media Publishers

Quality-Driven, Cost-Effective Recruiting Throughout North America, Europe, and the Pacific Rim. MBA Degree.

Strategic Talent Acquisition Executive recognized for success in building global staffing models and reducing time-to-hire and cost-to-hire for all organizations while consistently exceeding expectations for quality of hire. Successful collaborator and partner to other senior executives to meet operational staffing needs worldwide. A big-picture thinker with achievements in employment branding, M&A integration, HRIS, diversity, and vendor management.

- **10K Annual New Hires.** Created novel talent acquisition strategies to attract new hires worldwide for Dyson's diversity-focused recruitment and staffing programs.
- **46% Growth in Employee Volume.** Brought KDF staff to 2200 in IT, HR, finance, science, research, sales, and support functions while reducing turnover 10%+.
- **$1M+ Search Firm Cost Savings.** Designed focused staffing strategy to deliver huge cost savings to Merck.
- **Innovative Social Media Strategies.** Attracted top talent by leveraging social media and web presence to strengthen employee branding for The New York Times.

PROFESSIONAL EXPERIENCE

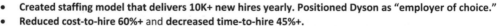

GLOBAL LEADER – TALENT ACQUISITION & DIVERSITY   2014 to Present

DYSON MEDICAL COMPANY *($16B medical technology manufacturer with 60,000 employees)* – Parkton, NJ

Recruited by Heidrick & Struggles to join Dyson in 2010. Declined that opportunity and recruited for the 2nd time in 2014. Accepted challenge to redefine talent acquisition strategy, design world-class global staffing processes, introduce advanced technologies, and implement critical diversity initiatives to facilitate continuous improvement. Manage a team of 10 direct reports in a 200-person department.

Cost-to-Hire -60%

- **Created staffing model that delivers 10K+ new hires yearly. Positioned Dyson as "employer of choice."**
- **Reduced cost-to-hire 60%+** and **decreased time-to-hire 45%+.**
- **Captured $15M in savings** over 3 years by restructuring and rebidding contingent worker program.
- Standardized recruiting and hiring from **20 different models into 1 single process.**
- Improved departmental **customer survey scores from 70% to 90% in 1st year.**
- Orchestrated implementation of **Workday solutions:** ATS cloud and mobile-enabled recruiting for worldwide markets; global talent acquisition dashboard with regional metrics for senior managers.

SENIOR DIRECTOR – STAFFING & OPERATIONS   2011 to 2014

KDF BIOTECH, INC. *($1.4B biotech company with growth from 1500 to 7000 employees in 3 years)* – Syracuse, NY

Built first-ever talent acquisition organization for fast-growing company (20% annual increase with 2nd most successful drug launch in US history). Created best-in-class-sourcing strategies and scalable recruitment and metrics-driven staffing models to meet growth demand with the very best candidates for the organization.

Cost-per-Hire -50%

- **Reduced cost-per-hire 50%** with online presence, social media outreach, and referral sources. Decreased reliance on contingent recruiters and orchestrated development of LinkedIn and Facebook pages.
- **Cut days-to-hire 30%** with preferred vendor list and new recruiting alliances.

Wendy Enelow, MRW, CCM, CPRW, JCTC • Enelow Enterprises, Inc. • www.wendyenelow.com

Note: Call-outs in the left margin highlight "wow" successes that are described in more detail in bullet points that are tightly written yet full of meaning and impact.

SENIOR DIRECTOR – STAFFING & OPERATIONS – KDF BIOTECH (continued)

- Created new executive recruiting function with predictable processes that **improved service level 50%.**
- **Implemented new Applicant Tracking System (ATS)** with improved metrics and reporting.
- Streamlined immigration processes, created relocation department, and expanded college recruiting.

DIRECTOR – GLOBAL STAFFING   2006 to 2011

STANWORTH PHARMACEUTICALS *($39M pharmaceutical research & manufacturing division)* – Princeton, NJ

Recruited to SP as part of new management/executive team brought in to turn company around, rebuild brand, and recapture market share. Crafted cost-effective recruiting and staffing models for employees, managers, and senior executives worldwide. Managed $15M budget, 5 senior recruiting managers, and 15 indirect reports supporting operations in 120 countries (with 50% of leadership in overseas locations).

Staffing Costs -15%

- **Orchestrated placement of 1000+ new hires** throughout North America, Europe, and the Pacific Rim.
- **Reduced staffing costs 15%** and **interview-to-hire ratio from 3 to 1.**
- **Decreased search firm volume 82%** and **saved $1.2M in annual hiring costs.**
- Managed complex **post-acquisition workforce integration** processes, including J&J's acquisition of SP. **Chosen to retain #1 talent management leadership position versus J&J incumbent.**
- **Improved intern conversion rate 47%** to further accelerate and strengthen talent base.

DIRECTOR – STAFFING   2003 to 2006

MEDIA PUBLISHERS *(1.6B+ in revenue with employees in the US & Europe)* – New York, NY

Designed and launched recruiting initiative that freshened brand to connect with next-generation leadership as publisher moved into digital technology. Devised creative sourcing strategies to address hiring shortfalls.

Time-to-Fill -37%

- **Cut time-to-fill 37%** (93 days to 58 days) with new messaging, marketing, and outreach.
- **Created innovative college internship and recruitment programs** targeted to top-tier business schools.
- **Drove Chairman's diversity initiative** with new dashboard showing cultural representation by business and highlighting underrepresentation of key populations to be targeted recruitment candidates.

DIRECTOR – STAFFING   2000 to 2003

SBT FINANCIAL SERVICES *($24B in revenue with employees throughout the US)* – New York, NY
Promoted from Manager of Staffing to Director within first year of hire. Managed $5M budget and 25 direct reports across 4 US locations. Met high-volume staffing and training needs with innovation and creativity.

Cost-per-Hire -50%

- Conceptualized and launched recruitment plan to **attract 800 new hires within 8 months.**
- **Reduced cost-per-hire 50%** by redesigning sign-on bonus program and other key recruiting functions.
- **Addressed $13M annual knowledge loss** by understanding and resolving issues related to high turnaround among women and minorities.

Early Professional Career: Promoted rapidly through increasingly responsible **operations management and HR generalist positions with CONWAY-DAVIS HEALTH CARE.**

EDUCATION

Master of Business Administration (MBA) – Princeton University – NJ
Bachelor of Arts (BA) – Labor Relations – State University of New York (SUNY)
Executive Studies at Center for Creative Leadership | Six Sigma Green Belt Certification

Martin Christopher, MA, PMP

Berkeley, CA | 510-255-2016 | mchristopher@comcast.net | linkedin.com/in/mchristopher

Change Management Leader

Fifteen years of experience delivering smooth transitions, product launches, and systemic corporate change in complex business environments. Passionate about working with people—building relationships, fostering self-sufficiency, guiding the implementation process, and supporting teams to succeed and sustain changes. Strengths:

Stakeholder Management	Training Development & Delivery	Change Impact Assessment
Cross-Cultural Communication	Success Metrics & Analytics	Meeting Facilitation
Project Management	Ambassador Networks	Change Management Methodology

Professional Experience

NEW DIRECTION LEADERSHIP, San Jose, CA   2011 – Present
Company providing consulting and support services to clients facing change and transition

Senior Consultant (2014 – Present) | **Consultant** (2011 – 2013)
Change Management | Stakeholder Management | Impact Assessment | Communication | Project Implementation

Consult with key clients, including Shell Oil (company's #1 client). Conduct comprehensive assessments of stakeholders and assess potential impact of change; then develop change management strategies to meet objectives while minimizing disruptions to staff and operations. Manage all aspects of change delivery, including communication, training, performance support, ambassador networks, and stakeholder relationships.

- Exceeded company expectations for wide-ranging Shell project, achieving 90%+ satisfaction rating through careful deployment of technical and process changes impacting 55K employees in 70+ countries on 4 continents.
- Led 10 project managers to implement Early Injury Management project in 5 countries.
- Customized Shell's change methodology curriculum and delivered training to business managers.

EXCELLENCE GROUP, Alameda, CA   2010 – 2011
Provider of staffing solutions, HR consulting, and change management consulting to medium to large firms

Senior Consultant
Strategy Development | Change Management | Team Building | Meeting Facilitation | Methodology Documentation

- Directed change management for highly successful launch of major product at utility, involving pilot group of 75K customers. Exceeded target expectations and expanded to include 1M customers. Great reviews from client.
- Led change management for re-launch of challenging utility customer website. Coordinated activities among technology, customer service, marketing, and product departments and strategized stakeholder engagement. Managed production and delivery of training, communication, and performance support materials.
- Built change management methodology for large technology client. Authored and published a widely adopted change management roadmap for the company.

SAN JOSE STATE UNIVERSITY, San Jose, CA   2005 – 2011

Adjunct Professor | College of Organizational Development
Teaching | Change Management | Organizational Behavior | Curriculum Development | Diverse Student Population

Developed curriculum and taught 4 courses per year to diverse group of working-adult students aged 21-65. Communicated organizational behavior theory in a manner that enabled students to apply it in their workplaces. Consistently received excellent reviews in student surveys, rating in top 12% of faculty.

Pauline Thaler, MA, CPRW, CEIP • True North Resumes • www.truenorthresumes.com
Note: Resume structure, content, and presentation all highlight and promote an extensive consulting career. Keywords prominently positioned under each job title increase visual impact and readability.

Martin Christopher | 510-255-2016 | mchristopher@comcast.net

INSPIRE CONSULTING, El Cerrito, CA   2003 – 2005
Change management, project management, meeting facilitation, and training to non-profits and IT companies

Principal
Change Management | Strategic Planning Facilitation | Training | Appreciative Approach | Process Implementation

- Developed change management strategies for large-scale program revamping back-office processes at TTM Systems. Trained staff for optimal transition. Program achieved 15% reduction in operating costs.

- Used Appreciative Approach—building on organizational strengths—to facilitate strategic planning for mid-sized child services non-profit. Delivered 5-year plan embraced by board of directors, managers, and employees.

- Redesigned and trained staff on service delivery processes for the Alameda Family Group. Lowered operational expenses by 25% and improved customer experience.

CALIFORNIA TRANSPORTATION GROUP, San Francisco, CA   1999 – 2003
State-wide organization providing emergency roadside service; $15M in annual revenue

Director, Planning & Performance Improvement (2001 – 2003)
Strategic Planning | Service Quality | Leadership| Balanced Scorecard | Cultural Change |Training | Process Re-Design

Provided senior executive leadership to process improvement area. **Promoted to this position.**

- Achieved 15% reduction in operating expenses, while maintaining high service levels, by establishing a measurement system that encouraged performance improvement.

- Delivered $15M in cost reductions through opportunities identified by performance improvement teams.

Manager, Service Quality (2000 – 2001)
Headed quality initiatives—a first-time venture for the company. **Promoted to this position**.

- Designed and implemented a field office cultural change program impacting 150 supervisors and representatives. Resulted in faster decision-making and increased customer satisfaction during a time of staff reductions.

- Initiated and managed team that delivered training to 100 service managers in quality and process improvement. Resulted in more than 100 local-based process changes and 8% reduction in operating expenses.

Manager, Member Relationship Management (1999 – 2000)
Managed a staff of 85, supporting delivery of 3 major systems replacements and launch of new member product.

- As program manager for launch of Service Plus, reported directly to senior management and coordinated technical staff and product managers in launching mission-critical product that exceeded revenue targets by 22%.

- Created enterprise member relationship strategy—a blueprint on how to deepen product relationships with members, which was presented and endorsed by senior management and board of directors.

———————————————— **Education and Training** ————————————————

M.A., Management – John F. Kennedy University
B.Sc., Business Administration – State University of New York at Albany – Dean's List, Graduated with Honors
Project Management Professional (PMP) – Project Management Institute
Certified Facilitator – AchieveGlobal / Zenger Miller
Certificate in Marketing – University of California at Berkeley Extension Program
Certificate in Effective Leadership and Communication – Dale Carnegie

Jordan Ramsey, LPN

(580) 781-7810 ◆ jordan.ramsey@yahoo.com ◆ Ada, OK 74820

Licensed Practical Nurse

Eight Years of Experience in Hospital and Skilled Nursing Settings

◆ **Service-driven** LPN combining strengths in comprehensive health assessments, accurate documentation, and relationship-based care to provide top-level nursing services in fast-paced settings. **Eager to secure a full-time LPN position; available for all shifts.**

◆ Dedicated member of multidisciplinary healthcare teams known for excellent clinical skills; ability to remain calm under pressure; and strengths in making swift, correct decisions in emergency situations while sustaining diligent focus on compliance and quality.

PROFESSIONAL EXPERIENCE

ADA REGIONAL HOSPITAL / NEUROLOGY FLOOR, Ada, OK
Licensed Public Nurse, 2016–2019

Delivered pre-operative and post-operative care that included:

Patient Assessments & Documentation ◆ Pre- / Post-Brain Surgery Observation/Care ◆ Tracheotomy & Chest Tube Care ◆ Wound Dressing & Care ◆ Post CVA / TIA Observation & Care ◆ IV Medication Administration ◆ Neurological Assessments ◆ G-Tube Feedings & Care ◆ Catheter / Tube Insertion ◆ Seizure, Back & Neck Care ◆ Post-Operative Care

- Supported doctors and patients before and after brain, seizure, back, neck, trauma, and orthopaedic surgeries.
- Ensured comprehensive care and accurate compliance with prescriptions, diets, and therapy.
- Assessed, monitored and documented patient progress, symptoms, and vital signs on each visit.
- Supervised nurse aides, providing clear instruction to ensure accurate and compassionate nursing services.
- Recognized for precise attention to detail in patient assessments, with notable strengths in neurological assessments.

MIDTOWN HEALTH CENTER, Ada, OK
Certified Nurse Aide, 2011–2016

Provided high-quality nursing assistance to residents:

Patient Care & Safety ◆ Vital Signs & Patient Monitoring ◆ Medication Administration

- Delivered dependable and compassionate care to multiple patients while sustaining a remarkably positive attitude, guided by a true concern for each individual and a deep passion for nursing.
- Assessed vital signs, performed lab draws and glucose checks, and provided pre- and post-operative care.
- Assisted residents with activities of daily living: meals, bathing, dressing, grooming, and use of assistive devices.
- Maintained thorough patient records and updated healthcare team on patients' status.
- Complied with HIPAA standards in all patient documentation and interactions.

EDUCATION & LICENSURE

OKLAHOMA CITY COLLEGE, Oklahoma City, OK
Licensed Practical Nurse (LPN), State of Oklahoma, 2016
Nurse's Aide Program, 2011

Irma Rojas • Resume Secrets Online • www.resumesecretsonline.com

Note: First bullet point in summary ends with objective and availability for unique presentation. Keywords at the beginning of each job description showcase specific expertise and knowledge most related to job objective.

BARBARA DOORE, PA-C

203-448-2284 | BarbDoore@gmail.com

PHYSICIAN ASSISTANT
Committed to Delivering Optimal Patient Care

Caring and intuitive young professional with hands-on experience assisting, monitoring, and managing the day-to-day patient needs in collaboration with and under the supervision of physicians. With a true love for caring for people, dedicated to playing a part in improving each patient's health and learning something new every day. *Flexible schedule for shift work.*

CERTIFICATIONS AND LICENSURE

Connecticut State Physician Assistant (PA) License — 2017 to Present
New York State Physician Assistant License — 2017 to Present

Drug Enforcement Administration License — 2017 to Present
National Provider Identifier License — 2017 to Present
Connecticut Controlled Dangerous Substance License — 2017 to Present

National Certifying Committee for Physician Assistants (NCCPA) — June 2017 to December 2019
AHA Advanced Cardiac Life Support (ACLS) — 2016 to Present
AHA Basic Cardiac Life Support (CPR) for Healthcare Providers — 2014 to Present
New York State Child Abuse and Neglect Recognition — November 2014

AREAS OF TRAINING & EXPERIENCE

- Patient Health Assessment
- Post-Op/Procedure Notes & Orders
- Pharmacology
- Patient Care & Safety
- Patient & Caregiver Communication
- Anatomy & Physiology
- Daily Patient Rounds
- Post-Procedure Patient Management
- Perioperative Care
- Medical Prescriptions
- Research Data Collection & Analysis
- Medical Microbiology

PROFESSIONAL EXPERIENCE

ST. PHILIP'S HOSPITAL via Trusted Care Associates | Melville, NY   June 2017-Present
Physician Assistant, Emergency Medicine

Serve as sole PA in 12-bed fast-track area of emergency department, providing patient care in conjunction with a physician. Order imaging, labs, medication, and specialty consults. Perform minor procedures, including laceration repairs, incision and drainage of abscesses, joint reductions, and splinting.

In ER, work alongside physicians to care for more critical patients requiring intensive workups. In both roles, admit patients to the hospital for further evaluation and care.

ADDITIONAL EXPERIENCE

Research Technician, UNIVERSITY OF CONNECTICUT | Storrs, CT (2015–2017)
Research Assistant, UNIVERSITY OF CONNECTICUT | Storrs, CT (2014–2015)
Volunteer, UNIVERSITY OF CONNECTICUT | Storrs, CT (2012–2014)

PEER-REVIEWED PUBLICATIONS

Smith, Shannon C., Doore, B., Thomas, L., Waters, E., (2014, May). *Does the Method of Contraception Correlate to the Rate of Yeast Infections?* Poster session presented at American Academy of Physician Assistants, New York, NY, May, 2017

COMPUTER SKILLS

Proficient in Microsoft Word, Excel, PowerPoint, and EMR used on clinical rotations.

EDUCATION

Master of Science in Physician Assistant Studies
NEW YORK INSTITUTE OF MEDICINE
Melville, NY
May 2017

Bachelor of Science in Kinesiology Movement Science option
UNIVERSITY OF CONNECTICUT
Storrs, CT
May 2013, *With Honors*

Schmidt Honors College
Dean's List (7 semesters)

Phi Eta Sigma Freshman Honor Society

Health and Human Development Honor Society

Phi Kappa Phi Honor Society

• • •

Laurie Berenson, CMRW, CEIC, CPRW • Sterling Career Concepts, LLC • www.sterlingcareerconcepts.com

Note: Shaded boxes pop critical keywords, educational credentials, and professional affiliations. Distinguishing list of certifications and licenses is prominently positioned while professional experience is concisely yet comprehensively presented.

MARIE DAVID, PHARM.D.

301-671-8910 • mdavid@email.com • Jefferson, MD 21755

CLINICAL PHARMACIST

Versatile and patient-centered professional with extensive experience in clinical pharmacy operations. Esteemed drug information resource, respected member of interdisciplinary healthcare teams, and valued contributor to organization-wide task forces. Proactive problem solver with unwavering drive for service excellence.

RESULTS SNAPSHOT

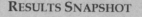

| **20% increase** in patient satisfaction | **10% growth** in monthly survey scores | **60% reduction** in 30-day readmissions | **15% savings** in formulary expenses |

Areas of Expertise

- ☑ Patient Counseling
- ☑ Order Verification & Processing
- ☑ Formulary Management
- ☑ QA/QC
- ☑ Medication Therapy Management (MTM)
- ☑ Anticoagulation Therapy
- ☑ Pharmacokinetic Dosing
- ☑ Drug Utilization Review (DUR)
- ☑ Staff & Student Training
- ☑ Process Improvement

Professional Credentials

- ☑ Pharmacist License – Maryland #111111
- ☑ Pharmacist License – Virginia #222222
- ☑ Member – American Pharmacists Association (APhA)

Computer Skills

- ☑ MS Office Suite
- ☑ Epic
- ☑ Pyxis
- ☑ Allscripts Healthcare Solutions
- ☑ Sunrise Clinical Manager

PROFESSIONAL EXPERIENCE

Clinical Staff Pharmacist | UMBC Hospital, Baltimore, MD, 2005–2019

Delivered pharmaceutical care within high-volume heart failure, CCU, internal medicine, and vascular surgery areas. Reviewed and verified orders, dispensed medications, and presided over daily anticoagulation and pharmacokinetically dosed drugs. Functioned as patient advocate and provided personalized counseling on medication therapies.

Advised medical staff on drug selection, dose, interactions, and monitoring as well as formulary protocols. Managed inventory, performed medication reconciliation duties, aided with discharge planning, and attended transition rounds.

- As member of Readmission Reduction Team, **decreased 30-day readmissions by 60% and propelled patient satisfaction by 20%** through:
  - Enhanced reviews for non-compliance and financial barriers
  - Improved medication reconciliation and patient education practices
  - Set-up of continued care prior to discharge
- Contributed to taskforce that **delivered steady increases in HCAHPS survey scores (10% each month)** concerning patient education in 3 areas: new medications, side effects, and discharge/home care plans.
- **Expertly controlled formulary with 100% compliance** to department budget and internal/external regulations **while cutting costs by 15%.**
- Mentored 3–6 pharmacy residents, interns, and students, **ensuring academic and professional goals were achieved and inspiring patient-focused attitudes.**

EDUCATION

Pharm.D. – University of Virginia, Charlottesville, VA
Rho Chi Society Member

B.A. in Chemistry – University of Maryland, Baltimore, MD

Natalie Winzer, CARW, CRS+HM, CRS+HR • iHire, LLC • www.ihire.com

Note: Results snapshot showcasing specific and measurable achievements adds an entirely new and very effective dimension to this resume. Strategic page design keeps the resume to 1 page without forfeiting any information.

Jack W. Smith

San Diego, CA 91942 • 542-555-1234 • jwsmith@yahoo.com

TARGET: GOVERNMENT & MILITARY BUSINESS DEVELOPMENT
Specializing in Healthcare Products & Support

Professional Profile

Competitor: Driven to succeed in every phase of life. One of youngest sailors to assume and fulfill executive responsibility for personnel health and welfare, budget and finance, equipment, and training.

Communicator: Able to interact with a diversity of people, from a sick child in a hospital to a 2-star Admiral in an executive briefing.

Relationship Builder: Consistently create trust, build positive relationships, and form alliances while maintaining an aggressive can-do drive for business.

Medical Products Knowledge

➢ 10 years of experience as a US Navy Independent Duty Corps Medical Department Manager.

➢ Extensive experience in medical equipment testing, assessments, acquisitions, and training.

- Medicine
- Pharmaceuticals
- Medical Equipping & Training
- OSHA Requirements
- NAVOSH Requirements
- International Networking

- Government & Military Sales
- Contract Management
- Foreign Military Sales
- Presentation Prep & Delivery
- Relationship Building
- Top Secret SCI Security Clearance

Professional Experience

US Navy, 1997 – Present

Senior Advisor for Division Clinics
Naval Health Offices, Valley View, CA   2015–2019

Oversaw staffing, training, and professional development of 384 personnel across 10 clinics throughout California, impacting the service and care of more than 90,000 individuals.

➢ Built partnerships with various departments; established a new training program and formal process for mentoring and promoting personnel.

➢ Prepared the organization for the Joint Commission on the Accreditation of Healthcare Organizations (JCAHO) review; received accreditation with outstanding scores.

➢ Revised personnel management practices, improving efficiency and workforce satisfaction.

➢ Oversaw emergency medical planning and coverage for the US Navy's El Centro Airshow. Ensured all medical equipment, staff, and procedures were in place and ready to respond if necessary.

Linda Gibson, M.A., CPRW • CareerHelm, LLC • www.careerhelm.com

Note: Military-to-civilian transition resume uses expanded summary section to highlight skills in demand in the healthcare products and services sectors. Early military career is briefly yet effectively summarized.

Senior Medical Director
Medical Division, Afghanistan   2014–2015

Senior advisor to executive staff.

- ➢ Engaged in policy planning and review as a member of the Board of Directors.
- ➢ Managed movement of personnel and equipment throughout the country – guaranteed constant mission readiness of surgical units across 6 locations, including very remote operating bases.
- ➢ Oversaw the rotation of 300+ personnel every 6 months.
  - Initiated and conducted team focus groups, successfully improving communication.
  - Developed and implemented standardized training program – improved efficiency, built team cohesion, and achieved seamless transitions.

Senior Medical Master Chief
Navy Command, Waterside, VA   2013–2014

Directed efforts in staffing, training, and equipping the organization. Provided oversight and decision making for all medical training.

- ➢ Wrote and established training protocols and selected medical training equipment.
- ➢ Guided the organization's move toward the use of advanced simulation equipment.
- ➢ Selected medical equipment and supplies for 100+ medical departments.
- ➢ Oversaw credentialing for 150+ medical providers.

Senior Medical Department Representative

Provided medical care, administration, and oversight of health and safety issues for up to 200 personnel.

Naval Studies Institute, Sunset, FL   2010–2013
Explosive Ordnance Unit X, International Locations   2009–2010
USS Shippensburg, Virginia Beach, VA   2006–2009

US Navy Hospital Corpsman   2003–2006

Served and trained at various duty stations and schools, including US Navy Dive School and Naval Medical Center San Diego Pediatrics ICU.

Education

Bachelor of Science in Health Sciences
San Diego State University, San Diego, CA   2011
Summa cum laude

KAITLYNN D. BRIDGES

265 S. Jackson Avenue Apt. 2 ◆ Ontario, CA ◆ (626) 454-0231 ◆ kbridges145@gmail.com

Nonprofit Program Coordinator with 10+ years of experience in program administration, case management, and special event planning.

Special interest in women's empowerment and sustainability issues.

Skills Profile: Hard-Worker ◆ Team-Player ◆ Self-Starter Compassionate ◆ Dependable ◆ Quality-Driven ◆ Client-Focused

> *"I've come to believe that each of us has a personal calling that's as unique as a fingerprint – and that the best way to succeed is to discover what you love and then find a way to offer it to others in the form of service."*
> *– Oprah Winfrey*

RELEVANT EXPERIENCE & KEY HIGHLIGHTS

PROGRAM ADMINISTRATION: *Staff Management & Development, Program Implementation*

- *Staff Management & Development*: Recruited, interviewed, and selected student workers based on program needs and objectives. Conducted interactive training sessions for all new hires and provided one-on-one support throughout the entire onboarding process. Created and monitored job performance criteria, providing coaching and counsel in areas of need.

- *Program Implementation*: Oversaw the independent studies and work experience program, teaching multiple-subject courses for 9th-12th grades, and creating individualized lesson plans as requested. Researched fitness and health concepts for teen girls and developed and implemented new program ideals. Instructed physical education classes weekly and recommended meals based on new criteria.

CASE MANAGEMENT: *Productivity & Client/Customer Relations*

- *Productivity*: Managed a high-volume workload in both an administrative and case-working capacity. Exceeded program requirements and achieved a QA/QI score of **90%** or above monthly. Prepared reports specific to program objectives, submitting data to senior leaders.

- *Client/Customer Relations*: Mentored and academically advised **100+** at-risk youth, successfully leading more than half to GED graduation. Supervised and interacted with program participants daily, fostering a healthy and progressive live/work/play environment for all.

SPECIAL EVENTS PLANNING: *Event Execution & Communication*

- *Event Execution*: Delivered weekly program services and planned, organized, and led large-scale events such as conferences, summer/winter camps, and community outreach activities. Exercised effective crisis and crowd control measures, decreasing frequency of harm and injury to staff and program participants. Traveled overseas and helped host a conference in London, England.

- *Communication*: Spoke to youth groups of **25–500**, articulating program objectives and empowering individuals to get involved and take lead. Partnered with internal and external stakeholders, ensuring all program objectives were achieved by all and within specified parameters.

WORK HISTORY

Hedgewick Claims Management, **Claims Specialist**, Placentia, CA (2014–2016)
Joan Lewis School, **Academic and Work Experience Coordinator,** La Verne, CA (2010–2014)
Premier Staffing Company, **Auditor,** Downey, CA (2010)
David and Marybeth Youth and Family Services, **Youth Residential Counselor,** La Verne, CA (2009)
Joy Christian School, **Instructional Aide,** West Covina, CA (2007–2009)
Joy Community Church, **Program Intern/Youth Leader,** West Covina, CA (2005–2007)

EDUCATION

Bachelor of Arts, Psychology, **California State University,** Fullerton, Fullerton, CA (2009)

Siti Williams, ACRW, PHR, MPA • Career Cultivators • www.careercultivators.net

Note: Functional structure allows this return-to-work candidate to showcase experiences from a diversity of paid and volunteer positions. This resume is a precise example of when a functional format is the right choice.

LUCINDA SALE

Miami, FL • 305-246-9753 • lucinda.sale@gmail.com • LinkedIn Profile

NONPROFIT EXECUTIVE

Entrepreneurial • Innovative • Growth Focused • Mission Driven

Committed to increasing scope, influence, and impact of organizations that empower and support others. Collaborative and action oriented—balancing thoughtful decision-making and inclusive leadership.

Performance Highlights

- Grew funding **35%** and number of children served **102%** in 3 years as Executive Director, Birth & Beyond.
- Led the most successful capital campaign in the history of the Ladies Who Lunch (**$3.2M** in 1 year).
- Consistently recruited high-profile **business and community leaders** as effective and engaged board members.
- Created numerous **first-of-their-kind** programs and national models.
- Strengthened operational performance by introducing **corporate management practices, metrics, and accountability.**

Notable Awards and Recognition

Pinnacle Award, Dade County Chamber of Commerce, 2014 • *100 Inspirational Women of Miami,* Photo-book by Sam Smithers, 2012 • Miami Heat Hot Heroes Award, 2011 • Miami Beach Association Volunteer of the Year, 2010

PROFESSIONAL EXPERIENCE

EXECUTIVE DIRECTOR • Birth & Beyond–Florida • 2014–2017 • Miami, FL
National nonprofit providing children in need with essentials to thrive at home, school, and play.

Recruited to lead the organization's flagship operation—$3.86M annual budget, 36 staff. Provided visionary leadership to expand operational reach, increase state-wide influence, and drive market success across all functional areas. As member of the National Leadership Team, supported organization's national growth plans to open 3 additional sites by 2018.

Visionary Leadership

- **Formed South Florida Board of Directors,** in 90 days recruiting 12 influential C-suite leaders representing a cross-section of Miami-area businesses, nonprofits, and communities.
- **Drove market analysis and strategic planning** to focus efforts on areas of greatest need and greatest opportunity. Pursued and secured grant funding aligned with strategic objectives:
    - **$500K grant** from Smith Family Foundation to seed growth in Central Florida.
    - **$500K grant** from XYZ Corp. to support fulfillment of mission and thought leadership in Florida.
- **Created first Corporate Advisory Council** to expand engagement and corporate strategy.
- **Conducted first-ever impact study,** establishing benchmarks for the organization's core programs and initiatives.
- **Convened inaugural Summit on Poverty,** a deep dive into thought leadership, collaboration, and the importance of essential goods featuring presentations and conversations with experts in medicine, social services, and philanthropy.

Operational Performance

- **Doubled the number of children served,** from 64,000 in 2013 to 129,000 in 2016.
- **Grew annual revenue 35%,** from $2.85M to $3.86M, in 3 years. Shifted development focus to major gifts and exceeded fund-raising goals every year.
- **Added mission-aligned programs and partnerships.** Initiated research partnership with Florida Women's Health to measure organizational impact, first of its kind; created partnership with West Miami Community Health Center.
- **Revolutionized internal decision-making.** Pushed daily decisions to mid-level managers to build bench strength and to free executive team for strategic leadership.

Louise Kursmark, MRW, CPRW, JCTC, CEIP, CCM • Best Impression Career Services • www.louisekursmark.com

Note: Highlighting substantial and quantified achievements, this resume for a nonprofit executive clearly conveys value while also identifying the soft skills and sense of mission she brings to her work.

LUCINDA SALE

305-246-9753 • lucinda.sale@gmail.com • **Page 2**

EXECUTIVE DIRECTOR • Kickstart for Kids—South Region • 2013–2014 • Atlanta, GA
National organization that recruits/trains college students to work with preschool children in low-income neighborhoods.

Invigorated development, program management, and community engagement for organization's largest and most progressive region. As member of National Operating team, contributed to organizational strategy, policy, and growth plans.

- **Expanded regional footprint,** opening 3 new sites in Alabama and Florida.
- **Strengthened and diversified Board,** introducing new co-chair model that balanced internal and external focus.
- **Created strategic development and targeted donor plans.** Secured major gifts from Disney Foundation and PNC Bank.

EXECUTIVE DIRECTOR • Ladies Who Lunch • 2007–2013 • Miami, FL
Day shelter for homeless and needy women and children in the Greater Miami area.

Recruited by board to raise organizational profile, diversify funding base, and manage change. Guided organization through major transitions and initiatives, including first-ever comprehensive program evaluation; total facility renovation; new funding model; and comprehensive strategic planning process.

- **Restrategized a planned relocation,** after learning first week on the job that a majority of volunteers and clients were resisting the new location. Convinced Board to conduct a space analysis that led to decision to renovate.
- **Executed $3.2M capital campaign (7% above goal)** in recessionary economy. Partnered with high-profile corporate leader who helped determine ideal timing and ultimately chaired the successful year-long campaign. Managed 6-month renovation that expanded space and deeply satisfied all stakeholders.

DIRECTOR OF COMMUNITY RELATIONS & PUBLIC POLICY • Farm Up • 2004–2007 • Coral Gables, FL
National model for engaging young people in personal and social change through sustainable agriculture.

Assumed newly created position with challenge to raise the profile of the organization at local, state, and national levels.

- **Developed first Neighborhood Food Council,** now a national model for local engagement in food systems work.
- **Launched inaugural Florida Food conference,** in collaboration with local hospital. Delivered keynote presentation.
- **Partnered with community-based groups and state** to acquire land and greenhouse for urban food production.

Prior Corporate & Academic Experience
- **MANAGER, CORPORATE TRAINING & BUSINESS ETHICS** • Austin Enterprises • Indianapolis, IN (*Largest holder of long-term-care facilities in the US*): Introduced behavior-based interviewing, performance management, and supervisory skills training curriculum that boosted hiring skills 80% and reduced managerial turnover by 25%.
- **VP, SALES AND MARKETING** • Medical Staffing Solutions • Indianapolis, IN *(Medical staffing agency serving the healthcare industry)*: Increased employee database 50% in first year and grew market share 25% in second year as part of start-up/management team for specialized staffing agency.
- **REGIONAL DIRECTOR** • National Marrow Donor Program—Central Region • Indianapolis, IN *(National nonprofit)*: Built donor center into #1 in the nation for donors of color. Designed recruitment/retention program for collegiate donors that is still the industry standard.
- **ASSOCIATE DIRECTOR, INSTITUTIONAL ADVANCEMENT** • Alcorn State University • Fayette, MS: Advanced through positions as Director of Recruitment and Admissions, Director of Public Information, and Director of Public Relations.

EDUCATION

MA Journalism, with Honors • Indiana University–Purdue University, Indianapolis, IN
BA English, with Honors • Alcorn State University, Fayette, MS
Graduate, University of Miami Executive Leadership Program, Miami, FL

KEVIN RUSSELL

404-671-9813 | kevinrussell@gmail.com
LinkedIn.com/in/KevinRussell | Atlanta, GA 30316

EXECUTIVE DIRECTOR

Organizational Transformation | Leadership Development | Change Management
Repeated success injecting a culture of excellence to unlock the potential of organizations

Service-oriented leader who leverages a collaborative approach to inspire organizational greatness and a dedication to shared goals. Catalyst for positive, well-organized change with the ability to uncover opportunities for innovation and define the path forward.

CORE COMPETENCIES

Executive Leadership	Organizational Development	Strategic Planning
Team Building & Leadership	Cultural Transformation	Fund Raising & Development
Program Development	Data-driven Improvement	Communication

CAREER SUMMARY

ST. JOHN'S LUTHERAN CHURCH   Atlanta, GA | 2015–2019
EXECUTIVE DIRECTOR

Challenge: Reenergize an organization that had experienced a 50% decline in membership

Led organization through a collaborative and comprehensive redevelopment initiative. Put the people, policies, and structure in place to align operations with the organization's vision, mission, and values. Supervised 6 employees and hundreds of volunteers on 6 major program teams.

- **Halted membership losses** and achieved 15% growth in 3 years. Positioned organization for added expansion.

- **Restructured the Board of Director's governance model** to remove the Board from day-to-day operations. Initiated discussions that resulted in full buy-in of the Board to shift from a management to an advisory role.

- **Orchestrated strategic planning process** that incorporated member questionnaires, community demographic surveys, and group interviews to uncover gaps in existing programs.

- **Launched new teams** to advance the organization's mission and better serve the membership:
  - *Marketing:* Created first formal marketing team with volunteer writers, graphic artists, and communication professionals. Oversaw rebranding to align logo, tagline, and other elements with the mission and vision.
  - *Guest Services:* Organized volunteer team dedicated to welcoming and following up with potential members.
  - *Community Relations:* Developed or strengthened partnerships with 10+ organizations to provide mentoring, financial assistance, and other support to the community.

- **Hosted the Global Leadership Summit** to equip 150+ business and nonprofit leaders in the metro Atlanta area. Oversaw all event planning functions, including public relations, advertising, hospitality, technology, and more.

- **Led a $1 million capital campaign** to fund operational budget and capital needs.

GRACE LUTHERAN CHURCH   New Orleans, LA | 2008–2015
MEMBER OF THE EXECUTIVE TEAM

Challenge: Expand, redevelop, and manage 4 core program teams to further the organization's mission

Worked with senior pastor to develop and supervise the marketing, community outreach, adult learning, and care ministry programs. Managed team of 10 employees.

- **Expanded programs and added new initiatives** to better serve members and increase community engagement.

- **Co-managed the organization's strategic planning process** to develop a 5-year plan.

- **Introduced a passion for innovation and excellence** in a highly change-averse environment.

Michelle Swanson, ACRW, NCRW, CERM, CJSS, CPRW • Swanson Career Solutions • www.swansoncareersolutions.com
Note: All content—keywords, job titles, accomplishments, and other details—is written to best position this pastor for successful transition to a secular nonprofit leadership role.

KEVIN RUSSELL Page 2 | 404-671-9813| kevinrussell@gmail.com

SALEM LUTHERAN CHURCH Atlanta, GA | 2004–2008
EXECUTIVE DIRECTOR

Challenge: Grow an organization within a rural community with a declining population
Led program development and capital improvement initiatives. Managed 3 employees and dozens of volunteers.

- **Achieved 50%+ growth in a stagnant community** through a multifaceted outreach program.
- **Restructured the organization's relationship with the Board** and injected a culture of excellence.
- **Shifted the organization from an inward to an outward focus.** Instilled a dedication to investing in the community, which solidified relationships with key community organizations.
- **Directed major capital improvement projects.** Managed budgets and organized teams of volunteers.

CHRIST LUTHERAN CHURCH Charlotte, NC | 2001–2004
EXECUTIVE DIRECTOR

Challenge: Redevelop an organization on the verge of closing its doors
Brought in to turn around organization with declining membership base and serious funding and leadership issues.

- **Initiated study of community demographics.** Achieved growth despite resistance to change among leaders.

COMMUNITY LEADERSHIP: BOARD OF DIRECTORS

JEFFERSON CHAMBER OF COMMERCE Atlanta, GA | 2016–2018
BOARD OF DIRECTORS: Joined this newly formed Chamber to support economic redevelopment and member recruitment initiatives. Participated in early stages of the development of a Leadership Academy.

ST. BERNARD COOPERATIVE MINISTRY Atlanta, GA | 2015–2018
BOARD OF DIRECTORS: Served on the Board of nonprofit providing food, financial aid, and counseling to people and families in crisis. Acted as Division Leader for a capital campaign that raised $5 million in funding to create an innovative sustainable development program and expand existing emergency assistance services.

EDUCATION & CREDENTIALS

Executive Program for Nonprofit Leaders — STANFORD GRADUATE SCHOOL OF BUSINESS, Stanford, CA
Experiential lab to strengthen the leadership and management capacity of nonprofit practitioners

- **Program Topics:** Nonprofit Sector Trends, Governance, Strategic Planning, Social Impact, Resource & Fund Development, Financial Management, Private–Nonprofit Partnerships, Negotiations, Organizational Change, Human Resources, Volunteer Management, Advocacy in the Public Interest, Marketing & Communication

Professional Doctorate in Leadership (D.Min.) — CONCORDIA SEMINARY, St. Louis, MO
5-year program that prepares leaders to revitalize organizations and nonprofit challenges

- **Emphasis**: Theory and practice of organizational development and restructuring, change management, and coaching for results

Master's Degree (M.Div.) — CONCORDIA SEMINARY, St. Louis, MO
Bachelor's Degree (BA, Psychology) — GEORGIA STATE UNIVERSITY, Atlanta, GA

Professional Memberships: Association for Research on Nonprofit Organizations and Voluntary Action (ARNOVA), National Council of Nonprofit Associations, Society for Nonprofits

Cherilyn Randall

cherilyn@gmail.com   Las Vegas, Nevada   (406) 123-4567

Cocktail Server

Resort ... Casino ... Restaurant ... Nightclub ... Winery ... VIP Parties

Playful approach to unsurpassed service and world-class entertainment
BUILD BRAND VALUE AND CUSTOMER LOYALTY THROUGH ATTENTIVE SERVICE
F&B Delivery – Guest Service – Publicity Photos – Product Promotion

Mixed Beverage Knowledge	– Seven years' casino, hotel, winery, bar, and catered event service
Complaint Resolution	– Champagne, wine, liqueur, beer, and specialty cocktail knowledge
Inventory Control	– Creative French pleat, standing fan, and single pocket napkin folds
Up-Selling and Cross-Selling	– Aloha, Squirrel, and Sable POS to convey drink orders to bartenders
High-Volume Sales	– Cash and personal bank controlled, counted, and reconciled accurately
Wine and Food Pairing	– Fun-filled ambiance created through lighthearted guest interaction
Personal Bank Management	– Regulations respected prohibiting service to minors and intoxicated persons

Work Experience

Cocktail Server
MGM GRAND HOTEL AND CASINO, Las Vegas, Nevada, 2015 – present

— Ensure safe, fast service for large, VIP, and private parties in bars, nightclubs, gambling areas, dance floors, lounges, restaurants, and poolside at Las Vegas' largest destination resort.
— Employ high energy and flexibility to deliver orders throughout the resort and provide prompt room service.
— Check patrons' identifications to ensure compliance with corporate standards and state alcohol regulations.
— Manage refrigeration units, beer taps, draft towers, and dishwashing systems to ensure well-timed service.
— Built strong rapport with bartenders, bar backs, runners, servers, and slots managers through professional service and positive communications.

Server and Tasting Room Manager
DESERT RAT WINERY, Palm Springs, California, 2012 – 2015

— Managed tasting room pouring of award-winning wines from French-American hybrid wine grapes.
— Served wine at high-profile, no-host tasting parties, fundraisers, weddings, and receptions of 10–250 guests.
— Managed sales, deliveries, and invoicing for wholesale, grocery, restaurant, and retail accounts.
— Improved company's competitive position in the fine wine industry by cultivating new business via cold calling that increased sales and wine club sign-ups.

Education

TIPS Alcohol Certification – TAM Alcohol Server Training
College of the Desert General Education Diploma, Palm Desert, California

Cheryl Minnick, M.Ed., Ed.D., NCRW, CCMC • University of Montana-Missoula • www.umt.edu

Note: The graphic makes the resume—and instantly tells readers who this job seeker is before they read a word. Content expresses an excellent blend of both professional skills and personalized approach to customer service.

SUZANNA "SUE" SALAZAR

720.930.9933 | suesalazar@gmail.com | Denver, CO

SENIOR LEADER & HOSPITALITY TURNAROUND CHAMPION

I combine a fierce passion for customer service with ability to improve marketing, branding, operations, sales, and much more for hospitality venues: family-owned businesses, large lodges and resorts, multimillion-dollar chains.

THE SUE PROMISE — To each employer, I make a personal guarantee of improvement in at least 3 key areas:

CUSTOMER EXPERIENCE: I identify what motivates customers and guests to travel to the area. I then improve and train management and staff to provide excellent customer service, striving to make every stay a great experience.

REVENUE AND PROFIT: I diagnose unnecessary drains on resources, enhance service offerings, implement new programs, and ensure the numbers get back into the black — and then I show management how to keep them there.

OPERATIONS, MARKETING, AND BRANDING: I overhaul any weak branding messages and examine and act on local market opportunities. I also specialize in strategizing for long-term results while driving consistency across the board.

HOSPITALITY LEADERSHIP EXPERIENCE

DIRECTOR OF OPERATIONS — WHITE WOLF RESORT LODGE — DENVER, CO   2015 – 2019
RESULTS OF TENURE: REVENUE IMPROVEMENT: $72M — WINTER OCCUPANCY IMPROVEMENT: 24%

White Wolf Resort Lodge Statistics: 1500 rooms, 25 meeting rooms, and 3 restaurants

CHALLENGES: Brought on board to identify and solve an annual decline in winter occupancy and sales for ski lodge and resort. Recognized a severe lack of training among staff and virtually no programs or partnerships in place.

ACTIONS: Instituted several training programs for seasonal hires and a best practices management program for resort leaders. Overhauled operations, financials, and management team for the ski lodge. Developed partnerships with nearby tourist shops and an attraction to promote additional traffic to the restaurants.

DELIVERING THE SUE PROMISE: Remained a firm part of White Wolf Resort Lodge through 4 winter seasons, personally interviewing skiers and new seasonal staff to ensure that everything operated smoothly. Captured $20M in new revenue during the first winter season from record-breaking event hosting and attendance.

DIRECTOR OF MARKETING AND BRANDING — SCENIC VALLEY HOTEL — FLAGSTAFF, AZ   2013 – 2015
RESULTS OF TENURE: PROFIT INCREASE: 389% — SUMMER OCCUPANCY IMPROVEMENT: 78%

Scenic Valley Hotel Statistics: 450 rooms, gift shop, and family-run restaurant

CHALLENGES: Hired in a final effort by this family-run hotel to bring it out of a severe profit loss and identify the causes behind a complete lack of customers to the hotel, gift shop, and restaurant.

ACTIONS: Rebranded outdated hotel and restaurant with new, eye-catching desert theme to attract Grand Canyon tourists without alienating local loyal residents. Redesigned gift shop, partnering with a major local chain to carry their items.

DELIVERING THE SUE PROMISE: Optimized the e-commerce platform to allow room service delivery directly from the restaurant, bringing the restaurant back into the black in 9 months from this change alone. Coordinated with hotel leadership to implement new sales programs, bringing in hundreds of new guests each year. Stayed on an extra 8 months to ensure that hotel, gift shop, and restaurant were firmly in the black and rapidly improving.

Laura Gonzalez, ACRW, CPRW • Masterwork Resumes • www.masterworkresumes.com
Note: Unique summary statement—"The Sue Promise"—and illustration of that promise in each job description make for a personalized resume. Quantifiable successes from early career are included without aging the job seeker.

DIRECTOR OF OPERATIONS — SOUTH PROPERTY MANAGEMENT — AUSTIN, TX   2010 – 2013
RESULTS OF TENURE: SUMMER OCCUPANCY IMPROVEMENT: 35% — RESTAURANT PROFIT INCREASE: $150K+

South Property Management Statistics: 3 hotels (2000+ rooms), 6 restaurants, 2 attractions, gift shop, and water park

> **CHALLENGES:** Recruited by senior management to improve occupancy for all 3 hotels and to overhaul operations at a restaurant boasting 2 Michelin stars. Discovered a lack of staff knowledge and motivation at all venues.

> **ACTIONS:** Implemented a training program to help staff members sell hotel customers on the famous and unique experience of the restaurant. Collaborated with other senior management to create a team sales incentive program for hotel staff. Improved attraction, gift shop, and water park staff knowledge of hotel offerings.

> **DELIVERING THE SUE PROMISE:** Spearheaded a new culture of teamwork and communication among venue staffs and management. Played key role in the Michelin restaurant capturing several "Best in Texas" recognitions. Developed long-term strategies, new concepts, and initiatives for the hotels to ensure that occupancy will continue improving.

GENERAL MANAGER — THE BEAUMONT INN — TULSA, OK   2006 – 2010
RESULTS OF TENURE: INN REVENUE IMPROVEMENT: 35% — RESTAURANT REVENUE IMPROVEMENT: 78%

The Beaumont Inn Statistics: 200 rooms and family-run restaurant

> **CHALLENGES:** Hired by family to salvage a third-generation inn and a new restaurant that was unsuccessful from the very start. Identified a severe lack of training of restaurant staff and no real marketing for the inn.

> **ACTIONS:** Brought on a new executive chef and restaurant manager. Trained front-of-house staff on best practices for customer service in the food industry. Implemented a marketing plan revolving around partnerships with local businesses.

> **DELIVERING THE SUE PROMISE:** Launched the restaurant with a new grand opening, attended by the Mayor of Tulsa. Trained family on managing marketing programs so that the inn can be handed down to the next generation.

PAST RELEVANT HISTORY

Held numerous roles in the hospitality industry, and nearly every possible role in hotels and resorts. Built a solid career from the ground up, honing an understanding of the inner workings of hospitality organizations.

KEY RESULT HIGHLIGHTS:

> **REVENUE AND/OR PROFIT IMPROVEMENTS:** 15% profit (lodge), $26K+ revenue (hotel), 50% profit (hotel)
> **OCCUPANCY IMPROVEMENTS:** 10% (resort), 23% (lodge), 47% (hotel), 73% (hotel)

EDUCATION, CONTINUED TRAINING, AND MEMBERSHIPS

DEGREES:
MS IN HOSPITALITY MANAGEMENT — UNIVERSITY OF LOUISIANA
BS IN HOSPITALITY AND TOURISM (DOUBLE DEGREE) — UNIVERSITY OF LOUISIANA

CONTINUED TRAINING:
CERTIFIED HOSPITALITY SUPERVISOR (CHS) — AMERICAN HOTEL INSTITUTE — 2017
CERTIFIED HOSPITALITY TECHNOLOGY PROFESSIONAL (CHTP) — AMERICAN HOTEL INSTITUTE — 2013
HOTEL MANAGEMENT TRAINING — AMERICAN HOSPITALITY ACADEMY — 2011

MEMBERSHIPS:
SOUTHERN HOSPITALITY GROUP — SINCE 2009
AMERICAN HOSPITALITY ACADEMY — SINCE 2005

Henry Davis

Sarasota, FL 34242 • 941-833-9448 • henrydavis88@gmail.com • linkedin.com/in/henry-b-davis

Account Cultivation & Management | Sales & Customer Service | Project Management

Proven account management skills complemented by commitment to customer service that goes above and beyond

Highly resourceful, proactive, and customer-centric professional with track record of consistently exceeding customer expectations, driving business growth, and inventing ways to attract, delight, and retain key customers.

Professional Experience & Accomplishments

MONACO'S PIZZA | Sarasota, FL   2017–Present
Sales/Customer Service Manager

Recruited to return to Monaco's to revitalize sales following 2 years of declining performance.

- **Developed recommendations to improve service and enhance menu.** Achieved immediate 11% jump in add-on sales following introduction of new line of desserts.
- **Trained in-store and delivery staff in customer service,** leading to rapid decline in service complaints.
- **Built relationships with area businesses** to drive large sales for corporate lunches and celebrations.
- **Established preferred-account status** with 3 of Sarasota's largest employers (PGT Industries, Venice Medical Center, FCCI Insurance Group) and created exclusive employee rewards program.
- **Reversed sales decline in 6 months and achieved consistent sales growth in every quarter thereafter.**

SPECIALTY LIGHTING GROUP | Venice, FL   2015–2017
Project Manager, National Accounts

Managed customer service/coordination of strategic accounts—including Hard Rock Café, Moe's Southwest Grill, Collective Brands—for high-end corporate/commercial lighting firm (30+ employees, privately held). Account management expanded to include Saks Fifth Avenue and Subway (40,000 stores worldwide).

- Collaborated with sales manager to develop custom lighting solutions meeting architectural specifications; **added value by tailoring "cost-and-design" service contributions to individual customers.**
- **Expertly managed numerous concurrent responsibilities and deadlines.**
- **Cultivated relationships with customers, vendors, and architects** in new construction market.
- **Met customers' urgent deadline requirements,** managed procurement, expedited logistics, negotiated costs/delivery dates, priced custom orders, and sourced product from manufacturers.
- **Go-to resource** to other project managers; developed strong technical knowledge of product features.

MONACO'S PIZZA | Sarasota, FL   2014–2016
Customer Service/Delivery

Hired to **bring customer service skills** to startup establishment. Key member of team that quickly launched Monaco's to success built on reputation for quality, service, and customer attentiveness.

Education: UNIVERSITY OF SOUTH FLORIDA | Tampa, FL – **Bachelor of Science, Marketing** (2014)
Graduate of *Muma College of Business* (AACSB-accredited program) with minor in Political Science

Jan Melnik, M.A., MRW, CCM, CPRW • Absolute Advantage • www.janmelnik.com

Note: Chronological format is retained, while return to former employer is explained in a way that substantiates this job seeker's value. Use of bold print throughout draws visual attention to the most important information.

JASON F. KARL

304-846-8412 | www.linkedin.com/in/jkarl | jasonfkarl9@gmail.com

GLOBAL DIRECTOR OF MARKETING & BUSINESS DEVELOPMENT

Translate customer insights into highly differentiated products and programs for leading brands

Key Accomplishments:

✓ **Captured market segments for global enterprises and startups,** planning and executing social/new media marketing to increase solution sales, secure venture capital, and position companies for sale.

✓ **Secured multimillion-dollar contracts in Europe, the US, and Asia,** leveraging a gift for languages to negotiate business customs in 50 countries and build relationships to springboard new opportunities.

✓ **Turned around profitability in key business segments,** using financial background to focus on the bottom line and co-location with R&D/manufacturing to create integrated teams within matrix organization.

✓ **Rejuvenated direct reports and marketing teams to produce top results** across multiple segments and geographies, energizing employees, partners, and suppliers to track and capitalize on technology trends.

Master's in Marketing | MBA in Finance | Conversational German & Spanish; Beginner Japanese

PROFESSIONAL EXPERIENCE

CARESTREAM, USA & UK

Brought in to grow revenue and give equipment manufacturer a competitive edge in mature market. Developed long-term diversification plan, identifying market opportunities and presenting business case.

Director of Marketing & Business Development (2013–Present)

Drive product development and portfolio management with R&D and technical groups. Optimize OEM relations, branding, solutions marketing, collateral, website, sales, and trade show strategy. Accountable for P&L and budget.

Business Growth: Turned around 3-year declining US and European revenue.

- Increased revenues and profit 30% by expanding sales to existing customers and acquiring 2 OEM long-term supply contracts in North America and Japan.
- Stabilized Kodak account in first 6 months to snag $2 million annual contact and additional $2 million contract in the UK, delivering product family that outperforms incumbent supplier at 40% of the cost.
- Added $18 million in revenue in 5 years by leading product development of 4 product families and 2 product line extensions, translating OEM specifications into wins.

Product Development: Refined and implemented business strategies to deliver "Lowest Total Lifecycle Cost" equipment systems to global customer base.

- Directed product development to address global dealer network need, creating universal processing systems that increased flexibility to meet needs of multiple OEMs.
- Led launch execution – media communications, trade shows, artwork, content development, and collateral design.
- Strengthened global partnerships with OEMs and dealers, ushering equipment throughout lifecycle, from conceptualization to design, manufacture, and technical support.

JFK STRATEGIES, Philadelphia, PA

Built management consultancy from the ground up, providing customer intelligence and focusing across global product line management phases, from ideation to launch and international expansion.

Founder & Principal (2011–2013)

Consulted on product line/market segment strategy, KPI tracking, B2B and B2C social media marketing, website design, SEO, content and direct marketing, CRM, lead generation, customer-centric solution selling, and market launch.

Marie Zimenoff, M.Ed., NCRW, NCC • A Strategic Advantage • www.astrategicadvantage.com

Note: Subheadings in the job descriptions reinforce keywords while focusing on the skills and accomplishments that matter most. Mention of 2 Master's degrees and language skills is a perfect way to close the summary.

JASON F. KARL

Key Impacts: Delivered results for clients in the US, Canada, Europe, and Asia across diverse industries, including aircraft and printing systems manufacturers, industry trade associations, and SaaS remote proofing.

- Implemented social media marketing programs for several B2B and B2C clients, managing brand and engaging customers through Facebook, YouTube, blogging, customer surveys, and monthly e-newsletters.
- Secured 2nd round of venture capital funding for Israeli tech startup.
- Won 2 profitable OEM contracts for NES Worldwide, prompting a partnership offer from the principals.
- Developed pricing and launch plans for Canadian SaaS supplier to Global CPGs, positioning company for sale through extensive competitive analysis and recruitment of strategic partners (sub-brand managers).

HEWLETT-PACKARD, Norwalk, CT / Fort Collins, CO / Eschborn, Germany

Advanced steadily within $2 billion new business venture within Hewlett-Packard.

Worldwide Packaging Market Segment Manager (2009–2011)
European Packaging Segment Business Development Manager (2005–2008)

Transformed business from product focus to solution approach, directing marketing strategy, value-based solution mapping, and sales analysis/plans for 5 global regions. Managed technical assistance group and market analysts.

Global Product Launch: Outpaced competitors by training US sales leaders and creating plans for 4 global managers, partnering with OEM competitors and initiating organic R&D programs and strategic acquisitions.

- Led global NPD team that launched 3-time GATF award-winning printing system, identifying needs across value chains and developing roadmap that delivered brand promise worldwide.
- Increased segment-specific solution sales 40% in 5 years. Developed global business plans for package solutions and piloted new product development programs and alliance partnerships with global OEMs.
- Designed advertising content to maximize brand exposure and composed segment-specific marketing materials, customer messaging, and website that supported brand promise to global CPG companies.

Global Sales Leadership: Stepped in to gain traction in global market segment, leading product management, manufacturing, and European business development from regional headquarters in Germany.

- Grew new product sales 215%. Strengthened relationships with CPG, packaging, and converting companies, and created 5-year product portfolio that aligned with R&D spend/timing.
- Translated message into sales leads and training, delivering sales presentations in German and Italian and demonstrating solution pitch for regional segment sales that addressed pain points for European CPGs.

Worldwide Product Manager, Chemistry & Equipment (2003–2005)

Promoted to lead total lifecycle management for 6 portfolios with 185 products. Saved millions by standardizing suppliers, training, and logistics.

Product Development Leadership: Increased profitability of $75 million business 10% in 2 years through manufacturing consolidation, portfolio reduction, and regional pricing alignment.

EDUCATION

Marketing Strategy Certificate – Northwestern University Kellogg School of Management
MBA, Finance & Marketing – Rochester Institute of Technology Saunders College of Business
BA, Liberal Arts Concentration – Colorado State University

Steven Sanchez

(510) 400-0404 | stevenpsanchez@gmail.com | www.linkedin.com/in/stevenpsanchez | Berkeley, CA 94704

BUYING & MERCHANDISING PROFESSIONAL
Versatile E-Commerce Expert • Motivating Team Leader • Outstanding Negotiator

Competitive, accomplished professional with track record of reducing costs, identifying and capturing opportunities, and building strong alliances in all internal departments and with vendors.

☑ Purchasing	☑ Merchandising Strategy	☑ Negotiations
☑ Team Leadership & Development	☑ Category Strategy	☑ Vendor Relationships
☑ Project Management	☑ Inventory Management	☑ Cost Containment / Profit Growth

"Steve's attitude is terrific and contagious. He fears no obstacles, is eager to accept any challenge, and has a desire to win."
– Excerpt from Performance Review from Martin Miller, COO and Direct Manager at SwimSavings.com

PROFESSIONAL EXPERIENCE

BUYER ▪ SwimSavings.com   **2016–2019**
Leading online retailer in swim goods, known for cutting-edge e-commerce marketing.

Built buying function from ground up as company quickly grew from start-up to 300 employees. Reported directly to Chief Operations Officer as company's first Buyer, then to General Merchandise Manager. Hired, managed, coached, and mentored 5-member cross-functional team. Managed 9 divisions, including the largest (Competitive Swim), and key accounts representing >80% of total revenue.

Negotiated all contracts and exclusive deals. Researched market and competitors, performing biweekly competitive price analysis and addressing MAP issues. Forecasted demand to maintain optimal inventory levels. Fostered communication with all internal partners, including Marketing, Operations, Finance, and Customer Service.

Buying & Merchandising
- Opened 140 new vendors in 4 years, generating an additional >$3.5M YOY sales in 2016–2017 alone.
- Renegotiated payment terms with largest vendor from net 30 to net 90 within first month after hire.
- Analyzed and negotiated successful multimillion-dollar off-price opportunities, resulting in large increases in margin. Negotiated favorable prices, ship windows, and payment terms.
- Negotiated special promo list of 24 items with largest vendor, dramatically increasing margin and profitability on top sellers with minimal effort.
- Negotiated with accounts as company opened business in Canada, gaining participation from 90% of vendors.

Business & Team Leadership
- Drove increase of 136% in total sales across 9 divisions managed.
- Proposed and launched cycling division that netted $174K in sales during first year, overcoming traditional resistance of cycling vendors to dotcoms.
- Met or exceeded all KPIs, including inventory turn, gross margin, and in-stock percentage of top performers.
- Seamlessly managed vendor communication and coordination during 2 moves as company grew.
- Developed employees through weekly meetings and upgraded team's specialized knowledge through weekly assignments. Retained leadership of team throughout tenure as company grew to 4 levels of Buyer positions.

ASSISTANT BUYER ▪ WheelerBike.com / Wheeler Bicycle Works, Inc.   **2014–2016**
Fast-paced and customer-driven online bicycle business.

Held purchasing responsibility for soft goods and accessories inventory. Introduced purchasing procedures and systems that improved financial performance. Handled large-dollar purchasing negotiations and vendor relationships.

- Increased inventory turn by implementing just-in-time (JIT) ordering.

EDUCATION ▪ Bachelor of Arts in Communication, 2014 – Kennedy University, Monterey, CA

TECHNICAL SKILLS ▪ Microsoft Excel (advanced), Word, and Outlook; Google Analytic; JIRA issue tracking

Thea Kelley, CEIC, CPRW, OPNS • Thea Kelley Career Services • www.theakelley.com

Note: Testimonial in summary instantly establishes credibility, and long tenure with SwimSavings.com showcases success in 2 relevant fields: Buying & Merchandising and Business & Team Leadership.

DAVID M. LETWAT

davidmletwat@gmail.com ♦ Bloomingdale, IL 60117 ♦ 847-123-4567 ♦ www.linkedin.com/in/davidmletwat

Director of Marketing Communications | Senior Marketing Executive
Fanning the flames of strong brands to spread like wildfire

Energetic leader who uses both left- and right-brain thinking to build programs that resonate with global customers and generate significant revenue. Known for transparent and clear communications and marketing success strategies that include:

♦ **Partnering with C-level executives to consistently elevate brands to #1**: Grew Bolez brand preference 300%—went from #4 to #1 within top 12 market leaders. Established Kanzer Tools as top 3 preferred brands in 4 new markets. Catapulted Viper to #1 selling consumer paint line nationwide.

♦ **Implementing innovative technologies to improve lead generation**: Added $34M+ to pipeline by establishing marketing automation platform.

♦ **Developing comprehensive global metrics dashboard system to track KPIs:** Gained $2M sale by evaluating campaign performance and redirecting outreach programs to optimize effectiveness in emerging market.

> *"David understands the most difficult thing to prove and accomplish in business-to-business marketing – ROI."*
>
> – Missy Palmer,
> Managed David at Bolez, Inc.

INTEGRATED MARKETING IMPACT & RESULTS

BOLEZ, INC., Naperville, IL   2011–2019
#1 market leader of electrical and fiber-optic interconnection systems. $3.6B revenue. 36K employees. 100K products.

DIRECTOR, GLOBAL MARKETING COMMUNICATIONS
Budget: $7.2M. Reports: 17. Agencies: 18.

Developed and executed global go-to-market strategies to position company as premier interconnect solutions provider. Transformed department from reactive to a proactive unified global team.

<u>IMPACT</u> – **Shifted company perception to market leader—7%+ above competition.**

♦ **Brand Management** – Grew net promoter score (NPS) 4 points over 2 years to move from #4 to #1 brand in electronic components and interconnect solutions category.

♦ **Global Integrated Marketing Communications** – Decreased marketing spend 15% with implementation of international integrated industry marketing plan. Led multiple successful campaigns, including:
  - ✓ Increased commercial vehicle sales 247% ($66M) within 18 months.
  - ✓ Skyrocketed CRM pipeline for mobile products 48% ($7.8M to $12.4M) in only 3 months.
  - ✓ Boosted organic growth of medical global business 27% in 1 year.

♦ **Content Management** – Cut content development time 50%, dropping from 8 to 4 weeks, and increased repurposing of existing content 500% with implementation of new global content strategy process.

♦ **Analytics** – Raised desired customer activity 64% by spearheading effort to develop marketing dashboards to track KPIs.

♦ **Public Relations** – Earned 4x ROI by developing first global media relations program across 16 countries.

> *"He provides crystal-clear direction to his team, treats them as equals, and holds them accountable to the same exacting standards David holds himself to."*
>
> – Patrick Esposito, Reported Directly to David

♦ **Talent Management** – Identified key staff, with 9-box evaluations, to receive management training and mentored other staff through multiple promotions.

Continued

Michelle Robin, NCRW, CPRW, G3 Coach • Brand Your Career • www.brandyourcareer.com

Note: Infusion of candidate's brand in every part of the resume creates a cohesive message of consistent success and strong performance. Third-party testimonials further substantiate expertise and value to next employer.

INTEGRATED MARKETING IMPACT & RESULTS – CONTINUED

KANZAR TOOLS, INC., Chicago, IL   2006–2011
157-year-old manufacturer of professional hand tools. $175M revenue. 1.2K employees. 2.5K products.

DIRECTOR OF MARKETING & COMMUNICATIONS
Budget: $3.5M. Direct Reports: 7.

Brought marketing team in-house and expanded more into retail environment. Attracted attention of Julia Roberts for leather tool bag to the point that production could not keep up with demand.

<u>IMPACT</u> – **Moved Kanzar Tools into top 3 preferred brands in 4 new strategic markets after collaborating on development of first 3-year strategic marketing plan.**

♦ **Channel Marketing** – Gained $8.5M in incremental sales across traditional and retail channels with strategic marketing promotions and award-winning POS merchandising programs.

> *"David's organizational skills and attention to the many details kept it all working well, producing excellent results and coming in on budget."*
> – Adam Smith,
> Managed David at Kanzar Tools

♦ **Product Marketing** – Exceeded sales plan 58% for 20 new key product launches over course of tenure.

♦ **Brand Building** – Grew brand awareness from 0% to 40% in aviation market within 5 years and generated $1.6M in incremental revenue from Indy Racing League (IRL) sponsorship program.

♦ **Customer Loyalty** – Crushed membership goals 50% within first year of implementing first-ever (and industry-first) customer loyalty program; continued 15% annual growth.

ADDITIONAL BRAND-BUILDING CAPABILITIES

Viper, Marketing Manager (2 years) – Led American Tradition to <u>#1 consumer paint line</u> in U.S. by orchestrating joint-venture program with Lowe's and the National Trust for Historic Preservation.

Luna Lighting, Manager, Marketing Communications (4 years) – Negotiated and launched cross-marketing partnership with Disney and Lutron Electronics, leading company to become <u>#1 recessed and track lighting manufacturer</u>.

Jupiter Lighting, Director, Marketing Communications (2 years) – Exceeded sales forecasts up to 140% and achieved <u>#1 ranking in industry</u> with marketing launch of new product lines.

Farrell Manufacturing, Manager, Marketing Communications (3 years) – <u>Grew brand awareness 200%</u> through $1.3M national ad campaign.

AFFILIATIONS & VOLUNTEERISM

♦ **CMO Collective** (2015–Present) – Member

♦ **Business Marketing Association (BMA)** (2011–Present) – Co-chair Program Planning

♦ **Chicago Innovation Awards | Innovators Connection** (2017–2019) – Program Director

♦ **Frost & Sullivan Marketing World Advisory Board** (2009–2014) – Program and Content Advisor

♦ **Digital Collective** (2006–2012) – Member

♦ **Color Marketing Group** (2005–2008) – Executive Vice President, Board of Directors, Chairperson

♦ **Boy Scouts of America** (2007–2013) – Eagle Advisor, Adult Leader

♦ **Tri-City Challenge League Baseball** (2015–Present) – Manager

EDUCATION

B.A. in Visual Communications, Northern Illinois University, DeKalb, IL

KATE MONTGOMERY, MBA

San Antonio, TX | kmontgomery@myemail.com | 210-246-0845 | in

SENIOR DIGITAL MARKETING EXECUTIVE

RETAIL OPERATIONS - OMNI-CHANNEL STRATEGY — E & M-COMMERCE INNOVATION — BRAND ARCHITECTURE

■ ■ ■

15+ years of experience championing marketing, branding, and advertising strategy for digital commerce,
online, and social media spaces to drive YOY sales and client growth and exponential ROI.

CORE COMPETENCIES

✓ Digital Delivery Infrastructure	✓ Mobile & Social Media	✓ Market & Consumer Intelligence
✓ Lead Generation	✓ Relationship Management	✓ Stakeholder Engagement
✓ Virtual Sales Leadership	✓ SEO, SEM & Web Analytics	✓ Talent Acquisition/Development
✓ Integrated Marketing	✓ Budget Management	✓ Direct Marketing

NOTABLE ACHIEVEMENTS

❖ Generated $1.2M in sales through successful launch of an online beta version of web loans processing e-commerce site, complemented by extensive digital and email marketing efforts. *JS Financial Services*

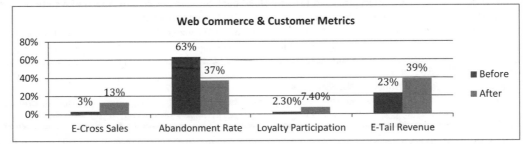

❖ Secured 28% customer acquisition growth for HSBC Bank and 17% web revenue growth for Best Buy. *RMS Connect*

❖ Delivered a 21% sales increase in 9 months by designing qualitative and quantitative research programs to understand customer needs, test new campaign tactics, and measure customer experience. *Reid Insurance*

❖ Drove 32%+ increase in online revenue for national retailers Whole Foods, Best Buy, and Walgreens by developing innovative social media, mobile commerce, and SEO/SEM programs targeting key customer segments. *RMS Connect*

PROFESSIONAL EXPERIENCE

JS FINANCIAL SERVICES, SAN ANTONIO, TX   **2016 – PRESENT**
VICE PRESIDENT OF MARKETING & DIGITAL STRATEGY
Oversee all retail, digital, e-commerce, branding, and marketing communications in addition to internal communications and employee training programs. Founded the inaugural digital marketing group and architected a comprehensive strategy to integrate digital technology into existing marketing establishment.

- Boosted operating margins 18% by eliminating professional fees and strengthening internal capabilities.
- Increased online web visits 132,000 and leads 80,000 monthly by rolling out new e-commerce platform.
- Slashed consumer website abandonment rate 53% by overhauling web functionalities.
- Integrated traditional with digital marketing plans, emphasizing sustainability and cost effectiveness.
- Drove comprehensive corporate rebranding effort, integrating efforts with J. Walter Thompson Worldwide and cross-functional executive committee.

Tiffany Benitez, CPRW, CARW • Resume Bridges • www.resumebridges.com

Note: Modern presentation, use of graph to demonstrate multiple metrics, and other visual cues clearly demonstrate that this job seeker is a current digital marketing pro.

KATE MONTGOMERY, MBA | kmontgomery@myemail.com | 210-246-0845   PAGE 2

REID INSURANCE & FINANCIAL SERVICES, SAN ANTONIO, TX   2014 – 2016
VICE PRESIDENT OF MARKETING
Delivered strategic marketing leadership to add revenue and define/refine corporate brand recognition. Built and deployed retail merchandising, digital marketing, and CRM marketing efforts; played a key role in branding, public relations, omni-channel advertising, and media communications. Oversaw internal staff and external agencies.

- Catapulted sales 42% by harnessing targeted e-loyalty promotion, taking advantage of innovative e-commerce platform equipped with mobile and social media components.
- Netted $5.6M in added incremental sales by identifying 3 strategic product offerings developed from in-depth market analysis, consumer intelligence, and mystery shopper programs.
- Increased brand awareness 27% in 1 year by formulating and executing a compelling brand promise and USP.

RMS CONNECT, DIGITAL MARKETING AGENCY, DALLAS, TX   2010 – 2014
VICE PRESIDENT OF DIGITAL MARKETING
Developed digital marketing and communications strategy for corporate customers. Partnered directly with clients to assess and respond to consumer needs and architect high-impact, targeted solutions. Led the full range of e-commerce, mobile, and integrated web/social planning.

- Produced 18% growth in commercial accounts for Frost Bank Texas by differentiating client's brand messaging.
- Secured 28% increase in mortgage loan sales for HSBC bank through design and launch of a suite of customized social media and mobile marketing programs aimed at Tier I commercial customers.
- Increased Walgreen's e-commerce sales $9.25M in 9 months through online customer acquisition tools.
- Grew agency gross revenue from $0 to $63M in 4 years, leveraging digital marketing strategies.

ADVANCED DEVICES, AUSTIN, TX   2003 – 2010
DIRECTOR OF GLOBAL CHANNEL MARKETING (2004 – 2007)
Promoted to global channel marketing role with oversight of public and government relations, promotions, and communications as well as a $9.3M annual budget. Developed and managed 24-member staff.

- Created $600,000 in press coverage through a CEO speaking tour with key government and corporate officials.
- Served on a 12-member brand council tasked with restructuring and revitalizing brand and forging links with key international markets using strategic government relations and contract bid plans for China, Russia, and India.
- Grew profit margins 29% in 9 months by developing and launching a globally standardized CRM system.
- Increased retail revenue 27% via cooperative retail advertising partnership with Microsoft, Acer, Dell, and HP.

DIRECTOR OF MARKETING COMMUNICATIONS, AMERICAS (2003 – 2007)
Recruited by producer of advanced integrated circuitry to build the Latin American marketing region as a distinct, fully scaled entity. Directed marketing, promotions, and advertising at the head of 27 staff accountable for $76M in annual new business and delivery of the highest market share companywide. Managed $6.5M annual marketing budget.

- Fostered 35% regional sales growth through introduction of CRM-driven customer loyalty program.
- Catapulted market share from 13% to 33%, delivering the highest market share within 3 years.

EDUCATION

Master of Business Administration in Marketing, Jefferson University, San Antonio TX
Bachelor of Arts, Jefferson University, San Antonio TX

PROFESSIONAL AFFILIATIONS

American Marketing Association | Digital Marketing Association

JOEL PHILIPPE
Design Engineer

Joel.Philippe@mail.com
970.310.4153
Linkedin.com/in/JoelPhilippe

Inventive technology product developer with 15+ years' experience leading product development, from conception through commercialization, while meeting customer and business needs.

Lead product development teams, launch products, and fix field equipment, consistently providing outstanding customer service in high-pressure, time-sensitive situations.

Multi-Platform Strategies
Product Design & Vision
Thin Film & Solar Knowledge
Team Management
Relationship Building
Business Development
Customer Solutions

CAREER HIGHLIGHTS

- **Design lead** for 60kW and 120kW bi-polar dual magnetron sputtering DC accessory supply.
- **Project manager and design lead** for 500kW solar inverter project, resulting in product compliance and emergence into new target markets.
- **Oversee $5.6 million in design architecture annually**, ensuring customer requirements, reducing material costs, verifying designs, validating test results, and mentoring engineers and technicians.

EXPERIENCE

Honeywell   2003–Present
Global producer of commercial and consumer products with 132,000+ employees

Member of Technical Leadership, Thin Film Unit

Establish product vision and manage product delivery from conception through discontinuance. Relationship manager for key customer accounts and product customization projects.

2015–PRESENT

- **Spearheaded design that launched company into new customized market.** Served as design lead for 60kW and 120kW bi-polar dual magnetron sputtering accessory to DC sputtering supply.
- **Manage cross-functional development team** of 15 employees focused on meeting product specification, cost goals, and manufacturing schedules.
- **Effectively resolved a $4 million customer product issue,** ensuring continued customer relationship and future equipment purchases.

Member of Technical Staff, Renewable Energy Unit

Invited to join solar division to lead product architecture and design for new business unit. Contributed to business development strategy that included immersion into new target markets. Directed engineering validation testing, ensuring regulatory compliance and performance specifications.

2012–2015

- **Designed 500kW solar inverter system,** ensuring product release that met market demand.
- **Oversaw hardware design projects,** including development, testing, DFMEA, PFMEA, and worst-case stress analysis, resulting in manufacture-ready products and timely product releases.
- **Supervised cross-functional team of 5 technical personnel** on solar inverter projects.

"Joel excels when working with teams and customers. He is talented across a number of technical disciplines and applications." – B. Lewis, Honeywell Senior Development Manager

Ruth Pankratz, NCRW, CPRW, MBA • Gabby Communications • www.gabbycommunications.com

Note: Creative design, career highlights, and endorsements set this resume apart and instantly generate interest from hiring managers. Large shaded box at the top visually demonstrates the candidate's design expertise.

Joel.Philippe@mail.com
970.310.4153
Linkedin.com/in/JoelPhilippe

JOEL PHILIPPE
Page 2 of 2

Hardware Design Engineer

Mentored new department engineers and technicians in methodologies, issue resolution, and company processes. Coordinated engineering product validation testing activities, switch network verification, control loop analysis, thermal validation, and specification testing, resulting in product release to production.

2008-2011

- ⅄ **Invented and designed new method for arc handling** in vacuum deposition process for a 400kW sputtering supply, resulting in awarded patent.
- ⅄ **Researched solar inverter compliance requirements for European market**, effectively creating new European company product offerings and new market share options.
- ⅄ **Investigated 20kW DC generator product issue** at international customer site, determined root cause, and implemented hardware corrective action, solidifying customer relationship.

Design Engineer I

Coordinated hardware designs and validation of power supplies to meet product specification performance requirements, UL certifications, and CSA safety requirements.

2003-2008

- ⅄ **Analyzed and interpreted test information,** resolving design-related problems and providing solutions to senior engineers.
- ⅄ **Problem-solved and evaluated power and control sections of power conversion systems** used in plasma process equipment, resulting in customer solutions and stronger product offerings.

EDUCATION & PATENTS

Master of Business Administration, Colorado State University, 2017
Power Electronics Certification, University of Colorado, 2004
Bachelor of Science, Electrical Engineering, University of Colorado, 2001

Patent US 751498B5, System and Method for Managing Power Supplied to a Plasma Chamber

"Joel takes personal responsibility and positively influences others." – L. Sanford, Honeywell Director of Engineering

CANE WEINSTEIN

Dallas, TX 75001 | 214-600-0398 | cweinstein@gmail.com | **Linked in**

VICE PRESIDENT OF PRODUCT MANAGEMENT

PRODUCT DIRECTION, STRATEGY & ROADMAP | GLOBAL PRODUCT LAUNCH | M&A LEADERSHIP

Direct Agile teams in developing innovative SaaS solutions & multiplatform software products for millions of users.
Assume end-to-end ownership of product lifecycle by defining and driving strategic development & growth.

TRUSTED PRODUCT EVANGELIST WITH SHARP BUSINESS ACUMEN offering 20 years of experience conceiving, developing, and launching innovative products totally aligned with company's overall strategy and goals. Passionate about developing game-changing products and delivering double- and triple-digit revenue increases through innovation, cutting-edge technology, and best-practice Agile methodologies.

APPROACHABLE LEADER WITH STRONG OPERATIONAL BACKGROUND: One of 10 executives charged with driving SaaS-based transformation for GianTech. Led large-scale initiatives for core product offerings and new services for healthcare and IT industries.

SUCCESS SNAPSHOT	
Skyrocketed Revenue Growth:	$204M → $1.1B+
Integrated 4 Acquisitions Valued at:	$50M → $100M
Launched Products Valued at:	$450M
Drove Software Portfolio in Africa:	34% → $300M
Managed Cross-Functional Teams:	Worldwide
Built Best-in-Class PM Department:	12 → 158 People

SIGNATURE SKILLS & COMPETENCIES	Multi-Product Portfolio Management ▪ Strategy Development & Enterprise Solutions ▪ Product Definition & Requirements ▪ Roadmap Development ▪ Product Engineering ▪ Global Product Launch ▪ Startup/Development ▪ P&L ▪ Stakeholder Engagement ▪ Strategic Partnerships ▪ Team Building & Mentoring ▪ New Market Identification ▪ Product Lifecycle Management ▪ Change Management ▪ Performance Management ▪ Mergers & Acquisitions

EXECUTIVE EXPERIENCE & MILESTONES

GIANTECH INCORPORATED   2010–2018

VICE PRESIDENT, PRODUCT MANAGEMENT | MEDISYSTEMS HEALTH DIVISION | 2015–2018

Fast-track promotion through 11 years of increasingly responsible, mission-critical technology leadership positions, based on record-breaking growth and consistent on-time, on-budget delivery of multimillion-dollar projects.

As VP, Product Management, provided strategic direction, growth management, operational oversight, and team leadership for MediSystems Health product management. Charged with delivering robust and cohesive strategies to provide foundation and guidance for effective, ground-breaking use of SaaS across company. Moved division from a "research" mentality to a market-driven commercial success model. Drove next-generation solutions in healthcare and life sciences markets.

Increased Revenue by $896M to $1.1B → Development Budget: $56M → Technology Integration Budget: $70M
Worldwide Responsibilities for MediSystems Health Products → Team of 12 Direct and 143 Indirect Reports

— **Turned around 12% YOY loss to 23% YOY gain** using innovative solutions and business models.
— **Introduced GianTech's first cloud-based offerings in healthcare** and managed first business unit to implement technologies in an FDA-regulated quality management system.
— **Drove successful launch of 6 major products** by leveraging organic development, the synergy created by new assets, and the commercialization of research work.
— **Improved time-to-revenue recognition for SaaS contracts 50%** and **raised customer satisfaction 15%.**
— **Served as trusted advisor to business unit executive** responsible for defining and implementing the new operating model for GianTech. Owned implementation strategy and execution of core cognitive technologies with vertical-based solutions.

Irma Rojas • RSO Resumes • www.rsoresumes.com
Note: This well-designed resume focuses on strong achievements that are highlighted in crisp bullet points—all 1 or 2 lines in length.

CANE WEINSTEIN

DIRECTOR OF PRODUCT MANAGEMENT | SOFTWARE GROUP, AFRICA | 2013–2015

Promoted based on track record of success in defining order and structure out of chaos. Developed overall SaaS strategy for Africa, identified growth markets, and led design and rollout of market-specific products.

Increased Software-Based Revenue 34% to $300M → 12 Countries in Continental Africa → Team of 12 GMs & Staff

— **Achieved double-digit software revenue growth** in 2014 while opening **22 new accounts** for GiantTech software business.

— **Drove localization and a 34% growth of the GianTech software portfolio** by creating a model of sustainability and growth in Kenya, Nigeria, Ghana, South Africa, and Tanzania.

— **Collaborated with local regulatory agencies** to define a strategy that would work across political boundaries.

— **Achieved 100% retention** of culturally and geographically diverse local teams.

CHIEF OF STAFF TO GENERAL MANAGER | 2012–2013

Selected for executive training program based on ability to lead and grow a product-based business as well as overall business knowledge and top executive potential.

— **Coordinated all external messaging** for events with 5000+ attendees, driving $400M+ in validated pipeline.

— **Spearheaded concept and creation of "brand-of-the-future" demo** for top-to-top meetings with GianTech CEO.

— **Facilitated the closure of a $90M cross-brand software deal.**

PROGRAM DIRECTOR, PRODUCT MANAGEMENT | 2010–2012

Led cross-functional team that defined the Commerce-as-a-Service product and purchasing system for GianTech's Global Advantage, paving the way for all future such assets to be defined and purchased through the online ordering system.

Revenue Growth: $450M → Global Responsibilities → Team of 9 Direct and 36 Indirect Reports

— **Smoothly transitioned from executive position** in smaller company to leader in organization with 400K employees.

— **Drove proposal to secure $9.1M in funding** from Cloud Incubation Board for Commerce-as-Service product solution set.

— Overachieved the 2-year acquisition case, attaining **125% of business case** and **incremental $80M revenue** in first 6 months.

— **Defined and completed MaxData acquisition** and led initiative to recruit and retain top talent from MaxData.

DEF INCORPORATED (NOW A DIVISION OF GIANTECH)   2006–2010

VICE PRESIDENT, PRODUCT MANAGEMENT

Revenue Growth: 10%–12% ($156M Annually) → Global Responsibilities → Team of 6 Direct and 21 Indirect Reports

— **Grew SaaS component of the business from 0 to 24%** through inorganic and organic development.

— **Retained 100% of employee product management teams** from 2 substantial acquisitions.

PRIOR EMPLOYMENT

GHI SYSTEMS, INC. | GROUP DIRECTOR

XPERT SOFTWARE CORPORATION | TECHNICAL TEAM LEAD, PREMIUM SUPPORT GROUP

SCIENCE DATA CORPORATION | SENIOR COMPUTER CHEMIST, SHIFT SUPERVISOR

EDUCATION

BACHELOR OF SCIENCE, CHEMISTRY

MARQUETTE UNIVERSITY | MILWAUKEE, WI

MICHAEL HOWARD

(512) 555-1212 ▪ howard.michaelp@ybase.com

www.linkedin.com/in/michaelphowardjr

CHIEF TECHNOLOGY OFFICER

- Envisioned, designed and managed $30M, 55,000-square-foot, tier-4 data center—largest construction project in organization's history.

- Revolutionized the way attorneys and law enforcement agencies interact with the state's judiciary, playing instrumental role in the design/buildout of TexFile, TexVault and Tex-Citation.

- Collaborated in design and implementation of the Texas Supercomputer Authority and the FBI Fusion Center.

- Chief technology consultant for TSA's Board of Directors.

FOUR-TIER ARCHITECTURE | IT DEPARTMENT TURNAROUND | DISASTER RECOVERY PLANNING
DATA & SYSTEMS MIGRATION | COMPLEX APPLICATIONS DESIGN | BUDGET MANAGEMENT
HIGH-LEVEL PROJECT MANAGEMENT & ROADMAPPING

ACHIEVEMENTS and EXPERIENCE

Chief Technology Officer   RETIREMENT SYSTEMS OF TEXAS | Austin, TX | 2013 to present

Oversee daily operations and budgeting of Texas' technology division while developing solutions for state agencies and other users. 141 indirect reports; 8 direct reports.

Challenge: Hired to turn around an IT department in disrepair.

Action/Result: Built thriving new department by enlisting outside programmers, implementing incentives to get "quick wins," rebuilding network and server infrastructure, and leading move into new facilities.

- Developed a $30M data center from the ground up. Manage and oversee data center operations with SOC 2 Type 2 effective implementation.
- Created a new revenue stream by starting technology support and consultation business within TSA.
- Led data migration from mainframe systems to SQL server/.net side.
- Effected time and cost savings by implementing new web portal for the health insurance plan.
- Collaborated with architects and engineers to develop major construction projects.

IT Operations Manager   CENTRAL JUDICIAL SYSTEM | Austin, TX | 2009 to 2013

Hired to manage and cultivate IT for judiciary system. Led restructuring of division to newer IT standards and created dozens of new applications for use by judicial system and law enforcement community.

Challenge: Innovate and automate the state's judicial processes and migrate from legacy systems.

Action/Result: Took over a small department of mainframe programmers, brought in teams to identify data elements to move from mainframes, and sold users on new technology and culture. Developed a fully integrated case management system, facilitating e-filing, electronic case status updates, and order entry.

- Cut costs by implementing Cisco VoIP system for 450 users and IPCC for multiple call centers.
- Boosted revenue and slashed costs with the implementation of TexPay–payment of traffic tickets and criminal fines online–and TexLync–subscription service for attorneys and law enforcement agencies.
- Implemented statewide network, engineering wiring and network for 254 locations, 5,000 users.

EDUCATION

BS Information Technology–IT Management ▪ Sam Houston State University, Huntsville, TX

Alexia Scott, CPRW • A-Winning-Resume • www.a-winning-resume.com

Note: Great graphic, combined with headline, captures immediate attention and communicates who this job seeker is and what he does. In each position, Challenge and Action/Result tell a compelling story.

BEN MARTIN

303-230-5605 • benmartin789@yahoo.com

PHYSICAL & NATURAL SCIENCE MANAGER | METEOROLOGIST

Air Force Weather Officer – Current Top Secret Security Clearance – National and International Exposure
(includes 4 years specializing in complex Arctic Region)

15 years' experience interpreting worldwide atmospheric and space weather conditions to support enterprise planning, resource sustainment, and contingency response activities.

— Software Proficiency —

Unidata Gempak Analysis & Rendering Program (GARP)
PC Weather Products HURRTRAK ■ AccuWeather Galileo ■ QuarkXPress ■ ESRI ArcInfo
Microsoft Office and Access ■ Adobe Systems and Photoshop

HIGHLIGHTS OF VALUE OFFERED

"His analysis was invaluable in accurately shaping the organization for future mission evolutions."
— Major General Matthew Solomon, USAF

➤ **ENVIRONMENTAL PLANNING (POLAR FLIGHTS):** Spearheaded winter use of polar flight route, saving $340K in fuel and 96 flying hours. Synthesized multi-source statistical data to analyze weather patterns, address risk management issues, and recommend best routing options.

➤ **CONTINGENCY RESPONSE (VOLCANIC ERUPTIONS):** Analyzed atmospheric data and plume information from volcanic eruption in Finland, developing forecasting tool to plan >600 mission-critical flights between Europe and Iraq during 2-month period European airspace was closed to normal air traffic.

➤ **IMPACT ASSESSMENT:** Evaluated meteorological, oceanographic, solar, and space environmental effects to provide impact assessments on effectiveness and survivability in response to nuclear warfare scenarios.

➤ **TIME-CRITICAL ANALYSIS:** Evaluated historical data and provided real-time support for coordination of multiple air-to-air refueling events for 3 aircraft conducting 25-hour, 11.5K-mile round-trip flight.

PROFESSIONAL EXPERIENCE

UNITED STATES AIR FORCE   2003 – Present

US AIR FORCE EUROPE – Henderson Barracks, Belgium
Senior Meteorological and Oceanographic Officer, 2017 – Present

Choreograph cohesive delivery of weather support by 40 weather officers stationed throughout the European region; provide planning and mission oversight as the Air Force liaison to joint service European Command.

- **Organized and managed short-notice deployment of 15 staff to Ukraine** to coordinate influx of emergency response personnel, aircraft crash investigators, and recovery crews following civil airliner crash.
- **Developed European theatre catastrophic contingency weather support plan,** collaborating with senior joint service meteorological staff to gather information and address all potential military scenarios in Europe.
- **Provided critical operational weather support to 2-month international mission,** ensuring safety and effectiveness of >20 ships tasked with neutralization of the Iranian chemical weapons capability.

US AIR FORCE EUROPE – Joint Base Gricignano, Italy
Current Operations & Analysis Branch Director, 2015 – 2017

Coordinated all Air Force assets in European theater with deputy responsibility for 24-hour Command and Control Center for aviation assets operating in 105 nations in Asia and Europe.

- **Reduced weather-attributed mission failure rate of unmanned aircraft to <5%** by acquiring, installing, and integrating a $2M state-of-the-art radar capability at remote forward location in less than 2 weeks.

Melanie Brassfield, ACRW • Career Wordsmith, LLC • www.careerwordsmith.com

Note: "Highlights of Value Offered" instantly communicate this job seeker's versatility and performance in often high-stress and dangerous situations. The addition of a reference to start that section makes it even stronger.

- **Coordinated establishment and oversight of command and control structure** providing mission and logistics support, including transportation of forces, delivery of 2M pounds of cargo, and provision of air-to-air refueling services, to international coalition forces conducting anti-terrorism operations in Northwest Asia.
- **Shaped planning and conduct of unmanned aircraft operations** that eliminated more than 10 major terrorist threats in remote areas of Asia; identified weather hazards, analyzed optimal timing to maximize impact and reduce operational risks, and provided critical input to decisions on airfield basing.

253 AIR AND SPACE OPERATIONS CENTER – Fort Geneva Air Force Base, GA
Weather Plans Division Director, 2012 – 2015

Led small team, integrating actionable real-time weather analysis into mission planning and operational support for more than 900 worldwide transportation flights.

- **Generated 30% time saving** in delivery of 1.7K military vehicles to combat zones, leveraging weather analysis to drive risk management decisions associated with aircraft routing.
- **Simultaneously orchestrated weather effects planning** for troop surge in Iraq and humanitarian relief efforts in Pakistan, providing advice that ensured timely delivery of personnel and >4K tons of equipment.
- **Enabled operational risk analysis** of >20 remote Southwest Asian airfields, developing Airfield Weather Analysis tool to track and analyze locational weather patterns and implications.
- **Created comprehensive hurricane impact timeline and assessment**, driving planning for 314 evacuation sorties from 12 bases in response to Hurricane Giselle.
- **Achieved 100% grading on bi-annual audit** of 100+ weather-related systems, processes, and procedures.

5 OPERATIONS SUPPORT SQUADRON – Henderson Air Force Base, AK
Weather Flight Commander, 2009 – 2012

Directed combined military-civilian team of 15 weather forecasters and observation staff, providing mission-tailored operational weather support to 3 aviation squadrons and a range of Army and National Guard units.

- **Increased mission efficiency 20%,** using tide and fog trend analysis to drive flight scheduling.
- **Strengthened unit forecasting capabilities**, acquiring $450K mobile meteorological observation system.
- **Ensured ongoing protection of $7B assets**, implementing base-wide contingency weather warning system.
- **Repaired fractured and disenfranchised staff**, improving previous audit rating of 78% to 94% during first year in position; awarded "Best Weather Unit" in Pacific Air Force ahead of 11 other organizations.

652 WEATHER SQUADRON – Yunam Army Installation, Republic of Korea
Weather Support Unit Manager, 2008 – 2009

Led team of 12 staff, delivering meteorological and oceanographic analysis in support of strategic decisions, daily sensor optimization on $90K U-2 flights, and intelligence gathering activities throughout the Korean theater.

UNITED STATES STRATEGIC COMMAND – Offutt Air Force Base, NE
Meteorological Operations Deputy, 2005 – 2008

Managed comprehensive training program. Overhauled curriculum to reduce certification time for weather officers performing atmospheric weather analysis, space effects planning, and impact assessments for US nuclear activities.

EDUCATION AND RELEVANT TRAINING

Master of Public Administration – Troy University, AL
Bachelor of Science (Meteorology) – San Jose State University, CA
Intermediate Leadership and Management – Air Command Staff College
Weather Officer Training – United States Air Force

WILLIAM EMERSON

770.555.1234 • WillamEmerson@memail.com • linkedin.com/in/williamemerson

COMMERCIAL ELECTRICIAN
Operations – Repair – Maintenance

Resourceful Troubleshooter • Team Player • Self-Starter • Clear Communicator

Electrical Systems Professional with exemplary reputation for delivering bottom-line results and consistently exceeding expectations in a fast-paced environment.

✓ Auditing	✓ Estimating	✓ Project Management
✓ Electrical Coding	✓ Installing	✓ Quality Assurance
✓ Electrical Engineering Design	✓ Planning & Scheduling	✓ Technical Inspection

PROFESSIONAL EXPERIENCE

UNITED STATES AIR FORCE, Aviano Air Force Base, Italy   2015–Present
ELECTRICAL SYSTEMS TECHNICIAN

Perform preventive maintenance on electrical power-generating equipment that supports $4.3B infrastructure; provide maintenance on 11,000-foot runway that supports 21 aircraft valued at $458M. Direct maintenance on 254 fire alarm and safety systems and 11 traffic-control devices. Service 3 electrical substations and 117 miles of prime distribution network to sustain Air Base.

HIGHLIGHTS OF ACCOMPLISHMENTS

Electrical Operations, Repair & Maintenance

✓ Averted taxiway closure by rerouting 2000-foot airfield circuit in 3 hours instead of 6. **Payoff: Ensuring no aircraft diversions or mission delays.**

✓ **Installed $270,000 airfield instrument-landing system (ILS)**—7 grounds and 1000 feet of cable. Logged 120 man hours.

✓ Replaced 24 assault-approach fixtures, **reducing base operation inspection time by 25%.**

✓ Provided electrical backup to D-well installed panel and powered chlorination system, **restoring potable water operations.**

Project Leadership

✓ Inspected 18-wing organization as member of Environmental, Safety, and Occupational Health Compliance Assessment and Management Program (ESOHCAMP) team. **Payoff: Identified 6 hazardous material findings and curtailed health hazards for 2,500 personnel.**

✓ Served as the lead for the Child Development Center's exterior lighting upgrade; installed 15–100 watt ballasts, **enhancing safety for 350 CDC staff members.**

✓ Revamped section of Arc Flash program and oversaw 17 personnel. **Managed $44,000 in safety gear and safeguarded 34 technicians.**

ENVIRONMENTAL FIELD CONSULTANTS, Atlanta, GA   2013–2015
ENVIRONMENTAL FIELD TECHNICIAN

Conducted asbestos, lead, and mold survey investigations, abatement oversight and air sampling; prepared reports. Developed blueprints for construction drawings, housing, and public schools. GA certified inspector.

EDUCATION and TRAINING

BS FINANCE • University of Maryland   Expected 2019
AS MECHANICAL AND ELECTRICAL TECHNOLOGY • Community College of the Air Force   2016
ELECTRIC SYSTEMS TECHNICAL TRAINING • Sheppard Air Force Base, TX   36 credit hours, 2015
MICROSOFT OFFICE (Word, PowerPoint, Excel) • Sheppard Air Force Base, TX   2015

USAF Honor Guard, 2016–2017

Cachet Prescott, CPCC, PHR, SHRM–CP • Career Cachet • http://careercachet.com

Note: Military-to-civilian transition resume starts with a summary that instantly positions this job seeker within the commercial sector. Strategic use of bold print in accomplishments draws attention to what matters most.

CASSANDRA LEE

728.977.3837 • Cassandra.Lee@yahoo.com

PRODUCTION AND MATERIAL SUPERVISOR

Earned multiple Achievement Awards.
Fluent in Chinese (Taiwanese and Mandarin) and English.

Electronic & Semiconductor Assembly	Schematics	Production Processes
Clean Room Operation & Maintenance	Supply Chain Management	Low Error Production
Project Planning & Management	Expediting / Procurement	Customer Support
Cost Containment & Profit Growth	Staff Training & Supervision	Lean Manufacturing

— 2017 Performance Evaluation: "Fully Successful or Above" in all categories —

EMPLOYMENT • PRODUCTION and ASSEMBLY (8 Years)

Production Manager   Composite Industrials   South Norwalk, CT
- Supervised production workers and hired/trained 100+ new staff for this $25B corporation.
- Engineered Safety Management program that decreased lost productivity 250% in first year.
- Optimized workflow to improve output and exceed company goals and customer expectations.
- Attained company targets, attributing to an average 10% annual growth.
- Chaired weekly supervisor meetings to ensure communication of value-added processes.

Production Planner
- Achieved objectives, ranging from $3.5M to $4M in sales per quarter.
- Planned, scheduled, and established production timetable to meet industrial plant deadlines.
- Worked with vendors to ensure product was available on time and at competitive cost.
- Monitored material inventory, tracked production, and reviewed factors affecting calendars.
- Controlled production overtime, employee hiring, and rehiring.

Production Supervisor   Leviton, Inc.   Melville, NY
- Supervised, organized, and provided training to production workers.
- Maintained production schedules for 250 floor operators, ensuring workflow optimization.
- Delivered accurate data during equipment upgrading and redesign process.

Assistant Production Supervisor
- Supervised and trained 30-50 employees in production of motion detectors.
- Trained assembly workers and followed schedule to fulfill shipment.
- Scheduled and assigned tasks to subordinates.
- Shipped orders timely to meet deadlines.

Material Handler / Line Leader   Conductor Manufacturing, Ltd.   Taiwan
- Conversed in English and Chinese when overseeing and distributing work to production floor team – 145 employees per shift operating 138 machines.

Andrea Howard • New York State Department of Labor • www.labor.ny.gov

Note: Return-to-work resume uses years of employment (instead of actual dates) to focus on skills and success and away from lack of current employment. Dual employment sections position her for opportunities in both fields.

EMPLOYMENT • OFFICE & TECH SUPPORT (7 Years)

Receiving Assistant   Ohio Department of Taxation   Columbus, OH
- Extracted documents for personal income tax vouchers using proprietary software.
- Received corporate tax vouchers and payments; verified data accuracy and signatures.
- Performed corporate tax return retrieval through database.
- Located alternate addresses through phone communications and web research.

Sr. Employment Clerk   Ohio Department of Social Welfare   Columbus, OH
- Interviewed claimants for claim details, ensuring compliance with state policies and laws.
- Calculated and processed manual monetary redeterminations according to policy.
- Responded to claimants' inquiries and resolved issues; answered 60–80 calls daily.
- Analyzed claims for possible errors and corrected deficiencies.
- Transmitted and logged daily postings for special projects.

Sr. Maintenance Operator   Lee Hung Technical Services   Taiwan
- Provided technical support and troubleshooting for computer systems.
- Repaired and maintained electronic systems and computer equipment.
- Aided specialists and engineers in maintenance of electronic equipment.

EDUCATION & TRAINING

BS Industrial Engineering – University of Bridgeport, Bridgeport, CT

Manufacturing

Federation of Taiwanese Manufacturers – 100+ hours of training in business and manufacturing

Certificate – Critical Skills for Supervisors in Manufacturing Industries

Technical

Certificate of Achievement in Dbase Programming – Informatics Institute of Computer Science

Certificate of USB Accounting – USB Software

National Trade Certificate – Sponsored by Toshiba

Certificate – Application Software for Administrative, Clerical, and Operational Staff

Certificate – Database Management – Southern Connecticut State University

Certificate – Research for Executive Assistants – Southern Connecticut State University

Management

Certificate in Supervisory Management – Taiwan Management Training Center

Certificate for Successful Supervision – Institute for Productivity Training, Singapore

---

Thomas P. Williams

1950 Oakville Avenue • Monroe, MI 48162

tomwms9@isp.com

313-555-1234

SENIOR MATERIAL MANAGEMENT PROFESSIONAL
— *Providing change management leadership while driving performance and profit* —

Proactive leader with expertise in material control and operations. Reputation for standardizing processes and implementing cost-saving improvements. Expertise in melding autonomous units into centralized structures. Talent for training and motivating employees to achieve common goals. Impressive 3-year global assignment.

COMPETENCIES

Material Process Control	Cost Avoidance	Gemba Walk
Supply Chain Management	Bills of Material	Global Transportation
Continuous Improvement	ERP/MRP	Leadership/Teaching/Mentoring
Inventory Control	SAP	Project Management
5S Methodology	JIT	Basic Portuguese

CAREER CHRONOLOGY

LEAR CORP./UNITED TECHNOLOGIES AUTOMOTIVE (UTA)/INTERNATIONAL COMPONENTS GROUP (ICG)
2001–2019
Navigated through several transitions of ownership.

Distribution Manager – Trenton Electrical Plant • Southfield, MI (2013–Present)

Scope: Distribution and material handling to support high-volume, low-mix product manufacturing in 1.1 million sq ft facility | Staff: 68 (118 at peak) direct and indirect reports

Maintained continuity in the face of a 60% turnover in labor over 6-year period resulting from changes in corporate structure. Adapted processes to accommodate subsequent labor reduction. Championed accuracy and adherence to JIT shipping schedules to sustain high customer ratings.

Performance Indicators:
➤ Surpassed delivery performance objectives 7 consecutive years, including all-time highs in 2015 for production (**100%**) and service (**100%**).
➤ Introduced continuous improvement strategies and changes in material flow, resulting in efficiencies of 20 heads within a 1.5-year time frame.
➤ Reduced external storage costs and improved productivity by relocating parts cribs on site.
➤ Launched line-side material delivery fed by metered routes.

Freight Payment & International Transportation Manager – Lear HQ • Detroit, MI (2010–2013)

Scope: Freight bill payment and international transportation services provided by third-party partners

Examined enterprise to identify improvement opportunities. Instituted electronic bidding process. Issued RFQs and purchased services. Garnered cooperation and acceptance from internal customers and vendor partners.

Performance Indicators:
➤ Served on team that drove 3rd-party partners to capture **$51M+** in cost avoidance and **$36M+** in freight savings over 2 years.
➤ Led team to develop centralized global transportation strategy that replaced previously dispersed, fractured system. Consolidated processes and reduced costs.

Janet Beckstrom, MRW, ACRW, CPRW • Word Crafter • www.wordcrafter.com

Note: Integration of multiple company names – resulting from various acquisitions and changes in ownership – into a single employer listing communicates long-term employment and avoids the appearance of job-hopping.

Thomas P. Williams (Page 2)   313-555-1234   tomwms9@isp.com

Incoming Business Manager – UTA Seating Plant • Sao Paulo, Brazil (2007–2010)

Scope: Inbound materials and processes encompassing receiving, material flow, and non-production materials | $4M+ budget

Tapped for 3-year overseas assignment. Challenged to revise outdated, unprofitable activities and institute standardized processes. Surpassed delivery performance and inventory objectives. Collaborated with Brazilian colleague to increase interdepartmental collaboration and build a cohesive team based on US work culture.

Performance Indicators:
> ➤ Implemented system improvements, resulting in **42%** increase in inventory turns, **42%** reduction in purchase parts days of supply, and **35%** reduction in purchase parts inventory.
> ➤ Launched consignment and sequencing center to support assembly plant in Argentina.
> ➤ Established marketplace storage and line-side delivery for specific sets of purchase parts.

Senior Analyst, Bill of Material (BOM) – ICG Electrical • Lordstown, OH (2003–2007)

Scope: Program and bills of material for 10 manufacturing plants

Spearheaded the move to centralize the BOM process for all plants. Trained new analysts in the North American Interior Systems Division.

Performance Indicators:
> ➤ Based on expertise, selected to conduct 3 weeks of training for division in Honduras.
> ➤ Traveled to UTA Sao Paulo plant to assist with resolving material planning issues associated with the launch of Lear's proprietary ERP/MRP system.

Unit Supervisor – Taylor Plant • Taylor, MI (2001–2003)

Scope: Bills of material and engineering change control for = manufacturing plant | Staff: 5 BOM analysts

Established and maintained BOM plant-wide. Coordinated engineering changes with manufacturing floor and materials group.

Performance Indicator:
> ➤ Standardized format and process for manufacturing engineering to communicate BOMs to analysts.

EDUCATION

INDIANA UNIVERSITY • Bloomington, IA
BS Business Administration – Business Logistics and Economics

Master-level course work in **Finance and Economics** — University of Toledo

LEON ADAMS

leon.adams@mail.com • 781-445-1251
LinkedIn.com/in/LeonAdams

MANUFACTURING ~ DISTRIBUTION ~ TRANSPORTATION OPERATIONS
2 Decades of Large-Scale Manufacturing, Enterprise Performance & Value Stream Management

- **Drive mission-critical strategies,** programs, and projects to deliver value, optimize global import/export operations, and ensure enterprise-wide profitability through supply chain management.

- **Advocate for best practices,** standardization, and continuous improvement in production planning, logistics, original equipment manufacturing (OEM), and material management.

- **Thrive in managing change,** aligning decision makers, mapping performance drivers, and assessing performance metrics across diverse functions.

☑ Import/Export Compliance
☑ Quality Systems Management
☑ Alliance Management
☑ Fiduciary Affairs/Reporting
☑ Process Improvements
☑ Change Management

PROFESSIONAL EXPERIENCE

MANUFACTURING & LOGISTICS, INC. – 1999–PRESENT

Augment or provide management oversight of logistics and manufacturing management for the world's leading manufacturer of construction and mining equipment, industrial turbines, engines, and locomotives. Jump-start operations, revitalize existing foundations, and streamline processes for national and international locations.

FACILITY MANAGER (Waltham, MA, 2017–Present) – Relocated to implement start-up strategies, link functional areas, and launch new Corporate Distribution Center. Participated in creating operational guidelines and hiring practices.

☑ Profit & Loss (P&L):
$6M Annual Budget

☑ Human Capital:
8 Direct Reports
50 Technicians
3PL & 4PL Providers

- Maintained 97.9% on-time shipping schedules for 2 consecutive years (2017, 2018).
- Implemented 5S workplace organizational methodology for the entire facility. Introduced lean manufacturing, Six Sigma to 4PL.
- Outperformed projections, saving more than $1.5M within first year of operation.
- Served as Safety Champion and recorded zero reportable accidents or injuries.

SHIPPING FLOOR MANAGER – PRODUCT DISTRIBUTION (Omaha, NE, 2013–2017) – Coordinated integrated logistical in support of global customer base. Championed value stream mapping process, orchestrated sourcing and manufacturing of machinery and delivery of heavy equipment to domestic and international dealers.

☑ Performance Gains:
$7M Cost Savings
45% Reduction
(Transit Time)

☑ Human Capital:
5 Direct Reports
$3M Export Contract
3PL Providers

- Wrote the Business Continuity Management (BCM) Plan; benchmarked productivity, implemented regulatory controls, and introduced compliance programs.
- Managed fulfillment process, invoiced dealers, scheduled on- and off-site equipment modifications, and directed large equipment tear-downs to accommodate vessel cuts.
- Managed contract alliances with one of the largest freight railroad networks in North America. Dealt directly with BNSF Transportation Coordinators, arranging dispatch, transportation, and movement of products to ports of exit.

Lisa Parker, CERM, CPRW, CEIP • Parker – CPRW • http://parkercprw.com

Note: Content maximizes keywords while also capitalizing on contributions and accomplishments. Visual presentation keeps the eye moving, satisfies the reviewer's need for excitement, and conveys the right message.

LEON ADAMS • Page 2   leon.adams@mail.com • 781-445-1251

TRANSPORTATION MANAGER (Omaha, NE, 2008–2013) – Developed integrated systems and controls, transportation plans, and processes governing all outbound and inbound shipments, including JIT delivery of materials and return of materials from suppliers.

> ☑ Cost Savings/Revenue
> **$4M Expedited Freight**
> **$6M Contract Carriers**
>
> ☑ Project Management
> **Strategic Planning**
> **Quality Analysis**
> **Resource Optimization**

- Managed multiple 3PL providers (trucking company, engine sub-assembly, modules, and cabs) and provided support for expedited requirements.
- Implemented new logistics center as Six Sigma Green Belt Lead.
- Directed critical vendors, implemented new strategies and freight transportation processes, streamlined use of authorized contract carriers, and reduced operating costs by millions within just 1 year.

ACCOUNT MANAGER (Omaha, NE, 2002–2008 – Leveraged network of relationships to increase yearly return on investment (ROI), improve profit margins, and generate savings for variety of national and international distribution centers and facilities. Participated in up to 8 Six Sigma projects yearly.

> ☑ Global Distribution
> **24 Facilities**
> **$53M Annual Spend**
>
> ☑ Quality of Service
> **Material**
> **Replenishment**
> **Material Flow**
> **Dealer Processes**
> **Production**

- Performed extensive supply chain planning in Mexico with on-site process improvements at 3 facilities. Integrated proven methodology to optimize processes and control the flow of materials to U.S.-based facilities.
- Established border crossing process and launched performance-based training programs for 100+ employees, with an emphasis on import operations.
- Resolved complex discrepancies associated with quality of service, efficiency, cost savings, and profitability.

ASSISTANT TRANSPORTATION BUYER (Omaha, NE, 1999–2002) – Managed multiple carrier accounts and contracts. Assessed the competitive landscape and negotiated scope of work, fair pricing, and transportation services.

- Exercised fiduciary responsibility in procurement of $45M in annual transportation services and solutions.
- Saved $13M over 2 years as Six Sigma Green Belt Lead on truckload bid project.

NOTABLE MENTION • PROFESSIONAL AFFILIATION

Authored Facility Standard Work Instructions for Occupational Skill Sets
2009 Chairman's Project Award Recipient

Member – National Transportation Club

EDUCATION • CERTIFICATION

BS, Major in Criminal Justice | BS, Major in Sociology
Northwestern University

Certified in Carrier Claims | Import & Export Customs Regulations
University of Idaho

Certified Critical Issues in Purchasing
Six Sigma Green Belt • Six Sigma Yellow Belt

Idar Janns

www.linkedin.com/in/idarjanns | Seattle, WA 95138 | 880.222.4444 | idar.jans@yomail.com

INTERIM COO ⊃ EXECUTIVE VICE PRESIDENT ⊃ SENIOR VICE PRESIDENT ⊃ VICE PRESIDENT GLOBAL PRODUCT ENGINEERING

AWARD-WINNING ENGINEERING EXECUTIVE and BUSINESS TRAILBLAZER
Igniting performance and driving shareholder value to unparalleled heights

BILINGUAL BUSINESS TURNAROUND TECHNOLOGY EXECUTIVE with expertise building top-performing companies and rescuing underperforming organizations through ingenuity, global collaboration, and unstoppable momentum.

Drove profitability by leveraging supply chain systems and partner ecosystems. Led organizations to exponential growth through product design, engineering, system manufacturing, and platform development. Competed with billion-dollar corporations and won major agreemetns with Fortune 500 companies.

Internet of Things • Utilities • Smart Grid • Transportation • Medical Devices • Electronics

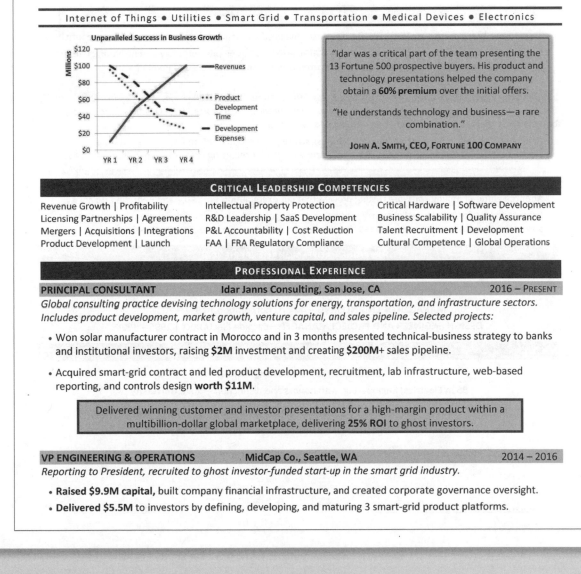

"Idar was a critical part of the team presenting the 13 Fortune 500 prospective buyers. His product and technology presentations helped the company obtain a **60% premium** over the initial offers.

"He understands technology and business—a rare combination."

JOHN A. SMITH, CEO, FORTUNE 100 COMPANY

CRITICAL LEADERSHIP COMPETENCIES

Revenue Growth	Profitability	Intellectual Property Protection	Critical Hardware	Software Development
Licensing Partnerships	Agreements	R&D Leadership	SaaS Development	Business Scalability	Quality Assurance
Mergers	Acquisitions	Integrations	P&L Accountability	Cost Reduction	Talent Recruitment	Development
Product Development	Launch	FAA	FRA Regulatory Compliance	Cultural Competence	Global Operations

PROFESSIONAL EXPERIENCE

PRINCIPAL CONSULTANT Idar Janns Consulting, San Jose, CA 2016 – PRESENT

Global consulting practice devising technology solutions for energy, transportation, and infrastructure sectors. Includes product development, market growth, venture capital, and sales pipeline. Selected projects:

- Won solar manufacturer contract in Morocco and in 3 months presented technical-business strategy to banks and institutional investors, raising **$2M** investment and creating **$200M+** sales pipeline.

- Acquired smart-grid contract and led product development, recruitment, lab infrastructure, web-based reporting, and controls design **worth $11M**.

Delivered winning customer and investor presentations for a high-margin product within a multibillion-dollar global marketplace, delivering **25% ROI** to ghost investors.

VP ENGINEERING & OPERATIONS MidCap Co., Seattle, WA 2014 – 2016

Reporting to President, recruited to ghost investor-funded start-up in the smart grid industry.

- **Raised $9.9M capital,** built company financial infrastructure, and created corporate governance oversight.
- **Delivered $5.5M** to investors by defining, developing, and maturing 3 smart-grid product platforms.

Maureen Farmer, CHRP, CCMC, CRS, CCS • Word Right Career • www.wordrightcareer.com

Note: Starting with eye-catching design elements and continuing through strong yet succinct content, this resume holds the reader's attention from beginning to end.

(MidCap Co., continued)

- Negotiated **multimillion-dollar** supply chain agreements and off-shore partnerships.
- Established regulatory and safety compliance. Managed DOE (**$2.2M**) and ARPA-E (**$4M**) government grants.
- **Won $700M** proposal with Global Top Search Engine—over competing billion-dollar companies.

VP GLOBAL ENGINEERING   **Grapton International, Sharpsville, PA**   2009 – 2014

$90M company producing safety-critical wireless automation and remote controls for railroads and industrial equipment. Reported to the CEO and led 140-person engineering team.

- **Directed design and release of 4 platforms and 18 new products** for safety-critical, wireless-enabled automation and controls, including M2M (cloud-based) for in-yard freight locomotives.
- Organized and executed cloud-based strategy for full product lifecycle management for **1M+ documents** and associated KPIs. Strategy was adopted globally across critical functions.

> Generated **$110M+ annual revenues** by releasing 3 major platforms and 6.2M+ lines of software.

- Transformed zero margin to **20+% EBITDA** by integrating product management globally—US, Europe, offshore.
- **Engineered successful sale of the company for $90M cash** by creating pitch strategy and delivering riveting presentation to the purchasers while being supported by investment bankers and equity partners.

MANAGER – SYSTEMS DESIGN   **Hampton-Strickford, Plainsville, IL**   2005 – 2008

Recruited to Aerospace Division of $69B Uber Technologies Corporation. Reported to CEO with 50 direct reports and $8M P&L. Served as pivotal player in winning $445M+ program for aerospace systems.

- **Achieved $1B award by creating winning business strategy** for product offering for Acme Avionics.
- Slashed product development times **35%** and set new record for recurring costs—**33%** net of previous costs.

> Drove profitability **$5.6B** in FY 2008 by using low-cost outsourcing strategies.

- Adopted game-changing software testing process that cut examination time **40%** and improved reliability.
- Executed plans for intellectual property protection and negotiated 10+ major development proposals for aerospace electronics, software, and test hardware with low-cost, high-value international suppliers.

PREVIOUS PROFESSIONAL EXPERIENCE

VICE PRESIDENT PRODUCT DEVELOPMENT – Maxim Electronics | 2003 – 2005

DIRECTOR OF ENGINEERING – Sunlife Power Systems | 2001 – 2003

MANAGER OF ENGINEERING – Amerix Corporation | 1998 – 2001

DESIGN ENGINEER AND PROJECT MANAGER – Carbide Electronics | 1995 – 1998

FORMAL EDUCATION ➲ EXECUTIVE TRAINING ➲ PATENTS

MS in Electrical Engineering – M.I.T.

BS in Electrical Engineering, with honors and distinction – **Duke University**

Corporate Strategy Development | University of Pennsylvania – Wharton School of Business

General Management for Technology Executives – Yale University

Patents: "Enhanced Source Power Control" | "Harmonic Sourcing of UPS" | "Integrated Energy UPS"

www.linkedin.com/in/idarjanns | Seattle, WA 95138 | 880.222.4444 | idar.jans@yomail.com

MOIRA MCQUAIG
OPERATIONS EXECUTIVE

- Innovating profitable strategies

CHIEF OPERATING OFFICER | VICE PRESIDENT, OPERATIONS

Achieve Best Outcomes: Modernization, Cost Savings, Revenue Generation

Innovative business strategist who implements global corporate projects with clearly communicated expectations and enterprising industriousness. Driver of business-focused continuous improvement initiatives, nurturing productive partnerships and building high-performance local and remote teams.

Particularly skilled communicator who excels in conveying vision, expressing passion, and mentoring excellence.

> " *Your leadership is even-keeled even in tumultuous times, keeps everyone calm and focused on tasks at hand, instills confidence, and allows us to do our job at the highest level possible.* (360° Review Excerpt)

Key Proficiencies

Visionary Leadership | Business-Focused Innovations | Organizational Effectiveness
Tactical Planning & Implementation | Strategic Resolutions
Change Management | People Management

Professional Experience

PhoneTech, Inc. | Duluth, MN | Since 2001

Vice President, Device Care | up to 650 global staff | up to $1B business   2015 – Present
Promoted to lead newly formed Device Care organization, comprising 50 outsourced repair facilities, 680 walk-in service centers, and 2 factories.

- **Merged 2 organizations** – Global Repair and Global Customer Care, successfully driving culture change and improving metrics to best in class in division that serves corporate clients, including major banks.
- **Met critical corporate goal,** leading cost optimization initiative that **achieved $39M savings target on time.** Solutions included closing factories, reducing headcount, outsourcing services, and negotiating tax concessions with state government.
- **Requested to speak at global conference** on topic of returns prevention/customer satisfaction.
- **Spearheaded cost-reduction project that realized 15% warranty savings within 1 year.** Organized cross-functional, silo-bridging teams to identify opportunities for savings from concept to delivery.

Senior Director, Customer Operations | 10 reports | 250 staff | $400M warranty reserve   2012 – 2015
Directed North American and European repair operations, including 10+ third-party repair sites.

- **Instituted a proactive operations mindset**, overcoming resistance, mentoring teams to plan and prepare rather than react, and driving "returns prevention" change to attain goals.
- **Built professional, confidence-inspiring partnerships** with carriers (Verizon, AT&T, Bell), leveraging influential presence to defuse escalations and communicate openly in difficult conversations.

... continues

Spearheading modernization and competitiveness

moiramc@moira.com | 555.555.5555 | linkedin.com/in/MoiraMcQuaig

Stephanie Clark, MRW, MCRS, MCIS • New Leaf Resumes • www.newleafresumes.com
Note: Notable about this resume—in addition to strong and succinct content—is the quotation in the Summary and the final paragraph on page 2—"a bit about me"—that shares interesting personal information.

MOIRA McQUAIG
OPERATIONS EXECUTIVE

Innovating profitable strategies

Page 2

Director, Carrier Quality Programs | 20 reports | $1M budget   2010 – 2012

- **Established new division and global team**, centralizing effort to reduce and prevent returns, with global responsibility for strengthening relationships with major business partners/carriers.
- **Slashed returns** globally, taking No Fault Found (NFF) rate **from 63% to less than 15%.**
- **Innovated cost-neutral solution**, sold idea to senior executive, and maintained an established, relationship-building, customer-service enhancing, and diagnostic toolset.

Project Manager, Mobile Business Unit   2008 – 2010

Realized gains in each project under management, including a quality improvement taskforce, churn analysis and reduction program, and retail customer improvement initiative.

- **Drove customer satisfaction improvements** by engaging customer experience usability studies and site visits; success led to promotion to helm customer experience improvements for global carrier partners.

Business Operations Manager, Mobile Business Unit   2006 – 2008

Spearheaded demand planning, forecasting, product launches, administration of legal contracts and amendments, day-to-day management and coaching of marketing team, and development and execution of marketing strategies.

- **Modernized product launch management**, implementing project framework that identified risk and drove stakeholder accountability.
- **Met 1:1 with COO** to discuss health of business and conducted executive demand-planning sessions monthly.

Senior Marketing Manager, Mobile Business Unit   2004 – 2006

Led marketing team in execution of retail, enterprise, small business, and online channel marketing strategies.

- **Employed critical skills in relationship building, negotiation, and engagement** to ensure product launches generated customer interest with effective advertising. Supported launches with thorough carrier training.

Carrier Marketing Manager, Mobile Business Unit   2002 – 2004

- **Introduced first smart phone** to the North American market, devising promotions geared to enterprise and retail customers. Ensured success with product knowledge training, sales incentives, and events.

Marketing Program Manager   2001 – 2002

Education and Professional Development

BS Business – Entrepreneurial Management, University of Minnesota, Honors – 2001
- Recognized with President's Scholar Award for graduating in top 10%.

... and a bit about me: I enjoy "bootcamp" exercise, read a ton of books, am into health and nutrition, and skied my way to head ski racing coach at Afton Alps. These activities keep me fueled and competitive!

Meeting improbable goals

moiramc@moira.com | 555.555.5555 | linkedin.com/in/MoiraMcQuaig

RASHIDA M. TOWER

404-249-7730 ▪ RashidaMTower@gmail.com

Equities professional seeking to transition back into

INSTITUTIONAL EQUITIES

Buy- and sell-side finance professional with a **Harvard MBA** and investor relations experience. Client service-driven and resourceful, with the ability to make sound decisions and meet tight deadlines. Strategic thinker with excellent analytical and communication skills. Series 7, 66, 86, 87 qualified.

▪ Quantitative Data Analysis	▪ Business & Financial Writing	▪ Client Relationship Management
▪ Investment Selection	▪ Industry & Competitive Analysis	▪ Institutional Equity Sales Support

— PROFESSIONAL EXPERIENCE —

WESTSIDE CAPITAL MANAGEMENT   Atlanta, GA
Associate Director of Research, 2009 to 2014
Hired for a newly created associate role to work for a senior research analyst and then promoted into her position when she left shortly thereafter. Covered stocks in industries ranging from medical devices to construction equipment for this long/short, value-oriented hedge fund with $400M under management.

- **Evaluated investment opportunities** using detailed financial models and proprietary analyses.
- **Conducted research** via field checks with industry consultants, company reps, and customers. Maintained ongoing relationships with industry contacts. Interviewed management teams and sell-side analysts.

MERRILL LYNCH SECURITIES   New York, NY
Associate, Equity Research, 2004 to 2009
Served as lead associate analyst for Applications Software coverage with primary responsibility for 9 stocks. Created equity analysis reports and financial models. Participated in company earnings conference calls and discussed investment ideas with internal sales force and institutional clients.

- **Led research-related due diligence** for pre-IPO investment banking clients. Responded to vetting requests.
- **Actively developed and maintained industry contacts** at analyst events, conferences, and trade shows.
- **Helped plan and organize Merrill's annual Software Conference,** attended by as many as 250 investment professionals. Moderated company presentations for institutional clients.

CAMERON ASSOCIATES, INC.   New York, NY
Account Supervisor, 2001 to 2004
Advised CEOs and CFOs on improving company reputations within the financial community. Served as investor relations consultant to global companies in retail, real estate, technology, and medical-device industries.

- **Achieved a 15% increase in equity analyst coverage for a homebuilding client** by presenting recommendations collected from surveying the financial community, including buy- and sell-side analysts.

— EDUCATION —

Master of Business Administration in Finance, Harvard University – 2004
Bachelor of Science in Journalism, New York University – 2001

Laurie Berenson, CMRW, CEIC, CPRW • Sterling Career Concepts, LLC • www.sterlingcareerconcepts.com
Note: Networking resume used for outreach to industry contacts will help this return-to-work mom find new opportunities. For 100% transparency, very first line of resume clearly states that she is reentering her profession.

David L. Bloth

889-352-0881 • dbloth968@gmail.com • LinkedIn Profile

SENIOR ACCOUNTANT • ACCOUNTING MANAGER • FINANCIAL ANALYST

Degreed Accounting Professional with 15+ consecutive years of fast-track promotion and top performance with 2 Fortune 500 companies.

"David is a professional who continuously strives to delight the client."
Thomas Simpson, Director
Accounting & Finance

"David holds himself accountable for achieving desired outcomes and has demonstrated the ability to appropriately prioritize multiple initiatives, a required skill for anyone who must balance an intense work schedule in conjunction with graduate studies."
Michaela Antonini,
Operations Manager

David's "technical ability is very good, his intellectual capability is strong, and he makes good use of data for decision making. He is also very capable in getting data from various sources, including BW and SAP. The quality of his work is very good."
Linda Parnello,
Accounting Manager

"David did an exceptional job in getting the project done early. Company generated tax benefits earlier than expected."
Robert Adams, CFO

ACCOMPLISHMENT HIGHLIGHTS

COST SAVINGS

- **Delivered multimillion-dollar tax savings** by managing the transfer of self-insured risk to onshore captive insurance domicile.
- **Minimized hours and expense** for external CPA firm by providing comprehensive reports and succinct explanations during onsite audit process.

PROJECT MANAGEMENT

- Recognized on performance review for completing Goldstar Platinum project well ahead of time, **allowing company to realize tax benefits even earlier than expected.**
- **Met/exceeded all milestones** on insurance renewal project.
- **Resolved a multitude of antiquated processes** and beat most milestones on year-long project to replace legacy cost accounting system.
- Known for regularly **delivering to fixed-time schedules,** often against steep odds.

PROCESS IMPROVEMENT

- Identified and rectified complex A/P–A/R system involving 2 subsidiaries, **reconciling after several years of being out of balance.**
- Restructured staff, resulting in a **28% decrease in staffing salary** while simultaneously increasing efficiency of the work flow.
- Customized process for managing outstanding receivables, **speeding turnaround** from key accounts.

STAFF SUPERVISION/TEAM BUILDING

- Chosen to **supervise staff of 9 professionals** after less than 1 year of employment.
- Trusted to **train treasury and accounting staff.** Exceeded expectations in developing favorable relationships with general ledger team.

FINANCIAL REPORTING AND ANALYSIS

- **Consistently met expectations** for timely monthly, quarterly, and year-end closings.
- **Expertly managed Sarbanes-Oxley compliance** to meet PWC requirements, resulting in audits with no comment.
- Repeatedly selected to **partner with PWC** based on keen ability to provide comprehensive reporting, documentation, and narratives to address concerns.

CHANGE MANAGEMENT

- Contributed significantly to **smooth transition of work** to facilitate acquisition.
- Recognized by management for ability to **adapt to an ever-changing environment.**

Vandette Anderson, CPRW • Not in Kansas Resumes • vandette@comcast.net

Note: The functional style of David's resume highlights strong qualifications as an Accountant while downplaying the fact that he has not worked for the past 6 years. Note the use of number of years instead of actual dates.

David L. Bloth • Page 2   889-352-0881 • dbloth968@gmail.com

CORE COMPETENCIES

Project Management	Account Analysis & Reconciliation	GAAP
Financial Analysis	Internal/External Client Relationships	SAP
Accounting Processes	Expense Review & Control	JD Edwards
SOX Compliance	Audit Review Procedures	MS Excel
Financial Statements	Records/System Automation	Negotiations
Budgeting & Forecasting	Organizational Cost Savings	Risk Management

PROFESSIONAL EXPERIENCE

Parwick & Hinton – Philadelphia, PA   13 Years

Financial Manager	5 Years
Consolidations Accountant	6 Months
Accounts Payable Supervisor	2 Years
Senior Intercompany Accountant	2 Years
Consultant (through Janson Handfield Smith)	4 Years

Initially engaged as a consultant for a 3-week reconciliation project to avoid a negative audit opinion. Subsequently awarded 9 contract extensions and ultimately offered a full-time in-house employment opportunity. During 13-year tenure, promoted 3 times.

Executed on a broad range of tasks:

- Developed and managed internal relationships, serving as a liaison for external vendors.
- Evaluated and managed company's insurance portfolio of claims and processes.
- Automated trial balance, ensured GAAP compliance, and validated integrity of financial statements.
- Made recommendations for workflow improvements.
- Supervised accounts receivable staff.
- Served as a trusted advisor to insurance director during annual negotiations with global insurance companies and brokers.

Glidden & Parsons, LLC – Chesapeake City, DE   9 Years

Financial Cost/Analyst	2 Years
Executive Auditor	3 Years
Staff Accountant	4 Years

Recruited to provide cost accounting support for 2 specialty plastic manufacturing ledgers. Recommended and facilitated transition from job costing to perpetual inventory system, resulting in decreased overruns along with improved current-state decision making.

EDUCATION

Bachelor of Business Administration – Major in Accounting
Ridell University, Harrisburg, PA

Mason Mack

San Francisco, CA 94101 ▪ 415.321.6702 ▪ masonmack@gmail.com

STAFF ACCOUNTANT/CERTIFIED PUBLIC ACCOUNTANT/TAX ACCOUNTANT

Offer superior customer service in all aspects of accounting.

Trusted accounting professional offering years of achievement upholding accounting and tax principles, accurately analyzing financial performance, and building sustainable relationships with clients. Combine background in finance and accounting with success in listening to customers, properly assessing their needs, and executing effective solutions.

~ Recent Accomplishment: Contributed to unprecedented 18% client base increase. ~
~ CPA Success: Completed all CPA exams, including FAR, AUD, REG, & BEC plus 150 credit hours. ~

Value Offerings:

- ❑ Creating & maintaining accurate financial transactions
- ❑ Reconciling complicated general & subsidiary accounts
- ❑ Embracing fast-paced environment to respond to client inquiries

- ❑ Building long-lasting client relationships
- ❑ Achieving high client referral rates
- ❑ Developing strong network capabilities

Expertise:

Retail Banking ~ Banking Management ~ Wholesale Finance ~ Commercial Finance ~ Business Banking
US GAAP ~ Audit & Tax Principles/Standards ~ Balance Sheet Preparation ~ Income Tax Withholding Reports
Profit & Loss (P&L) ~ Cash Flow ~ Bank Statement Reconciliation ~ Journal Entries ~ Tax Forms

Professional Background

Tax Solutions, Tiburon, CA
Firm offers accounting, tax, payroll, & business consulting services

Brought strong work ethic to accurately and efficiently handle clients' accounting matters, leading to referrals.

STAFF ACCOUNTANT (2017 – Present)

Selected to provide accurate monthly accounting and payroll services to ~35 clients across multiple industries, including medical, retail, and wholesale. Prepare all tax forms: individual, corporate, state sales, local, property tax, and payroll tax. Properly respond to IRS and other tax authority inquiries as needed.

- ▪ **Liability Reduction** – Decreased year-end tax liabilities by solving customer's tax issues with IRS and tax authorities and conducting accurate tax projection.

- ▪ **Meeting Critical Deadlines** – Avoided client penalties by diligently meeting tax deadlines and payroll services deadlines—ensuring clients' employees were paid on time every week.

- ▪ **Profitable Contribution** – Played key role in boosting profitability 15% by bringing in 18 new accounts and tax return clients based on referrals.

- ▪ **Million-Dollar Accounts** – Entrusted to work closely with owners of private businesses up to $1+ million. Offer personable, yet reliable service to diverse clientele.

KLB Accounting & Tax Services, San Francisco, CA
Company provides accounting & tax services

Successfully grasped accounting concepts, quickly learning "in's & out's" of entire accounting business.

ACCOUNTANT INTERNSHIP (2016 – 2017)

Provided monthly accounting and payroll services to clients primarily in the medical, retail, and wholesale industries.

- ▪ **Accounting Development** – Honed practical accounting skills, quickly taking hold of entire accounting process from beginning to end.

...Continued

Nancy Walkup, MHRLR, CEIP, CPRW, CCMC • Walkup Career Management, LLC • www.walkupcareermanagement.com

Note: Expanded summary brings to the forefront a diversity of notable qualifications and credentials. Shaded box at the beginning of each job description emphasizes the most notable contribution to each company.

Merrill Lynch, Los Angeles, CA
Global financial services firm; $2 trillion in assets

> *Established key relationships with customers: Enhanced customer loyalty, turned new customers into repeat customers, and drove referrals for company.*

PERSONAL BANKER/FINANCIAL REPRESENTATIVE (2012 – 2016)
Hired to develop existing customer relationships and continuously prospect for, identify, and capitalize on new opportunities. Assessed customer needs and recommended suitable products.

- **Customer Satisfaction** – Achieved 20% increase in customer satisfaction surveys by anticipating financial needs and goals and recommending appropriate products and services.

- **Revenue Enhancement** – Increased assigned portfolio revenue 25% in 6-month period.

- **New Customer Growth** – Established up to 20 new customers per month – far outpacing monthly, quarterly, and annual goals.

- **Top Performer** – Ranked in Top 5 on state assessment as a Registered Representative.

- **Customer Loyalty** – Turned clients into loyal, return customers by finding ways to save customer money with bank accounts, mortgage refinancing, and loan assistance.

Previous Employment: Cellular One, San Francisco, CA; **Assistant Manager** – Recommended wireless solutions and built and maintained long-lasting customer relationships by providing top-notch service.

Education & Other Credentials

Education	**Bachelor of Science in Accounting,** University of California, San Francisco, CA (2015)
Credentials	*CPA ~ Earned 150 credit hours required to sit for exam and successfully completed all 4 parts of exam (FAR, AUD, REG, BEC)*
	FINRA (Financial Industry Regulatory Authority): Series 6, 63, & Life Insurance
Additional Training	Extensive training and workshops in customer service, relationship building, banking/finance products, and terms and regulations.
Technology	Accounting CreativeSolutions, Ultra Tax CS, QuickBooks, Microsoft Excel, TaxWise
Volunteerism	Accounting Aid Society; provide free income tax services for low and middle-income households.

PHILLIP P. ANGLE, CPA

205-555-1212
phillippangle32@ymail.com
Birmingham, AL

CHIEF FINANCIAL OFFICER | VICE PRESIDENT OF FINANCE

- ☐ **Accomplished CFO** with a reputation for replacing stagnant operations, uncovering hidden solutions, and providing accurate data to stakeholders.

- ☐ **Helped save $500K a year in operating costs** by guiding software team to create a central dispatch platform/in-house app, eliminating 5 physical locations.

- ☐ **Saved $75K a year** by outsourcing network responsibilities and virtualizing servers with VMWare.

- ☐ **Restored largest customer's faith in company** by eliminating old accounting practices that had resulted in a $37K account discrepancy.

- ☐ **Slashed fuel costs 25% in one year** by implementing GPS tracking systems in vans.

Expertise in:

Software Development & Implementation | Actionable Financial Analysis
Investment Decisions ⬚| Audit Compliance | Conflict Resolution
Contract Negotiations | HR Benefit Negotiations

PROFESSIONAL EXPERIENCE

CHIEF FINANCIAL OFFICER | 2010 to present
ABC Equipment, Birmingham, AL
35-year-old industry leader in Point of Sale (POS) solutions and security products with 250 employees and projects in all 50 states

Improved processes, cut costs, and directed financial operations during a period of sustained growth; earnings before taxes (EBT) grew 350%+ in 4 years. Hired as Controller; promoted to CFO 2.5 years later. 22 direct reports.

- ☐ Designed and implemented a centralized dispatch platform, cutting invoice processing time by 92.5% and saving $150K+ annually in leases, utilities, and maintenance.

- ☐ Cut shipping costs 15%, eliminated $85K in annual inventory shrinkage, and saved $175K a year by relocating shipping hubs.

CORPORATE CONTROLLER | 2007 to 2010
The James Group, Inc., Birmingham, AL
Holding company formed in 1982 with 130 employees and gross sales of $32M

Directed all financial aspects of firm's operations and budgeting. Oversaw accounting staff at 9 locations, traveling to visit each facility several times a month to perform audits and provide expert guidance.

- ☐ Facilitated accurate comparisons of 5 John Deere dealership operations to other Deere operations in region and US by reformatting chart of accounts.

- ☐ Enabled Huntsville Honda/Yamaha manager to compare operations to others in user group by implementing new accounting and operating software.

EDUCATION

Bachelor of Science (BS) in Business Administration (Accounting)
Auburn University, Auburn, AL

Alexia Scott, CPRW • A-Winning-Resume • www.a-winning-resume.com

Note: Rare 1-page presentation for an experienced senior finance executive includes only the most recent 12 years of experience. Five wow achievements at the top instantly capture attention and communicate value.

PART VII:
Resources to Write, Format & Design Better & Faster

No resume book would be complete without practical resume development tools and resources.

On the following pages you will find:

- **Goal-Setting Worksheet**, a tool that will help you define your current career objective—the starting point for every successful resume.

- **Career Vault,** a structured guideline for gathering all of your resume information in one place so it's easier and faster to work with.

- **Dig-Deep Questions** to guide you in uncovering, quantifying, and writing about your accomplishments.

- **Verbs With Verve,** our favorite list of **403 Resume Writing Verbs** to aid you in writing with power and distinction—while avoiding repetition.

Goal-Setting Worksheet

Define Your Objective Before Writing Your Resume

As you read in Chapter 3, most modern resumes do not start with a "Career Objective" as was standard in years past. But that doesn't mean you don't have to think about your current career goals. In fact, the #1 step in resume development is to know your objective, because it determines *what* you write, *how* you write it, *where* you position it, and *why*.

Give some thought to these questions:

- What jobs combine your skills and your interests—what you do well and what you love to do?
- Look at job postings that interest you. Do you have the skills, experience, and qualifications the employer is looking for? Can you recall specific examples of when you've used those core skills?
- Do the salary range, benefits, working conditions, locations, and other details meet your needs? In other words, are your goals realistic?
- What industries are most intriguing to you? Do you have any experience in those industries? If not, how will you connect your background to a different industry?

Next, fill in the blanks below to create a clear objective statement and position yourself to appeal to your target audience.

Targeted Job Titles (Profession)

_____
_____
_____
_____

Geographic Preferences

_____
_____
_____
_____

Targeted Industries

_____
_____
_____
_____

Salary Requirements

_____
_____
_____
_____

Top Skills & Attributes to Showcase

_____
_____
_____
_____
_____
_____

Additional Requirements & Specific Needs

_____
_____
_____
_____
_____
_____

Career Vault

Capture Your Career Information Once—Use It Forever

To begin the resume writing process you must collect all of the data you'll need—everything from the basics of job titles, company names, dates of employment, and college degrees to more detailed information about job responsibilities, career achievements, special training, and more.

Your "Career Vault" becomes the single document for all of your data. You'll use it when writing your resume, completing applications, or otherwise providing information to employers, and to recall specific facts for a bio, profile, or other career document. Add to your Vault with every new position to maintain an easy-to-access record that you'll find valuable throughout your career.

> **PRO TIP: Answer all of the questions and record all of the data**—even if you don't think you're going to use all of the information you've assembled. You never know, until your resume is finished, what specifics you'll use and what you'll omit, so it's best to collect it all at the beginning.

Our recommendation is to create a Word file to capture all of this information and, when complete, make a backup copy. You'll never again have to go through the exercise of recreating all of the facts, figures, dates, and detailed data from your entire career. It's all safely stored in your Career Vault!

Job & Career Objective

You've read a lot about clarifying your objective in Chapter 3, and we hope that you've taken the time to complete the Goal-Setting Worksheet on page 227.

You now know that even though you most likely won't include an objective statement on your resume, your objective is the driving force that guides everything about your resume.

- Begin your Career Vault by writing down your current career objective, so that you're always focused on this important information.

Education

Create a comprehensive list of your education. It might include multiple items from the list below:

- Degree • Major • College/University Name • Location • Honors and Awards • Graduation Date (year only unless you're a graduating student or very recent graduate, in which case you would add the month)

- College Leadership, Sports, and Activities (only if you are a graduating student or recent grad, or if you did something in college that is truly noteworthy even many years later)

- Certification and/or License • Organization/Agency/College/University • Date (year only)

- Professional Training and Development Program • College/University/Organization • Location (optional and if important) • Date (year only)

Experience

For each position you've held, document the following:

- Job Title • Company • Company Description • Location • Dates (include months in your Career Vault; you may need them for a job application, although we don't recommend adding them to your resume unless you are a young professional or graduating student).

- Scope of Responsibility—Functions • Projects • Operations • Organizations • Budgets • Staff—everything that you are/were responsible for. Quantify as much information as you can—e.g., $2M project, operations in 14 states, $30M annual operating budget, staff of 47.

- Your Achievements and Success Stories. This is the material that will set you apart from the competition, so be comprehensive in documenting all that you've accomplished, contributed, improved, increased, reduced … all the ways that you've been valuable to your company, colleagues, customers, and other important stakeholders.

  As you are recording your success stories, at this point don't worry about writing tight, lean, and clean or otherwise writing with impact. You'll apply those lessons when you begin to work on your resume. For your Career Vault, include details and tell the whole story. Details *now* will jog your memory *later,* so that these stories will remain rich and meaningful when you refer to them in the future.

> **PRO TIP: Use a professional resume writing technique: CAR Stories.** CAR is an acronym for Challenge–Action–Result. Follow the CAR structure to describe each particular challenge, obstacle, or opportunity in your career; what actions you took; and what happened as a result. The specifics that you uncover will be valuable additions to your resume, LinkedIn profile, and interview responses.

Refer to Dig-Deep Questions on pages 231–32 for more ideas to help you identify, describe, and quantify your unique and valuable achievements.

Technology / Technical Qualifications

Create a comprehensive list of your technical skills, knowledge, and expertise: hardware, software, systems, telecommunications, new media, tools, equipment … whatever is appropriate to you and your career:

- If technical expertise is a prime qualification for your job (e.g., programmers, designers, some engineers and skilled trades workers), Technology Qualifications, Technical Qualifications, or Equipment Skills are particularly important and should be listed in detail.

- If you're an IT senior manager or executive, you may want to include a brief listing of relevant technologies (normally at the end of your resume), unless you have already interwoven them into your summary, job descriptions, and/or achievements.

- For every profession, if there is relevant technology (e.g., SAP in manufacturing) and you're experienced with it, be certain to mention it in your summary or experience.

Honors & Awards

Document the recognition you've received throughout your career:

- Name of Honor/Award • Reason for Award • Bestowing Company/School/Organization • Date

Project Profile

If you work in a profession or industry where projects are the mainstay, or you work as a consultant, you will want to capture all of these details:

- Name of Project • Date • Scope of Work • Project Partners • Budget • Outcomes/Results/Problems Solved (quantified as best as possible)

Professional Affiliations / Community Memberships

For every professional association and every community, nonprofit, or volunteer organization to which you belong now or have belonged in the past, list:

- Name of Organization • Committee or Board Positions • Achievements • Projects • Location • Date

Publications

Capture all of the data for each book, online or print article, white paper, or other publication you've written or where you've been featured:

- Title • Publisher/Magazine Name/Website Name • Co-Authors • Date of Publication • URL if published online (be sure to also capture and save a hard copy)

Public Speaking

For each presentation, record:

- Title of Presentation • Audience • Sponsoring Company or Association • Location • Date

Languages

List all languages you speak, read, and/or write, and your level of fluency.

For most people reading this book, English will be your primary language and is not necessary to state unless it is a particularly rare job search situation.

Personal Profile

It is rare to include personal information on a resume in the US. However, as you are creating your Career Vault, make a note of personal items that you might briefly list at the end of your resume. If you live and/or work outside the US, list whatever personal information is customary in that country.

Dig-Deep Questions

Uncover and Quantify Your Career Successes

Having difficulty identifying your achievements? Don't worry; you're not the only one. Use this compilation of thought-provoking questions to pinpoint your career highlights and successes that ultimately become the foundation and showpieces of your resume.

General Questions About The Company

- What is the company's primary line of business?
- What are its annual revenues and have those revenues increased during your employment?
- What markets or customers does the company service/supply/support?
- Is the company local, regional, national, or international?

General Questions About Your Position

- What is the scope of your responsibility; specifically, the daily business functions for which you are responsible?
- Do you have any management responsibilities for personnel, projects, functions, organizations, revenues, profits, or anything else?
- Have there been any particular challenges associated with your position?
- Have there been any specific opportunities associated with your position?
- Where you promoted from one position to another? How quickly? Based on anything in particular?
- Do you have budget or any other type of financial responsibility?
- What other departments or organizations do you "touch" as a routine part of your job?

Questions About Making Money

- Did the company's revenue increase during your tenure? If so, by what dollar amount or percentage?
- Would you say that the increase was average, above average, or phenomenal?
- Did you help impact (directly or indirectly) that increase? How?
- How did the company rank in comparison to other branches or to other competitors?
- Did market share increase? Were you directly or indirectly responsible or contribute in any way?

Questions About Saving Money

- Did you suggest any ways to cut costs in your team, department, unit, branch, or company?
- What were the before and after numbers or percentages of the savings?
- Were the savings significant in comparison to the total budget?
- Did the savings give you or the company a competitive advantage? If so, how, and what was the final result?

Questions About Saving Time & Improving Productivity

- Was there a reduction-in-force while you were there? Or, did you find yourself managing the work previously done by more than one person?

- Can you describe any tasks that used to take a lot longer to accomplish and what you did to streamline the process, function, or activity? Were the savings sustainable over time?
- What part did you have in reducing the time to complete these tasks?
- Did you regularly meet all your deadlines?

Comparisons With Your Performance

- How did you do in comparison to your competitors?
- … to industry averages?
- … to company averages?
- … to your predecessor in the position?

Questions About Performance & Overall Qualifications

- What are you most proud of?
- What did supervisors compliment you for?
- What do your performance evaluations say?
- What were your performance goals? Did you meet them? Exceed them? How does that compare to … (see comparison questions above)?
- What are you best known for?
- What do you do that others can't or don't do?
- What would "fall apart" or "slide downhill" if you weren't at your job for a week?
- What did you do that saved the company money or time?
- How did you contribute to the bottom line?
- Were you the first, best, or most effective in any particular function or organization?

Good "Support" Phrasing For Accomplishments

(If you didn't take the lead or can't take full credit for an accomplishment—but want to feature it on your resume)

- Contributed to …
- Partnered with …
- Co-managed with …
- Aided in …
- Helped to …
- Instrumental in …
- Member of 7-person task force that …
- Collaborated with department manager to …
- Participated on committee that …
- Supported a …
- Company-wide efforts led to …
- Departmental efforts led to …
- Selected for team that …

Verbs With Verve

Write with Power, Punch & Pizzazz!

Accelerate	Capitalize	Correct	Draft	Explode
Accentuate	Capture	Corroborate	Drive	Explore
Accomplish	Catalog	Counsel	Earn	Export
Accommodate	Catapult	Craft	Edit	Extricate
Achieve	Centralize	Create	Educate	Facilitate
Acquire	Champion	Critique	Effect	Finalize
Adapt	Change	Crystallize	Effectuate	Finance
Address	Chart	Curtail	Elect	Forge
Adjudicate	Clarify	Cut	Elevate	Form
Advance	Classify	Decipher	Eliminate	Formalize
Advise	Close	Decrease	Emphasize	Formulate
Advocate	Coach	Deepen	Empower	Foster
Align	Cobble	Define	Enact	Found
Alter	Collaborate	Delegate	Encourage	Gain
Analyze	Collect	Deliver	Endeavor	Garner
Anchor	Command	Demonstrate	Endorse	Generate
Apply	Commercialize	Deploy	Endure	Govern
Appoint	Commoditize	Derive	Energize	Graduate
Appreciate	Communicate	Design	Enforce	Guide
Arbitrate	Compare	Detail	Engineer	Halt
Architect	Compel	Detect	Enhance	Handle
Arrange	Compile	Determine	Enlist	Head
Articulate	Complete	Develop	Enliven	Helmed
Ascertain	Compute	Devise	Ensure	Hire
Assemble	Conceive	Differentiate	Entrench	Honor
Assess	Conceptualize	Diminish	Equalize	Hypothesize
Assist	Conclude	Direct	Eradicate	Identify
Augment	Conduct	Discard	Espouse	Illustrate
Authenticate	Conserve	Discern	Establish	Imagine
Author	Consolidate	Discover	Estimate	Implement
Authorize	Construct	Dispense	Evaluate	Import
Balance	Consult	Display	Examine	Improve
Believe	Contemporize	Distinguish	Exceed	Improvise
Bestow	Continue	Distribute	Execute	Increase
Brainstorm	Contract	Diversify	Exhibit	Influence
Brief	Control	Divert	Exhort	Inform
Budget	Convert	Document	Expand	Initiate
Build	Convey	Dominate	Expedite	Innovate
Calculate	Coordinate	Double	Experiment	Inspect

233

Inspire	Motivate	Project	Reorganize	Suggest
Install	Navigate	Project manage	Report	Summarize
Institute	Negotiate	Proliferate	Reposition	Supervise
Instruct	Network	Promote	Represent	Supplement
Integrate	Nominate	Propel	Research	Supply
Intensify	Normalize	Propose	Resolve	Support
Interpret	Obfuscate	Prospect	Respond	Surpass
Interview	Obliterate	Prove	Restore	Synergize
Introduce	Observe	Provide	Restructure	Synthesize
Invent	Obtain	Publicize	Retain	Systematize
Inventory	Offer	Purchase	Retrieve	Tabulate
Investigate	Officiate	Purify	Reuse	Target
Judge	Operate	Qualify	Review	Teach
Justify	Optimize	Quantify	Revise	Terminate
Launch	Orchestrate	Query	Revitalize	Test
Lead	Organize	Question	Sanctify	Thwart
Lecture	Orient	Raise	Satisfy	Train
Leverage	Originate	Rate	Schedule	Transcribe
Liaise	Outsource	Ratify	Secure	Transfer
License	Overcome	Realign	Select	Transform
Listen	Overhaul	Rebuild	Separate	Transition
Locate	Oversee	Recapture	Serve	Translate
Lower	Participate	Receive	Service	Trim
Maintain	Partner	Recognize	Shepherd	Troubleshoot
Manage	Perceive	Recommend	Simplify	Unify
Manipulate	Perfect	Reconcile	Slash	Unite
Manufacture	Perform	Record	Sold	Update
Map	Persuade	Recruit	Solidify	Upgrade
Market	Pilot	Recycle	Solve	Use
Marshall	Pinpoint	Redesign	Spark	Utilize
Master	Pioneer	Reduce	Speak	Verbalize
Mastermind	Plan	Reengineer	Spearhead	Verify
Maximize	Position	Regain	Specify	Win
Measure	Predict	Regulate	Standardize	Work
Mediate	Prepare	Rehabilitate	Steer	Write
Mentor	Prescribe	Reimagine	Stimulate	
Merge	Present	Reinforce	Strategize	
Minimize	Preside	Rejuvenate	Streamline	
Model	Process	Remedy	Strengthen	
Moderate	Procure	Render	Structure	
Modify	Produce	Renegotiate	Study	
Monetize	Program	Renew	Substantiate	
Monitor	Progress	Renovate	Succeed	

PART VIII:
Resume Index

This is one of the most valuable resources in the book—an index of all 90+ resume samples sliced and diced in countless ways. You can search by:

- **Industry or Profession:** Samples for jobs you've held in the past or those you are now pursuing.
- **Circumstance:** Resumes that have worked for those dealing with issues that put a wrinkle in the job search and resume development process—career change, military transition, and return-to-work.

In each category, you'll find the page numbers for relevant resumes.

Use the index wisely to find the right resume samples to guide you in writing, formatting, and designing a resume that works for you—that will help you *get noticed and get hired*.

Search by Industries and Professions

ACCOUNTING & FINANCE: Accounting • Auditing • Consulting • Corporate Finance • Economics • Financial Analysis & Reporting • Financial Services • Regulatory Affairs • Risk Management
Visit these pages for samples and ideas: 7, 48–49, 171, 219, 220–21, 222–23, 224

ADVERTISING, MEDIA & PUBLIC RELATIONS: Corporate Communications • Digital Media • Marketing Communications • Multimedia Advertising • Print Advertising • Outreach • Public Relations
Visit these pages for samples and ideas: 63, 111–12, 119–20

GENERAL BUSINESS: Business Administration • Change Management • Contract Administration • Consulting • Office Management • Process Improvement • Project Management
Visit these pages for samples and ideas: 58, 77–78, 157–58, 178–79

GRADUATING STUDENTS: Accounting • Advertising • Architecture • Biomedical Engineering • Business Administration • Economics • Financial Services • Industrial Engineering • Information Technology • Marketing • Media • Operations Engineering • Public Relations • Sales
Visit these pages for samples and ideas: 7, 63, 84–85, 89, 130, 143, 151, 153–54, 168, 169, 170, 171, 208

ENGINEERING & SCIENCE: Architecture • Biomedical Engineering • Construction • Defense • Electrical Engineering • Electronics • Environmental Sciences • Mechanical Engineering • Meteorology • Product Design & Engineering • Project Management • Skilled Trades
Visit these pages for samples and ideas: 84–85, 125, 144–45, 157–58, 168, 170, 201–02, 206–07, 208, 215–16

EXECUTIVE MANAGEMENT: Board of Directors, Business Development • Change Management • Consulting • Executive Leadership • Executive Negotiations • Global Business Affairs • Operations Management • P&L Management • Senior Management • Strategic Planning & Leadership
Visit these pages for samples and ideas: 12–13, 26–27, 28, 40–41, 42–43, 48–49, 50–51, 59–60, 90–91, 121–22, 126–27, 138–39, 144–45, 176–77, 186–87, 188–89, 191–92, 194–95, 197–98, 199–200, 203–04, 205, 215–16, 217–18, 224

HEALTHCARE: Biomedical • Biotechnology • Clinical • Healthcare Administration • Human Services • Nursing • Pharmaceuticals • Regulatory Affairs
Visit these pages for samples and ideas: 12–13, 26–27, 131–32, 138–39, 144–45, 153–54, 180, 181, 182, 183–84

HOSPITALITY: Event Planning & Management • Food Preparation • Food Service • Corporate Events • Guest Services • Hotel Management • Sales • Special Events • Tourism • Travel
Visit these pages for samples and ideas: 42–43, 82–83, 165, 190, 191–92

HUMAN RESOURCES: Employee Communications • Employee Relations • Hiring • HRIS • Organizational Development • Performance Management • Recruitment • Staffing • Training & Development
Visit these pages for samples and ideas: 174–75, 176–77, 178–79

MANUFACTURING & OPERATIONS: Distribution • ERP • Inventory • Logistics • Materials Management • Operations Management • Product Design & Management • Project Management • Purchasing • Quality • Shipping & Receiving • Skilled Trades • Supply Chain • Transportation • Warehousing
Visit these pages for samples and ideas: 32, 40–41, 58, 71, 90–91, 102, 160–61, 166, 170, 203–04, 209–10, 211–12, 213–14, 217–18

NONPROFITS, ASSOCIATIONS & GOVERNMENT AGENCIES: Association Management • Communications • Fundraising • Government Agency Operations • Government Relations • Membership Development • Nonprofit Management
Visit these pages for samples and ideas: 12–13, 126–27, 185, 186–87, 188–89

SALES & MARKETING: Account Management • Brand Management • Business Development • Client Relationship Management • Customer Service • Digital Marketing • Key Account Relationship Management • Marketing Communications • Market Research • Marketing • Merchandising • Regional Management • Retail • Sales • Sales Management • Territory Management
Visit these pages for samples and ideas: 17, 28, 82–83, 98, 103–04, 113, 121–22, 133–34, 137, 144–45, 169, 193, 194–95, 196, 197–98, 199–200

TEACHING & EDUCATION: Coaching • Corporate Training • Education Administration • Education Management • Organizational Development • Teaching • Training & Development
Visit these pages for samples and ideas: 96–97, 172, 173

TECHNOLOGY & TELECOMMUNICATIONS: Applications Development • Data Centers • Database Management • Digital Technology • Ecommerce • ERP • Hardware Engineering • Help Desk Operations • Information Technology • Multimedia • Network Administration • New Media • Social Media • Software Development • Telecommunications
Visit these pages for samples and ideas: 9–10, 33, 40–41, 50–51, 64, 72–73, 76, 89, 111–12, 121–22, 130, 133–34, 143, 151, 199–200, 201–02, 205, 215–16

Search by Career Circumstance

CAREER CHANGE
Visit these pages for samples and ideas: 33, 151, 153–54, 166, 188–89

MILITARY TRANSITION
Visit these pages for samples and ideas: 33, 157–58, 160–61, 183–84, 185, 206–07, 208

RETURN TO WORK: Long-Term Unemployment • Illness • Child and Family Care • Incarceration
Visit these pages for samples and ideas: 28, 32, 72–73, 165, 166, 185, 209–10, 219